PEACE AS PROCESS
Reconciliation and Conflict
Resolution in South Asia

PEACE AS PROCESS
Reconciliation and Conflict Resolution
in South Asia

Edited by
RANABIR SAMADDAR
HELMUT REIFELD

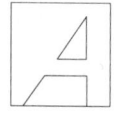

KONRAD ADENAUER FOUNDATION

MANOHAR
2001

First published 2001

© Konrad Adenauer Foundation, 2001

All rights reserved. No part of this publication may be reproduced or transmitted, in any form or by any means, without prior permission of the Konrad Adenauer Foundation and the publisher

ISBN 81-7304-397-3

Published by
Ajay Kumar Jain for
Manohar Publishers & Distributors
4753/23 Ansari Road, Daryaganj
New Delhi 110 002

Typeset by
Kohli Print
107 Radhey Shyam Park
Delhi 110 051

Printed at
Rajkamal Electric Press
B 35/9 G T Karnal Road Indl Area
Delhi 110 033

Contents

Preface
HELMUT REIFELD — 7

Introduction
RANABIR SAMADDAR — 11

I CONCEPTS

1. Value of Peace, Validating Peace
   RANABIR SAMADDAR — 21

2. Anthropology of Reconciliation
   PRADIP KUMAR BOSE — 45

3. The Mental Borders in South Asia
   SANJAY CHATURVEDI — 61

4. Interrogating Stereotypes: Women Making Peace
   RITA MANCHANDA — 81

II REGIONS

5. Regionalization as Peace Instrument: Western Europe
   HELMUT REIFELD — 101

6. Regionalization as Peace Instrument: Central Asia
   DEVENDRA KAUSHIK — 119

7. The New Search for a Durable Solution for Refugees: South Asia
   JAGATMANI ACHARYA and TAPAN K. BOSE — 137

8. Pluralist Politics under Monistic Design: Water Accords in South Asia
   DIPAK GYAWALI — 159

III CASES

9. Civil Societies in India and Pakistan and their New Peace Initiatives
   DAGMAR BERNSTORFF — 189

10. Possibility of Ethnic Compromise in Sri Lanka
    PARTHA S. GHOSH — 205

11. Nobody's Communiqué: Ethnic Accords in North-eastern India
    SAMIR KUMAR DAS — 231

12. Identity, Movements and Peace: The Unquiet Hills in Darjeeling
    SUBHAS RANJAN CHAKRABORTY — 253

13. Perspectives of the Indus Waters Treaty
    K. WARIKOO — 281

14. The Line of Control in Kashmir
    PAULA BANERJEE — 299

Contributors — 319

Index — 321

Preface

Since the worldwide turmoil of the years 1989 to 1991 and the subsequent ending of the Cold War, the interest in discussions on core values has increased considerably. In Germany, as in several other Western countries, an increasing interest in inter-cultural and cross-border dialogues can be traced. Peace is certainly still regarded as one of the most important among these over-arching values. In the course of the last decade, the value of peace has often been seen from new angles with new implications for conflict resolution. This affects the developing countries probably more than the developed ones, because about 90 per cent of all wars since 1945 were fought in developing countries. In many cases, these wars nullified all preceding development efforts and, furthermore, expenditures on emergency aid linked with militancy-related conflicts increasingly had to be incurred at the expense of long-term development.

Since the middle of the 1990s different German governments have tried to link traditional development cooperation with initiatives for conflict and crises prevention. Different kinds of support have been given. Among these, for example, there is the support for organizations with particular competence in disaster management or for those working for the integration of minorities in border regions. Another example is the support given to an independent media which puts special emphasis on information on democracy and human rights. A third form of support is for different kinds of exchange programmes, especially for younger people and those promoting dialogue.

The Konrad Adenauer Foundation has always had a profound interest in promoting dialogue programmes between ideologies, between cultures and between antagonistic interests. In many conflict situations the Foundation has taken the position that there are indigenous and culture-specific traditions of conflict resolution to be found among all conflicting groups. Democratic management of conflicts may well be handled and implemented in a variety of ways without fundamental principles being changed. The point is not to coerce other societies to accept the European way of life, but to find characteristic elements of human life that are capable of uniting people belonging to different cultures or countries. This might, in turn, serve as the essential starting point for any kind of dialogue, whether between or within cultures. This dialogue has to be pursued if we want to arrive at a stage when we can satisfactorily live together peacefully in a world increasingly prone to proliferation of hegemonies at different levels, from the community to the nation and beyond.

There is also another, more general reason for the profound interest of the Konrad Adenauer Foundation in wanting to induce and continue, under contemporary circumstances, a dialogue on 'peace as value' among different cultures, regions and 'civilizations'. It lies in the fact that today nearly all big political problems are global and globally linked. The understanding of other continents, countries and cultures is an indispensable precondition for cooperation. But understanding has to be based on a profound mutual knowledge of basic values, interests and unspoken assumptions. Therefore, a dialogue on 'peace as value' is a necessary answer to the process of globalization. It could help to increase confidence between nations, secure peace and should be regarded as a precondition for future policy.

A cross-cultural dialogue will undoubtedly help in modifying positively any negative cultural factors impeding the implementation of peace. It is due to differences in value codes and legal concepts that different cultures see conflict resolution in a different light. These value codes, in turn, are rooted in the terms of reference being applied. Democratic structures of conflict resolution can be developed everywhere, but these have to be developed within the particular culture and not to be transferred from one part of the world to another. A bridge of understanding can only be built by those who have acquired adequate familiarity with the fundamentals of other cultures and are willing and able to explain the fundamentals of their own culture and, if necessary, scrutinize them critically. A dialogue on peace as value may indeed contribute a great deal towards the implementation of conflict resolution.

One of the worlds most important regions in this context certainly is South Asia. The workshop out of which the contributions for this book emerged had investigated the main border conflicts of this region. The contributions are arranged in the present volume according to their approach as conceptual, regional or case studies. For comparative purposes, two other regions have also been taken into consideration.

The workshop was conceptualized and organized by the Konrad Adenauer Foundation in collaboration with the Calcutta Research Group, in particular Professor Ranabir Samaddar. To him and to all the other contributors, as well as to Bela Butalia for her excellent work as copy-editor, to Dr. Dagmar Bernstorff and to Professor Imtiaz Ahmad for their advice, the Konrad Adenauer Foundation would like to express sincere gratitude. The workshop was held in the splendid atmosphere of Darjeeling between 28 November and 2 December 1999. The papers included in this book were written with the aim of raising questions and exploring their possible implications. They seek to promote and carry forward the spirit of dialogue rather than end it with a final statement. In this respect the present book not only provides some useful information about South Asia but also hopes to be able to contribute to the promotion of a worldwide process of dialogue.

New Delhi   HELMUT REIFELD
17 September 2000

Introduction

Ranabir Samaddar

The editors wanted to give the title Peace as Value to this volume. But on being advised by those more knowledgeable about the ways in which publications should appear before the public, the volume comes out under the current title. Yet it needs to be emphasized that the fundamental strain of the book is treating peace as value. The writings in this volume, both theoretical notes and case studies, are based on the theme of ethicality of peace and an examination of some of the issues of conflict and co-operation in this region through the mirror of ethics. What is more significant is that these essays treat ethicality not as a fixed set of values and attitudes but as historically evolving.

The essays in the first section deal with some of the essential principles of peace studies, such as its historicity, the interim and contested terrain of peace, and its anthropological underpinnings. The second and third sections then unravel the nature of some of the contemporary conflicts in this region and elsewhere, to show how conflicts do not solve themselves owing to some intrinsic methods of conflict resolution. They call for new attitudes, new ways and interrogations of given paradigms. And in this deliberation the history of ethics and attitudes plays a great part. The moral is simple, yet worth repeating even after the hundred times it has been said. Men and women lay conflict to rest by striving for newer ways of accommodation on the basis of new understandings of values and principles. Dialogue plays a significant part in this historical transgression. It is appropriate therefore that the papers presented as first drafts of the essays in

12 | Introduction

this volume had been initally submitted as contributions to a dialogue programme.

If one were to look at the current literature on conflict and peace studies, the reason for undertaking the publication of this collection of essays will be perhaps clear. In the backdrop of the failure of realism and neo-realism to address issues of peace and justice in any significant way, there is now a strong revisionist current in international studies to bring these issues back at the heart of world history. These revisionist studies fundamentally adopt a liberal attitude in the sense that they concede the issues of rights, minimal justice, role and responsibility of the state on certain matters of human development, existence of different cultures, values and their legitimacies, global standards and morals, and finally the need to combine ethics and conscience with reality.[1] In the context of mass violence, terror and genocide, ethnic wars, and issues of equity and limits of markets in global economics and environment, issues of transitional justice, forgiveness in the face of vengeance, challenges to the patriarchal orientation of international studies, and finally changing concepts of rights and justice, the revisionist studies notwithstanding, the differences between individual writings in this corpus have gained attention. For these writings are speaking of differential morals, the power of pacifism, the need for an inquiry into the conscience of modern warriors, what Michael Ignatieff calls as 'the warrior's honor';[2] they are also speaking

---

[1] Some of these writings are John Rawls, 'Laws of Peoples' in Samuel Freeman (ed.), *Collected Papers of John Rawls*, Cambridge, Mass: Harvard University Press, 1999; Charles Taylor, 'Why Democracy Needs Patriotism' in Martha C. Nussbaum et al., *For Love of Country—Debating the Limits of Patriotism*, Boston: Beacon Press, 1996; Taylor, 'Cross-purposes—The Liberal Communitarian Debate' in Nancy L. Rosenblum (ed.), *Liberalism and the Moral Life*, Cambridge, Mass: Harvard University Press, 1989; Jurgen Habermas, 'Citizenship and National Identity' in J. Habermas, *Between facts and Norms—Contributions to a Discourse Theory of Law and Democracy*, Cambridge, Mass: MIT Press, 1996; Michael Walzer, *Just and Unjust Wars—A Moral Argument with Historical Illustrations*, New York: Basic Books, 1977.

[2] Michael Ignatieff, *The Warrior's Honor—Ethnic War and the Modern Conscience*, New York: Henry Holt and Company, 1998.

of the fallacies of political realism, the limits to the pursuit of realist notions of glory and power, and the role that place-based imagination has played in the politics of globalism. Since they question the politics of appropriation of scarce resources in state-consolidation, of borders, of accords (which Samir Das in this volume terms as 'nobody's communiqué'), the politics of the fictive ethnic cores that form the heart of the modern nation-states, and also since they raise the question of the fundamental patriarchal orientation of conflict management studies, the essays in this volume may be said to belong to this genre of revisionist studies.

The similarity of these writings with the emerging genre of revisionist studies I am speaking of herelies also in the fact that both are of a diffused disciplinary nature. John Rawls' argument regarding common laws of peoples, Charles Taylor's argument about combining patriotism with democracy, the meeting points in the liberal-communitarian debate, the recent resurrection of the notions of just and unjust wars by Michael Walzer, and above all Jurgen Habermas' plea for a constitutional republicanism—all combine political analysis with ethics, pragmatism with principles, and try to work round the issues that have proved in recent times the collapsing grounds of realism and neo-realism or alternatively of what many have thought of as 'utopia'. A rejection of the ways that marked international studies from the fifties to the eighties, the illustrious names which included men (noticeably very few women liked the approaches) like Hans Morganthau, Kenneth Waltz, and Zbigniew Brzezinski, and most singularly marked by the *Journal of Conflict Resolution*, is a common feature in these revisionist studies. The rejection has been possible only because the revisionist attempt has been launched from various angles—anthropological insights into ways of conflict resolution, ways of authority, to text-studies, hermeneutics, and studies of ethics and justice. A new genre of humanitarian law has also emerged questioning many of the received juridical wisdoms. The plan for this volume also emanates from such a diffused disciplinarian perspective. Probably peace studies cannot progress in any other way.

Yet there is a difference to be noted. Most of the revisionist works I have alluded to here are based on a *desire* to face the reality of attrition and war with morality, and spurred on by such *desire*, engage in construction of new ethical attitudes. The morphology of this new desire is unfortunately marked by an aversion to dissect the ways of contemporary power. Therefore the new ethic does not care to find out how principles of care, accommodation and understanding shape in history to become a counter-power to the established authorities intent on waging wars as a means of settling conflicts and continuing domination. The present volume takes off from the need to understand the historical grounding of the ethical orientation of peace. Therefore, unlike the bulk of the revisionist studies, this volume critically looks at the ways of power, the discourse of rights, traditional methods of conflict management, patriarchy in the discourse of international studies, the pattern of peace accords, the rise of regionalism as a site of conflict resolution, and several other related issues. The purpose is to combine criticism with new historical insights, or to inform criticism with new historical insights.

Conventional wisdom derived from Weberian insights has told us that with development, modernization and greater social communication there will be a reduction of conflicts owing to a lessening of differences. The contrary is taking place. Development is leading to underdevelopment elsewhere, both within a country and across the national political spaces. Modernization is generating new and more acute differences. New lords and new pariahs are appearing. Transition to a global(ized) society is proving to be as problematic as the transition from feudal economies to modern market economies. Violent patriarchal and neopatriarchal convulsions mark the peasant question today. The social structure of accumulation appears to be as imponderable an obstruction as the technical mode of accumulation. What the classical development theorists ignored was the factor of institutional dynamics of accumulation. We are faced with three traps—the Malthusian trap, the technology trap, and the ecological trap. And the severity of these three is compounded by the dynamic of accumulation that is based on an illusion that by keeping huge sections of the population at subsistence levels (the level itself is revised from time to time) accumulation can continue on the basis of an institutional management of popu-

Introduction | 15

lation, technology and environment.[3] If politics today therefore appears grotesque in form, the blame does not lie with the viewer. Avoiding the traps is like the exercise of managing a very grotesque dress whose one leg and one hand are long. While walking I may have to lean on one side so that the pant should be short on one leg. And to avoid tumbling into pit that can stare at me at any moment my shirt should have one hand short so that I can properly hold a branch. This is not an ill-imagined joke. While describing the travails of peace politics in her memoir, *This Side of Peace* (1996), the well-known peace activist Hanan Ashrawi mentions this popular Palestinian joke about the agonies of Palestinian life and predilections.[4] The internal faultlines generate ethnocracies, hate politics, industrial wars, recolonization, neo-patriarchal convulsions, and mass violence. The modern form of global and nation-state power despairs to rest comfortably on the dynamics of accumulation, as the social structure of accumulation gives it sleepless nights. A critique of the ways of power will have to be therefore historically informed. At the same time it will have to look out for signs of practices of accommodation, tolerance and democracy that are also generated from the faultlines in the power structure. Such a critical perspective will help us to understand that value is generated as the moral residue of practices and in turn can become the technology of a new being appropriate to a culture of friendship, justice, and understanding.

Few would deny the central issue of peace in our time when, as I have said, the faultlines in the current structure of global politics and economics makes peace a central pre-occupation of our leaders, planners and managers, but most of all the publics'. Yet, as we discovered in the dialogue that led to this book, peace studies lag behind developments in the world outside academic portals. The long history of peaceful action and thought has

[3] On this in the perspective of emerging conflicts, Ivan Ivekovic, 'Contemporary Ethnic Conflicts in a Comparative Perspective' in Ursula Oswald-Spring (ed.), *Peace Studies from a Global Perspective*, Delhi: Madhyam Books, 1999, pp. 186–251.

[4] Hanan Ashrawi, *This Side of Peace*, New York: Simon & Schuster, 1995, pp. 86–7.

scarcely been explored, and what is called the history of ideas and thought, pacifism and the ethics of accommodation have occupied a secondary place in a gallery where the most prized seat has always gone to bellicose thoughts and ideas. Themes of deterrence (nuclear and conventional) and collective and cooperative security have a psychological saliency that is at best explained by the long history that precedes our being today. As suggested earlier, in the face of such psychological saliency, only *desire, concern and care* seem to be the assuring and redeeming features that can generate the momentum for peace studies to transcend first, its official boundaries set by state practices of conflict and conflict management, and second the received difference between peace research and peace activism.

In the first case, the boundaries are set by a conceptual foundation that looks at peace as an absence of war; the most liberal example of such an approach is Kenneth Boulding's *Stable Peace*,[5] though he was gracious enough to admit the limits of his approach. Therefore such peace studies cannot explore what Galtung calls 'structural violence', and hence cannot suggest strategies either. In the second case, the difference is not surprising, for the difference is found in any human pursuit where academic and philosophical distinctions have a tendency to be disciplined at the cost of a study of practices that can provide clues to epistemic breaks and continuities in human pursuits. In this sense, peace studies originate not only from desire, concern and care, but also from a critical perspective that interrogates all ideas and actions that have sided with power, domination, discipline and authority.

As the essays in this volume show, peace studies are never peaceful, they are inherently volatile. They refuse to be confined to analysing wars, to the international scene only, or to issues of security. They quarrel with all perceptions that uncritically accept the power structures and assume symmetry between the powerful and the weak. Therefore peace studies are based on three principles. One, they are informed by an awareness of human rights and justice. Two, they are concerned with effect-

---

[5] Kenneth Boulding, *Stable Peace*, Austin: University of Texas Press, 1978.

ing changes in perceptions. Three, they are intended to enlarge awareness of social reality where strength is employed to maintain or enhance power at the expense of the weak.[6]

This is an immense task, which no single volume of writings on peace can exhaust. In basing this volume on essays of a differential nature, method, perspective and strain, we have attempted to convey the idea that peace studies cannot be monolithic. The only common refrain here is that these are meant as studies of practices of conflicts and accommodation which only can give us new insights into limits of realism; and by suggesting ways of becoming sensitive to reality, more than what realism can ever hope to convey, such studies of practices can offer us a way out of the binary of realism and ethicality. For, after all, morals are as real as eating food, grabbing wealth or hurting others in human life.

[6] For a concise discussion on the academic study of peace, James O'Connell and Adam Curle, *Peace Work to Do—The Academic Study of Peace*, Warwickshire: Berg Publishers, 1985.

I. CONCEPTS

Value of Peace, Validating Peace

Ranabir Samaddar

THE RATIONAL ARGUMENT

The cause of war, Thomas Hobbes had reminded us, was 'quarrel', and quarrel, in his view had three origins. Quarrel was first; and foremost; a result of competition or pursuit of gain; second, diffidence or a desire for safety; third, glory or a desire for recognition. Quarrel thus broadly signified *war of every man against every man*. Self-instinct for survival leads to the quest for power. Mankind is therefore perpetually compelled to seek power because it has to go to war for self-preservation. Honour, dignity, science, technology of control, peace, are all to be understood as expressions of power. The phenomenon of power is thus basic to humankind's experience of war and peace. The 'fear of death' leads man to strife, war, survival and to making compacts for peace.[1]

But if the instinct of self-preservation leads to war, alternatively to peace, how can mankind be sure that peace may be durable, for man by *nature* has to seek power, and therefore may relapse into war? We may have three solutions to this conundrum. First, the very aspects of human nature that cause war can be pressed in the service of peace, and this is what Hobbes seemed to have had in mind. Second, human nature can be changed, at least partly. We are reminded of Plato's *Dialogues* in this context. One can also remember in this context Marx, though

[1] Thomas Hobbes, *Leviathan*, ed. C.B. Macpherson, Harmondsworth: Penguin Books, 1972, Chap. 13.

in reference to any such possibility, he never spoke of human nature in the abstract. Human nature depended on the relations that man entered into, and the change in human nature depended greatly on the changes the structure of relations underwent. Third, as the *Federalist Papers* conveyed, a strong sense of rights and constitution can put the concerns of society above individual concerns, and thus can put a stay on war. War and peace are thus interchangeable. They defy solutions. They can be prevented, but as concepts relating to assumptions about power, they persist. Only the 'fear of death' keeps war at bay. Madison, who had said, 'ambition must be made to counteract ambition', went further by defining war as being of two types: one flowing from the will of government, and the other from that of society. In the former case, by changing the structure of government, war could be prevented. In the latter case while war could not be prevented, those who declared war would have to a submit to a law that those who were involved in war must pay for it.[2] Thus, fear, desire, reform, and cost and compensation principles are the elements that build peace that may any time slide into war. It in this unavoidable quandary, political philosophy tells, us that war and peace reside. We have no moral propositions here to discuss and decide. This is a world of the rational abounding with assumptions of power, fear and desire.

Unfortunately, about this rationality, or rather about its imperfection there hangs a tale. The point is, if war and peace are interchangeable, then why is it that only peace can be visualized as *absence of war*? Why cannot war be visualized as absence of peace? If peace is only in the mirror of war, shall we say then that war is the natural condition, and peace is what authority imposes? From Hobbes to the current arguments of *Pax Americana*, this seems the suggestion, though there is no answer to the inquiry as to why conflict, that natural product of power, fear and desire, should *naturally* lead to war and not adjustment, negotiation and understanding. The imperfection of interchangeability thus raises the basic question: must peace be seen in

---

[2] James Madison, 'Universal Peace' in M. Meyers (ed.), *Sources of the Political Thought of James Madison*, Hanover: Brandeis University Press, 1981, pp. 192–3.

the light of war?[3] Are these two concepts at all connected? Can there be a positive definition of peace that does not link to war for conceptualization? Revolt and rebellion have legitimacy in society because they override the binary. Even when ushering war they become widely acknowledged as a pathway to reconciliation and peace. The rational line of argument would however put it as the 'vigorous way to peace', in much the same way Hegel had spoken of the 'ethical health of the people' corrupted by 'prolonged calm', 'corruption in nations ... the product of prolonged peace' (Section 324, *Philosophy of Right*). This was like Immanuel Kant saying that long peace brought about a predominant commercial spirit and along with that 'low selfishness, cowardice, effeminacy'.

Since the rational argument has only made peace an ancillary of war, it is understandable why the thinking on peace whenever it appeared in its 'original form' had taken the line of *beauty, happiness, and goodness*. Religious philosophy particularly in its many forms has never held *reason* as a positive attribute. It is the neutral faculty that may serve wicked wills. Therefore the theme of peace is lodged in a 'longing', a 'desire' for the good, the beautiful. Saint Augustine had predicted that 'there will be a peace so good that no peace could be better, a peace so great that a greater would be impossible'. This phenomenology of the desire for peace subsumes within it the practice of war also.

Notice that there can be life without pain, but no pain without some kind of life. In the same way, there can be peace without any kind of war, but no war that does not suppose some kind of peace. This does not mean that war as war involves peace. But war, insofar as those who wage it or have it waged upon them are beings with organic natures, involves peace—for the simple reason that to be organic means to be ordered, and therefore, to be in some sense, at peace.[4]

---

[3] Once again we can look to Hobbes for the most apt definition, '... there is no such thing as perpetuall Tranquillity of mind, while we live here, because Life it selfe is but Motion, and can never be without Desire, nor without Feare, no more than without Sense'. *Leviathan*, Chap. 6.

[4] Cited by Peter Henrici in 'Two Types of Philosophical Approach to the Problem of War and Peace' in Peter Caws (ed.), *The Causes of Quarrel*, Boston: Beacon Press, 1989, p. 156.

But appeal to nature does not end with order. The immanent goodness is also crucial. We are told that 'anyone who grieves over the loss of peace to his nature loves itself, (because) . . . there can be no nature completely devoid of good'. 'If there were no good left, there would be no one to lament the good that has been lost.'[5]

So far, so good, but how does man feel happy? What is there in happiness that creates this longing for peace, a pacifist disposition, an inclination not to hurt, to understand, to appreciate, to approach quarrel with mediation? If appeals to immanent goodness have to be supplemented with logic that we have abandoned, we cannot be sure that peace will be inherent to society. This is admittedly a closed circle, from which we have to try to break out.

The closed circle is obvious when we see that commentators like Kenneth Boulding, though not always sympathetic to the rationalist-realist argument, are forced to concentrate on the dynamic nature of peace, and therefore emphasize that peace is a state of condition in which war is absent.[6] Given the fact that contradiction and conflict are not optional modes of social existence, the activity of peace invariably goes back to the issue of happiness. That implies *living how*, the happiness of having a vision, and therefore a capacity to exchange, interact, align, ally, befriend, in short to understand the difference. In an age of nuclear menace, fierce civil wars, massive migration, destitution, and a resurgence of statism, *living how* is a crucial lead to the inquiry of peace. In fact, the severity of war today has de-linked peace from war. Even the war-peace copula, which goes by the name of *security*, has been shattered to pieces. The psychology of conflict which is what security is all about has failed to re-anchor peace to security. Peace has become a maximalist concept, refusing to accept a minimalist version that stops with the master-idea of security. If indeed we are to offer a psychological explanation of peace, we have to go beyond Saint Augustine, and also beyond the modern exponents of the theory of security.

---

[5] Ibid.
[8] Kenneth Boulding, *Stable Peace*, Austin: University of Texas Press, 1978.

The Security Argument

Yet it will be worth our while to see how the peace argument fares when it is perched on the security tree. It begins with realist assumptions and then goes into a fierce psychological tailspin. To say the least, the results are intriguing. The realist argument will predictably say that to have peace is to have workable peace; for peace to be workable, it has to be sited in security considerations. Security implies security of one's body, body of the nation/state, and in a milieu of mutually accomplished total destruction, security of the body of the international. I leave aside for the time the possible objection to defining the *inter-national*—what this includes and excludes. But we can at least agree that security implies threats to security, therefore perceptions of threats to security. Perception is a matter of psychology, and so the security argument pitches the issue of peace on the ground of mutual invasion of *peace of mind*. After the twist, then, we find the peace argument taking a bizarre form. We are told that peace is achievable only when we do not have peace of mind.

The argument of *security as peace* is premised on conflicts and it is true that conflict studies in the form of conflict-management and conflict-resolution studies have contributed to security studies that are assumed to be peace studies as well. One of the notable phenomena in peace studies has been the rapid development of conflict resolution studies.[7] The theory, practice and skills of conflict resolution have taken off from behavioural and anthropological studies, system building programmes in the wake of managerial development in the field of arbitration, mediation, adjudication, and the practice of evaluation research. Starting as a managerial tool in the field of social conflicts, it became a matter of academic pursuit. Conflict-resolution programmes based in social and behavioural sciences and sometimes in the liberal arts get spread in the form of seminars, workshops, collaborative research, and foundation activities. Teaching conflict resolution has transformed an amorphous practice into a discipline. Curriculum, simulation, instrumental dissemination, and research combined into making a community

---

[7] On this Paul Wehr, *Conflict Regulation*, Boulder, Colorado: Westview Press, 1979.

of practitioners who became a part of the community of strategic analysts, security specialists, and conflict moderators. Conflict resolution could not keep itself distinct from conflict management and conflict moderation. The liberal arts and sociological dimensions of the theory and skills of conflict resolution were to be subsumed in the behaviouralism of statecraft. This is of course not to deny that the conflict resolution approach in many cases has led to the growth of peace studies. Experiences in community living, the academic anchorage to themes of social justice, and the emphasis on the training of mediation techniques have developed a field where peace has become an important element. But, at best this has given academic recognition to peace studies in the times of the Cold War and the subsequent years of the Washington consensus, and at worst it has become an appendage of conflict studies that in its turn had grown as an appendage of Cold War studies. In the development of disciplines, power, after all, has exercised a tremendous role.

The result is that even when peace studies, through the route of conflict resolution and conflict moderation studies, have been attentive to security concerns, interacted with strategic studies, and have attempted to engage the security lobbies in a dialogue —dialogue between peace and security—the result has not been encouraging. The security studies' lobby looks at peace studies academics and practitioners as upstarts or gatecrashers, men (these days some women) with a soft belly, too utopian, too amorphous, too impractical. More so because security specialists now occupy important positions inside the portals of power, they have developed an entrenched interested in prioritizing security among other concerns and this in the way they define security. Security studies is less a matter of study as an academic vocation, more a matter of getting a job. But this is a special job, one of being hired as consultant, writing reports and joining disarmament and security conferences, acting as negotiator in arms control dialogue, and finally becoming truly multinational, because the more one is a specialist in security matters, the more one becomes global. In this hierarchy of disciplines and fields where the leitmotif is power/knowledge, peace studies is the victim both as knowledge and as a depository of power. It is important therefore to know at least briefly the nature of security criticisms against peace studies. This will show whether the security route to peace studies is viable or not.

George Quester in an essay 'International-Security Criticisms of Peace Research' neatly outlines these criticisms. Peace researchers are too optimistic and unrealistic. They tend to assume that good things must go together. They think that domestic and international improvements are always linked, and that disarmament serves all the purposes of humankind. They redefine peace to include justice, and social improvement, and whatever other causes they favour. The result is that they remain confused about which particular problem is to be solved at a particular time. And all these they do or think because they hold that others, especially the security-specialists, do not understand the desirability of peace.[8] Quester has written,

> The assumption that domestic reform will lead to international peace or that one kind of international improvement will always support another kind of international improvement has emphatically not been endorsed by traditional European analysts of power politics. . . . When asked how they would choose between preventing nuclear war and preventing conventional war, many people who style themselves peace researchers will thus simply refuse to comment, regarding it as a moral betrayal even to acknowledge that such a choice might ever have to be made, arguing that there must somehow be a solution that would never give up on either agenda. Similarly, if asked to choose between eliminating poverty and eliminating war, the same researchers will again run away from the question, as if it were some kind of trap.[9]

Thus peace is security and must not be related to the ending of poverty, or any 'domestic' reform. By the same token, nuclear security is peace, conventional disarmament is a false pursuit. Yet this is not all.

[8] George H. Quester, 'International-Security Criticisms of Peace Research' in George A. Lopez (ed.), *Peace Studies—Past and Future*, special number of *The Annals of the American Academy of Political and Social Science*, vol. 504, July 1989, pp. 98–105.
[9] Ibid., pp. 99–100.

The peace studies approach seems to be on the verge of blaming our problems on an insufficient aversion to war among government officials and the establishment, and it extends this accusation to the people who work on national security, international security, or arms control.... The international-security community would normally counter that the disagreement is not about values or awareness or paradigms but about analysis.... For example, would the total nuclear disarmament of the Soviet Union and the United Sates make it less likely that a Qaddafi would seek nuclear weapons of his own, or would make it more likely? And what are we then to do about vertical and horizontal nuclear proliferation if there is no preordained linkage that all of these threats to peace recede in the same move?[10]

And then the final complaint that peace studies do not give enough importance to self-interest. Self-interest makes the 'fashionable' distinction between 'negative' peace and 'positive' peace meaningless. To attempt to make such a distinction

... is to use these words of our English language in a manner that substantially underrates the human priority of eliminating warfare, whatever its causes and whatever the remedy.... The crucial accomplishment in the advancement of arms-control reasoning comes with the open acknowledgement that now we must always care about the self-interest and motivations of our adversary.[11]

The comments are familiar. The underlying assumptions are worth noting in the context of this essay. In order to have peace we need to have a demon from whom we need (security and thus) peace. So we must have nuclear weapons, 'because Qaddafis may have them'. But the demonization is not enough as a peace strategy. It is necessary to believe in the pacific nature of state, officialdom, military officials, arms-control experts, and security specialists. Finally, peace is a phenomenon that is not rooted in any process, 'causes', and 'remedy'. In the security argument we have thus a return to psychology—we need justification for war in order to justify peace. In this play of psychology, to which all behaviouralism relapses, the realists are the most surreal. They inhabit the dual world of reality and fantasy. In fact, the real can appear real only by being unreal.

[10] Ibid., p. 102.
[11] Ibid., pp. 104–5.

The Disciplinarian Argument

The disciplinarian argument is about disciplining peace with the argument of security. The security *mantra* is however only one way of disciplining peace. What is significant is that peace, as an educational pursuit, has to be disciplined. We have before us the fate of many such pursuits in the past and recent past when pursuits were suitably disciplined. Women's studies is one example, and the formalization of a pursuit while lending solidity to human inquiry resulted in the impoverishment of the inner core.[12] Yet a mere acknowledgement of this is not enough. It is important to understand the need to discipline peace.

The uniqueness of peace studies at the present moment is that the pursuit has originated from a conjuncture of circumstances. Disciplining means cutting out traces, links, silencing the multiple, sometimes discordant and cacophonous, voices that arise from the circumstance of conjuncture in which peace studies as a vocation is sited. That is how disciplines originate, the effervescent field of differential traces is cemented into a solid structure of knowledge and an intellectual tool of power.

Peace studies is peace research, peace education, and peace action together. It is at a minimum level simply stopping violence, and particularly war, and at a positive level overcoming social injustice. Its locomotive had been earlier the traditional knowledge of society and increasingly now the newer ideas of justice, and newer movements for justice. Finally, peace studies depend on the knowledge produced from the local (sometimes called the grassroots) movements. As a concept it relies on global frameworks also. Peace vocation is thus at, what Chadwick Alger calls, the 'four crossroads'.[13] Can one merely study peace? Can one rest content with a prevention of war? Or, say, can one be satisfied with local knowledge while working for peace? These questions are invitations to take the multiplex character of peace studies with more seriousness.

[12] On the theme of emergence of disciplines, see Partha Chatterjee (ed.), *Texts of Power—Emergence of Disciplines in Bengal*, Minnesota: University of Minnesota Press, 1996, and Calcutta: Stree Pub., 1996.

[13] Chadwick F. Alger, 'Peace Studies at the Crossroads: Where Else?', *Annals*, op.cit., pp. 117–27.

If technologies of rule and violence are getting more and more complex, peace actions need a more secure foundation in studies and peace studies needs more researches into these technologies. To Johan Galtung, peace research is crucial, because:

> The danger is not that researchers also are interested in education and action. They should be, and thereby get some important feedback from the real world, from people who challenge the 'findings' and from a complicated reality that refuses to respond to actions in the way suggested by the research. Much more dangerous than this would be those who engage in education and action without any research basis and for that reason have a tendency to repeat their cherished ideas whether those of the establishment or the antiestablishment, trying to shape the world according to their dogmas.[14]

The problematic is then clear. Can a peace programme be deepened with research without being turned into another sterile pursuit? The skills of community organizers, social scientists, mediators, lawyers, pedagogues, teachers, and elders of society, are needed for enriching peace education. But peace produces its own practitioners and they pose a problem for peace, for peace is essentially a reflection of the conjuncture of circumstances and roads. It is therefore essentially an experiential act, and act of challenging values, a moral act.

The political agenda of turning peace into a fund-driven, curricula-based, university-incorporated vocation is *naturally* against such a moral act, though ironically it is the moral act that sets off the political agenda. In such institutionalization we have the seeds of a merger of peace studies and conflict-based programmes. In the conflict scenario, an endemic feature is not *conflict*, only the cataclysmic one is, and therefore peace defined as an end of a conflict cannot be concerned with endemic matters. Yet there is an irony also in this way of conceptualizing peace. For, in most of the conflict programmes, behaviouralism holds sway. Violence is a matter of human behaviour, of pathology, in other words endemic. It has to be cured. The stress is on non-violent behaviour, a non-violent resolution or moderation

---

[14] Johan Galtung, 'Twenty-five Years of Peace Research—Ten Challenges and Some Responses', *Journal of Peace Research*, 2 (2), 1985, p. 1985.

of conflict. In such lore of non-violence, justice is an outsider. In some very well intentioned academic programmes on peace, themes of non-violence, human nature, feminist education, pathological cure, and community restructuring, form the rainbow of peace. Birgit Brock-Utne in *Educating for Peace: A Feminist Perspective* shows how in the educational practices, aggression, competition and oppression of women are fostered in boys, and female-male differences make this world so violence-prone.[15] Thus even though in this case peace studies speak of *peace with justice*, peace is taken to be fundamentally *pacific behaviour*. The themes of *security as the core of peace* and of *right behaviour as the core of peace* are thus two sides of the same problematic of defining peace in an institutional format.

The problem is made acute when the behavioural is supplemented with the sociological. Thus we need peace because there is too much 'gruesome interracial and interethnic bloodshed'. As Stanley Tambiah (1997) says, 'Something has gone awry in center-periphery relations', there is 'collective violence among people who are not aliens but enemies intimately known'.

Ethnic conflict is a major reality of our time... thus upheavals... have become climactic in recent years, among them (are) the Sinhala-Tamil war in Sri Lanka, the Sikh-Hindu and Muslim-Hindu confrontations in Kashmir... the Chakma-Muslim turmoil in Bangladesh.... Most of these conflicts have involved violence, homicide, arson, and destruction of property.... The classic definition of the state as the authority invested with monopoly of force has become a sick joke.

We are told that easy access to technology of warfare and international fraternization among resistance groups, who have little in common save their resistance to the status quo in their own countries and who exchange knowledge of warfare, has led to increased violence.[16] In this scenario the pathological problem is

[15] Birgit Brock-Utne, *Educating for Peace—A Feminist Perspective* (New York: Pergamon Press, 1985), pp. 71–6. In this context, the writings of Gene Sharp are significant in their emphasis on non-violent behaviour, for example, *The Politics of Nonviolent Action*, Boston: Porter Sargent, 1973.
[16] These citations are from Stanley J. Tambiah, *Leveling Crowds—Ethnonationalist Conflicts and Collective Violence in South Asia*, Delhi: Vistaar Publications, 1997, pp. 3–6.

shown as acute with the addition of sociological explanations. Thus in this landscape violence is civil. The state does not feature, and even if it does so it does it in a minor way. In the rose tinted word processor every conflict is ethnic. Thus there is a 'Chakma-Muslim' problem in the Chittagong Hill Tracts in Bangladesh, similarly a 'Hindu-Muslim' problem in Kashmir. The nation-state or statism is not the prime root of violence, but ethnicity is. The road to peace is through a negation of particularisms, the state may now rest in comfort while peacemakers go about extinguishing fires of ethnicity.

The trap of routinization, banalization and formalization in this way springs on the theme of peace. The concern about universal destruction in the nuclear age had propelled the desire for peace; at the same time it has made this desire narrow, focused, and oblivious to the perennial social realities leading to conflicts and war. In the face of such a secular law and of growth of disciplines driven by exigencies of power, the idea is therefore of a 'powerful peacemaking',[17] that comes from a concept of experiential education. Experiences of community living, democratic decision-making, handling of ethical issues and organized protest against injustices are reconciled with social analysis, technical reasoning, and historical research. The nature of peace makes peace a living education.

Experiential education is thus not about the theme only, it is also about the way. 'There is no way to peace, peace is the way.' Peace studies is thus a matter of moral imagination, or more appropriately a matter of working against the themes of discipline and power with the imaginative tools of morality. Non-violence can be thus only one aspect of this experience; other important aspects are engagement, dialogue, and non-compliance with the rules of domination, a subaltern protest driven by the spirit of a collectivity. The political agenda of disciplining peace studies is actually about disciplining peace itself. As against this then experience becomes the basis of a counter-politics, a counter-culture around peace.

---

[17] George Lakey, *Powerful Peacemaking—A Strategy for a Living Revolution*, Philadelphia: New Society, 1987.

The Democratic Argument

The peace question, therefore gets pushed back to the issues of power, injustice, structural violence and war. If it was the threat of an impending nuclear catastrophe that raised the desire for peace, the growing understanding of human rights was also a factor. Awareness of a whole range of civil rights, rights pertaining to minorities, language, education, and work have either forced states to be more (or at least to some extent) participatory, or have broken the peace in non-participatory states. The social peace imposed by regimes in Turkey, South Korea, Singapore, Brazil, Nigeria, has increasingly faced protest with the growing awareness of rights. Today's peace question is thus unique in the history of peace. It builds not on social peace, but on contesting that peace.

The historicity of peace is thus to be noted. First, in the post-war era, international institutions have grown up that have provided some legal clarity to the notion of peace. Second, even those definitions are becoming antiquated in the context of the discourse of new rights. Redefining peace is thus becoming an imperative. Third, the relation of peace to democracy is becoming complex as the conduct of liberal democracy in matters of war and peace becomes more and more non-ideological and purely a matter of convenience. Fourth, causes and phenomena hitherto considered 'external' and 'internal', distinct from each other, are collapsing into one zone of unrest whose singular feature is the breakdown of states. Fifth, restoration of state and restoration of peace have become a single enterprise wherein peace building and state building have become the two inter-linked aspects of peace keeping. And, finally, all these take place in a historical situation that begins with the close of the Second World War; and then passing through the Cold War reaches the *Washington consensus* when the world is supposed to have reached the end of a conflict-ridden history and arrived at a consensus on the desirability and universal validity of market democracy. The historically irreducible nature of today's peace question thus rests in its uncomfortable union with democracy. It is important therefore to discuss some of these aspects in some details.

International Institutional Definition of Peace

The preamble of the Universal Declaration of Human Rights (1948) in the first paragraph says, 'Recognition of the inherent dignity and of the inalienable rights of all members of the human family is the foundation of freedom, justice and peace in the world'. And peace (and also freedom and justice) can be ensured when, the declaration says in the third paragraph, 'human rights' are 'protected by the rule of law', and in the fourth paragraph, there is development of 'friendly relations between nations'. Art. 3 says, 'Everyone has the right to life, liberty and security of person'. Art. 28 says, 'Everyone is entitled to a social and international order in which the rights and freedoms set forth in this Declaration can be fully realized'. And Art. 30 proclaims that 'Nothing in this Declaration may be interpreted as implying for any State, group or person any right to engage in any activity or to perform any act aimed at the destruction of any of the rights and freedoms set forth herein'. Peace as the space to enjoy the rights is thus a universal claim. The General Assembly in a resolution on 'Right of Peoples to Peace' adopted on 12 November 1984, declared, 'The peoples of our planet have a sacred right to peace'. Further, 'the preservation of the right of peoples to peace and the promotion of its implementation constitute a fundamental obligation of each State'. If this resolution is read with the injunction in the same resolution (A/Res/39/11) on the states to behave peacefully in resolving conflicts, the right to peace becomes clearer in import.

Yet in terms of the historical development of the notion of rights, peace defined as a right (to a space) to enjoy human development poses few problems. Proceeding from the Lockean notion of natural rights, rights have come to occupy primarily a juridical-political meaning, especially in the last two centuries. Yet we retain the notion of inherent rights and inherent justice. Even customary rights retain meaning though in a very reduced way. In such situation the notion of peace as right is perched precariously on the branch of justice and custom. If peace as right is justifiable legally, then the instruments of compulsion are not yet developed. The legal obligation of states is yet confined to rhetoric. The Helsinki Accord of 1975 is not a treaty law; respective countries have not ratified the specific obligations of states under it or under the Assembly resolution. The international law of security speaks of *jus ad bellum* that implies anticipatory self-defence, collective self-defence, reprisal as defence, and intervention. We have thus a quaint situation here. The first generation of rights was badly executed; the expectations that might have been fulfilled by a rigorous application of these, led to the development of the second generation of rights. Now this too remaining half-executed, the expectations have generated the need for another generation of rights. The category of third generation of rights to which the right to peace belongs thus hangs suspended between the traditional desire for end to *hostilities* that destroyed towns and villages, and affected human life, the new trend towards valorizing rights with a comprehensive notion of good life, and an accompanying low level of applicability of rights. Non-juridically conceptualized right indicates a democratic desire for a higher quality of life, and it also shows how much the later generations of rights depend on the applicability of the preceding ones. Thus peace as a comprehensive concept of disarmament, social justice, and democracy spans all the generations, and it seems that like all rights this one too depends on how much the history of popular struggles would make of it.[18]

Older Definitions and New Discourses

Indeed, one reason why peace appears as belonging to a new generation of rights is the inadequacy of some of the themes belonging to the concept of peace. The universal instruments of human rights and peace had to share place with regional instruments. Yet as democracy deepens, even this accommodation seems inadequate. We can take two cases of inadequacy of the available instruments of human rights—rights of the refugees and minorities.

The Convention of 1951 relating to the status of refugees

[18] I do not agree with David P. Forsythe who presents some compelling discussions on *Human Rights and Peace*, Lincoln: University of Nebraska Press, 1993, for ignoring that 'right' itself is a matter of historicity.

recognized the obligations of the contracting states to grant protection and set standards for treatment of refugees in the asylum states. It also established the principle of *non-refoulement* according to which persons may not be returned against their will to a territory where they may be persecuted. The institutional governance of the convention was assigned to the UNHCR (United Nations High Commissioner for Refugees) that was to encourage governments to subscribe to the convention, and make regional conventions also. It was to promote the grant of asylum to refugees. It was to secure due process of law in examining refugee applications and enforce international standards in the enforcement of legal status. And the UNHCR was to secure durable solutions also through voluntary repatriation or eventual grant of nationality of the country of residence. The protocol of 1967 enlarged the scope of the convention. The functions of the UNHCR increased. A separate category of internally displaced persons was recognized. The UN human rights machinery seemed to be paying greater attention to the condition of the refugees. The convention also led to regional initiatives. The Council of Europe recognized in 1994 that the refugee question called for a regional approach. Methods such as information-sharing, parliamentary attention, defining acceptable humanitarian standards for acceptance of refugees emerged as parts of a regional framework of refugee protection in Europe. The OAU (Organization of African Unity) convention of 1969 broadened the scope of definition of a refugee. The 1984 Cartagena Declaration of the Organization of American States took note of 'generalized violence' which may produce refugees. It seemed that the traditional arrangement was working well.

Yet, and as these developments in fact indicate, the system has virtually collapsed in the face of the unprecedented population flow in the nineties. The massive refugee flow, forced repatriation, the decline of liberal asylum practices, the creation of a *non-entrée regime* indicating the existence of a 'fortress Europe', and the security mentality overwhelming the refugee care regime have made the vision of 1951 inadequate for negotiating the population flow in the world of today. In any case the Convention of 1951 was intended for Europe, and did not consider the millions that were fleeing from homes in the wake of de-colonization, partition, and the emergence of new states. It is still unable to administer quick and proper care of the millions fleeing from ethnic violence and state terror. It is meaningless in the face of the structural adjustment policies that produce what the historian of indentured labour Hugh Tinker calls 'new slavery'. The phenomena of forced migrants, unwanted migrants and migrants of the underworld have made the demand for a more humane protection regime imperative.[19]

The situation as regards the international law on the minorities is similar. Though the protection of ethnic, religious, and linguistic groups has been one of the oldest concerns of international law on human rights, the task of ensuring minority rights has become only more and more complex. How does one define a minority? At least three definitions are before us, each reflecting a different facet of reality. Art. 27 of the UN Covenant on Civil and Political Rights mentions minorities in terms of rights. The Capotorti definition emphasizes the feature of 'non-dominance'. The Deschemes definition refers to a 'collective will to survive and whose aim is to achieve equality with the majority in fact and in law'.[20] So who is a minority? A group that is simply non-dominant? A group that not only suffers from domination, but also has a will? Or, one that enjoys certain rights? Does it need protection? Or does it self-determine? But self-determination is a right of peoples and not minorities. Several treaties erected the League system, and the UN started building

[19] On the theme of inadequacy of the refugee protection regime, the best is till date.

[20] Special Rapporteur F. Capotorti's definition appears in his *Study on the Rights of Persons Belonging to Ethnic, Religious, and Linguistic Minorities* for the UN Sub-commission on Prevention of Discrimination and Protection of Minorities, UN sales no. E 78, XIV.1; Canadian member of the same UN Sub-commission, Jules Deschenes' definition appears in his *Proposal Concerning a Definition of the Term 'Minority'* submitted to the Sub-commission and adopted by it 1985—UN Doc. E/CN.4/Sub.2/1985/SR.13–16. Reference to the legal texts are from, among others, Jean-Pierre Colombey (ed.), *Collection of International Instruments and Other Legal Texts Concerning Refugees and Displaced Persons*, Geneva: Division of International Protection of the Office of the United Nations High Commisioner for Refugees, 1995.

on that. Treaties on minorities in Poland (Versailles, 1919), Romania (Paris, 1919), Greece (Sevres, 1920), Upper Silesia (Geneva, 1922), Turkey (Laussane, 1923), and many others wrestled with ideas and clauses of cooperation, separation, self-determination, peaceful solution and guarantee. Yet events overtook these efforts in less than twenty years. And though the UN learnt from the preceding failures and made the obligation to protection wider through provisions of non-discrimination, yet minority rights seem to be as unsafe as they were. The provisions of non-discrimination were the institution of a sub-commission on prevention of discrimination and protection of minorities, prohibition of genocide, the covenant on civil and political rights, particularly Art. 27 of the Covenant, and the human rights committee (Arts. 28-45 of the ICCPR). Indeed, the Universal Declaration of Human Rights, the most significant document in the field of human rights, when passed in 1948 was conspicuous by its omission of a 'minorities article'.[21] Obviously the idea was that with universality of rights established, special care was secondary. That was non-discrimination. Wars, extermination of minorities, nationalist majoritarianism, ethnic cleansing, proxy insurgency, and great power backing of ethnic groups as a means of waging the Cold War made the UN system of universality a mockery.

The ghost of nationalism and great power politics is too strong to be exorcised by the discourse of group rights. On the contrary, as the 'cunning of history' would have it, group rights become the new front-paw of great power politics whether in erstwhile Yugoslavia or in Afghanistan. Clearly, conflicts overwhelm the structure of rights and peace. New discourses emerge, new generation of rights surface, only to become the terrain of new contests between democracy and the politics of domination. The new discourses therefore do not signify the arrival of the *final mechanism*, they only indicate that peace is a process, a process that is linked irrevocably and sometimes fatally to the processes of power and democracy.

[21] One of the most informed discussions on the minority issue in international law is by Patrick Thornberry, *International Law and the Rights of Minorities*, Oxford: Clarendon Press, 1991.

The Pacific Conduct of Democracies

We have to stop a bit before we hastily begin to conclude from the above that peace studies are therefore studies in democracy, for we must first address ourselves to the question, are democracies pacific? Democrats from Woodrow Wilson to Bill Jefferson Clinton have reminded us that democrats are peace loving, and therefore a world of democracy is inherently peaceful and safe for the people on earth. Immanuel Kant found a link between rights and peace—a view that had distinct traces of the Lockean attitude. The UN Charter also declares in Art. 55 that human rights are essential for friendly relation among nations. But what happens when democracies commit aggression or invade other countries for 'humanitarian reasons' (Kosovo), to overthrow autocracies (Grenada and Panama), to roll back communism (Nicaragua), or continuously arm themselves with nuclear weapons?

To keep peace, democracies may wage war. If democracies do not fight wars among themselves, they combine to fight war against others. In fact, this is almost a law of democracy that an ideological Calvinism goads democracies to launch wars against others. These wars may be overt, but are more often covert. These covert wars aim at overthrowing democratically elected governments (Mossadegh in Iran, Lumumba in Congo, Arbenz in Guatemala, Allende in Chile), or governments with very strong legitimacy (Castro in Cuba or Ho Chi Minh in North Vietnam). Thus existence of civil and political rights to a considerable extent may not fuction as a barrier to violence. On the contrary, the (alleged or real) absence or relative absence of civil and political rights in a country may become an occasion for other countries to wage war (the five-year war waged in Russia by the allied interventionist army after the Bolshevik revolution). But again, ironically when a democratic government is being overthrown by a fascist coup, and the most gross abuse of human rights is taking place, democracies may choose to remain neutral (e.g. the Anglo-French neutrality in the Spanish civil war). The club of democracies is indeed an elite club.

Therefore, ideology, forms of power, forms of weaponry, techniques of war (like covert operations, development of small arms, intelligence gathering) and the exclusivity/hierarchy of certain rights, are as important as the formal presence of democracy. Democracy as a theme of peace is thus not without problem. To put this succinctly, it means that peace as the signature-theme of democracy problematizes democracy. In an era of human rights rhetoric, do democracies advance the cause of peace? In a milieu where there is a strong hierarchy of rights is there a chance of peace being disturbed due to the hierarchy? Does right to property help peace? Second, what happens when in a context of globalization and Fund-Bank reforms, welfarism that was for long the domestic basis of peace, is eroded? Third, the present context is one of a rupture of relations between political democracy and ethnic politics, which no doubt has become an important cause of strife and violence today. Political democracy does not guarantee tolerance. Participatory rights and tolerance promote peace and in the absence of these two, democracy and civil and political rights may not be an adequate guarantee for peace. Finally, gross inequality destroys the legitimacy of a rule. An illegitimate rule cannot promote the culture of a non-pacific mode of resolution of conflicts. In short, illegitimacy dissuades dialogue.

The process is thus of contest, contesting the politics of exclusivity. But is that not what democracy is all about? As Partha Chatterjee in his book *The Present History of West Bengal* has said, *democracy is the politics of the governed*?

Double Restoration of State and Peace

The task of peace studies thus lands itself in the deep, in the inner region of the problematic of state-formation and particularly the formation of the modern state. Peace as I have tried to suggest in these preliminary remarks is a matter of history, of a process that is linked to the process of power, a matter of politics for justice, equity and plurality. This implies that peace remains inseparable from the problematic of power and authority that has always provoked the struggles for justice and a participatory politics. And here lies the irony of modernity. For, present in the architecture of that desire, known by the word *peace*, and provoked today by the most ruthless demonstration of power and authority ever in the history of mankind, is an important binary element called anarchy/order. Order produces authority, authority produces violence, and violence provokes the desire for peace. But violence breaks down authority also, and the breakdown of the historically admissible form of authority leads to a collapse of the state. This is recognized socially as anarchy, and the desire for peace gets the phantasmagoric form of a desire for lost authority, order, and thus the state. Thus in Afghanistan, Rwanda, Cambodia, Somalia, Lebanon, erstwhile Yugoslavia— in all these countries peace has been sought to be restored by restoring the state. The usual process has been a promulgation of a 'peace constitution' (much like reconstructing post-war Japan), talks, interim power-sharing arrangements, a multilateral peace-keeping army, elections under international supervision, and the *restoration of the state*. The breakdown of the state is a universal phenomenon, so is its restoration. I have termed this elsewhere as 'conditions of globalization and conditions of peace'.[22] Restoration of peace and the restoration of the state have therefore become the twin tasks of liberal democracy today. Together they present the strange spectacle of the politics of the modern.

The fact that the process of peace is now being governed by today's conditions of globalization has one more implication. If technologies of war have become global, so have technologies of peace. Modes of intervention by civil society, the democratic agenda linking up with the peace agenda, regionalization as a path to conflict-resolution, normative issues being articulated as issues of peace—these are *political* techniques of peace inasmuch as the question of war and peace itself has become intensely political, indeed to a degree unseen before. War is a matter of state. The modern state has ensured that peace also becomes a matter of state, its *raison d'être*. And yet, it is this condition of modernity that begins taking the agenda of peace beyond

---

[22] 'Conditions of Globalization and Conditions of Peace' in Ranabir Samaddar (ed.), Space, *Territory and the State* (forthcoming), first delivered as a seminar lecture on Geopolitics, Migration and the State, organized by the Maulana Abul Kalam Azad Institute of Asian Studies, New Delhi, March 1998.

the state by developing and widening the technologies of peace. Constituencies of peace emerge, as tools of peace make such constituencies viable. Peace in short becomes a durable programme, not because men (and women) are peace loving, but relations and technologies make such men a durable feature of society. That is why peace studies is perched on a critique of the condition of the state, of patterns of domination, of global hegemony, and of technologies that make permanent war a feature in today's globalized world. Strategies of peace are therefore based on the 'capillary' condition of peace today.[23]

Embedded Histories of Peace and Contests

In short, peace studies cannot be expected to produce a holy book of peace. Peace is not a settled concept. Being a problematic related to contests in society, peace studies problematizes peace. Peace studies cannot produce a manual of non-violent conduct for men (and women) that then gradually turns men (and women) into non-violent agencies. Peace studies is not a reformatory. Its pedagogic and programmatic aspects are intensely contemporary, historically conditioned. Emanating from contests, peace does not reside outside the reaches of power, an organized power as the state, but in its faultlines, in the contests that this power incessantly produces. Therefore, if we had been suffering from the earlier complaint that we have a history of war, but not of peace, we must turn our attention to the question of that *history*.

We do not have a history of that whose history we cannot anticipate. The anticipated history of peace must therefore lodge itself in the interstices of contests—contest between dialogue and

---

[23] Obviously I borrow the word from Foucault. But my intention here is different. Foucault links the capillary existence of power to the organization of political power and the transformed conditions of sovereignty. My argument has been that conditions of globalization make constituencies and technologies of peace and democracy widespread, distributed across several layers of political and civil society. And, this happens not because the state has almost collapsed and power resides in a capillary mode, but because of the emergence of new technologies of peace; and this, notwithstanding the most centralized existence of power in today's world of *Pax Americana*.

authority, state and sections of society, war and non-violent means, justice and power, and the established history of war and the silences in that received discourse. This anticipated history of peace consists of discrete moments to be recovered synchronically as the democratic moment will require. In its recovery and in its material form, peace is embedded in contests of various kinds. Contesting all values of authority by valorizing dialogue, peace acquires its own value.

The moment of peace is therefore a moment of contest. In one word, a *democratic moment*.

Anthropology of Reconciliation

Pradip Kumar Bose

CONFLICT AND RECONCILIATION

Social science, including anthropology, has uncovered more knowledge about war and conflict than about peace and reconciliation, just as psychology probably has yielded more insights into negative deviance (such as mental illness) than into positive deviance (such as creativity). Unfortunately, studies tend to be focused on wars as units of analysis rather than on periods of peace, and there is a tendency to define peace simply as 'non-war'. Thus peace thinking has had a tendency to become utopian and to be oriented towards the future: it has been speculative and value oriented rather than analytical and empirical. It is conceivable that this might change if research were to be focused more on peace than on war.

Anthropology of reconciliation generally comes as an appendage to the study of conflict and finds its relevance in an understanding of the functions of conflict and its expression. The anthropologist studies conflict as a multidimensional social process that operates in many different contexts and results in variety of consequences. Although theoretical attention to social and cultural conflict is relatively new in anthropology, ethnographers have long been recording instances of conflict occurring under a variety of guises. Such diverse phenomenon as witchcraft practices, feuds, factionalism, warfare, competitive games, contradictory values, and discord between spouses have been viewed as conflict or as the potential means of displacing conflict from one level of social grouping to another.

In each of these instances there are various reconciliation processes in operation governed by the social and cultural matrix of society. Conflict is discord; its opposite is harmony, reconciliation, which for many implies integration. Integration and conflict have often been discussed as opposites, and indeed, conflict has been equated with anomie—deviant, abnormal behaviour which impedes successful integration of society. The absence of conflict and presence of cooperation and coordination are sometimes used as indexes of integration and social stability. Conflict is more readily observable than integration. As a result, much of the anthropological discussion of integration or stability is implicit rather than explicit.

Anthropologists for quite some time never paid much attention to the question of disputes and reconciliation; this field only developed in the last fifty years. It was from that time that anthropologists began to publish detailed records of the course of disputes, from their origin to their attempted settlement and events that followed upon this attempt. However anthropologists of these societies were handicapped by the fact that by the time they were undertaking their fieldwork, colonizing powers had already suppressed indigenous modes of self-help. With the new rules and by establishing systems of organized authority, including their own dominant powers, the colonial power rendered unnecessary full dependence on the reconciliation through public opinion and its cross-linkages towards settlement. Hence the cases on which these anthropologists had to rely were often partial records from the past transmitted by contemporary untrained observers or recollections of disputes by aged informants.

One of the crucial questions that emerged from the very beginning in the study of the reconciliation process among indigenous populations by anthropologists was the meaning of the word 'law'. In any language most words which refer to important social phenomena—as 'law' obviously does—are likely to have several referents and to cover a wide range of meanings. We should therefore expect that the English word 'law', and other related words, will not have a single and precise meaning. If jurisprudence is full of controversy centring on how 'law' should be defined, the terminological disputes are increased when tribal societies with their very different cultures, are investigated. Since our own words for 'law' and related phenomena are already loaded with meaning, students of tribal societies run into difficulties as soon as they try to apply these words to activities of other cultures. Yet, on the other hand, how can we think or write outside our own language? Must anthropologists develop a special technical language, which some may confuse with jargon or should they conclude that it is misleading to try to discuss tribal law in the principal concepts of Western jurisprudence, and instead employ vernacular terms to describe the indigenous systems?

This problem is not specific to anthropology but a general problem in all social science. In general terms 'law' is viewed as social control through the systematic application of the force of politically organized society. However, if 'politically organized' implies the existence of courts, then there are societies without law. Thus Evans-Pritchard had stated that 'in the strict sense of the word, the Nuer have no law'. Yet in another book on the Nuer published in the same year he spoke of Nuer law and of legal relations and he described how people might recognize that justice lay on the other side in a dispute.[1] His pupil Howell followed him here in his *Manual of Nuer Law* (1954), stating that 'on this strict definition, the Nuer had no law....' He adds immediately: '... but it is clear that in a less exact sense they were not lawless',[2] and he states that he therefore uses the term 'law' rather loosely. Such pronouncements give enough indications that the system of dispute settlements that anthropologists encountered defied the standard format available in the West and required a more flexible approach.

The analysis of the reasonings of reconciliation mechanisms involves considering the types of social relations out of which dispute has emerged. Gluckman points out that in some of the

---

[1] E.E. Evans-Pritchard, 'The Nuer of the Southern Sudan' in *African Political Systems*, Oxford: Oxford University Press, 1940, pp. 293–6: contrast *The Nuer*, Oxford: Clarendon Press, 1940, pp. 160–5, 168.

[2] P.P. Howel, *A Manual of Nuer Law*, Oxford: Basil Blackwell, 1954, p. 95.

African tribes, where most transactions take place between closely related persons, usually kinsman or in-laws, disputes in such societies are qualitatively different from those where persons are linked only by contract or tort, as we find in modern societies.[3] In tribal societies where closely related persons are involved, the adjudicator may well try to adjust their dispute so that they should be able to resume their friendly relationship and it is a substantial advantage if all concur in the adjudication. In anthropological literature, those behaviours which proceed from and are indicative of conflict are also viewed as operating to resolve the conflict. If reconciliation is not achieved through routine procedures, the use of a third party to achieve settlement by arbitration, mediation, compromise, or adjudication is also likely. Certain institutional forms of reconciliation such as councils, courts, go-betweens, or 'crossers', perform these functions.

For instance, among the Yurok of California the parties to a dispute each appointed unrelated persons from different communities, who took evidence from them and other available sources conferred among themselves and with the parties and laid down a verdict. On the other hand the role of Ifugao 'go-between' is different. As Barton describes:

> To the end of peaceful settlement he exhausts every art of Ifugao diplomacy. He wheedles, coaxes, flatters, threatens, drives, scolds, insinuates. He beats down the demands of the plaintiff or prosecution, and bolsters up the proposals of the defendants until a point is renched at which the parties may compromise.[4]

He is more of a conciliator than an arbitrator. Among the Nuer a person called 'man of the earth' settles dispute by threatening to curse the disputing parties, and there is no suggestion that he listens to and weighs evidence. In fact he can be best described as a ritual mediator. One can make a grade of authoritativeness among the intermediary, the mediator, the conciliator and the arbitrator, and such a grade is related to the ranges of

---

[3] Max Gluckman, *Politics, Law and Ritual in Tribal Society*, Oxford: Basil Blackwell, 1977, pp. 169–212.

[4] R.F. Barton, *Ifugao Law*, California: University of California Publications, 1919, p. 94.

social pressure which back their actions, ranges of relationships between parties which, in turn, determines the specific procedure that will be effective.

Anthropologists have made significant note of the fact that reconciliation and control of conflict need not be identified with specialized political offices. There are viable, stable societies which lack central government and specialized political roles but which nonetheless have available other means of reconciling and regulating conflict. In such stateless societies a variety of institutions and personnel such as diviner and shaman may function as agents of reconciliation. Among the Dobu, sorcery is a socialized ritual that operates as the medium for a non-violent adjustment of opposing interests. The style of reconciliation derives from a society's structural principles of human association.

Among the Nuer of Southern Sudan, as Evans-Pritchard has shown in his classic study, the political institution of the feud is regulated through the mechanism known as the 'leopard-skin chief'.[5] The person is one of those specialists who are concerned, in a ritual capacity, with various departments of Nuer social life and nature and specially with the reconciliation process. The chief settles the conflict in terms of a complex process of sanctions, compensation and sacrifices for cleansing and atonement. If one gets the impression that the chief judges the case and compels the acceptance of his decision to the feuding parties then nothing could be further from facts. The chief is not asked to deliver a judgement; it would not occur to Nuer that one was required. He appears to force the aggrieved party (for instance, the kin of the dead man killed by others) to accept compensation by his insistence, even to the point of threatening to curse them, but it is an established convention that he shall do so, in order that the bereaved relatives may retain their prestige.

What seems really to have counted are the acknowledgement of community ties between the parties concerned, and hence of the moral obligation to settle the affair by the acceptance of a traditional payment, and the wish on both sides, to avoid, for the time being at any rate, further hostilities. It is not difficult to

[5] E.E. Evans-Pritchard, *The Nuer: A Description of the Modes of Livelihood and Political Institution of a Nilotic People*, Oxford: Clarendon Press, 1940.

comprehend that feuds are more easily reconciled the smaller the group involved. When a feud occurs within a village, general opinion demands an early settlement, since it is obvious to every one that were vengeance allowed corporate life would be impossible. At the other end of the scale when conflict occurs between primary or secondary sections of a tribe, there is a little chance of an early reconciliation and owing to distance reconciliation process takes more time. Nevertheless, since the feuding parties, as a rule, have frequent social contacts, so eventually the mechanism of the leopard-skin chief has to be employed to prevent their complete dislocation. The leopard-skin chief does not rule and judge, but acts as a mediator through whom communities desirous of ending open hostility can conclude an active state of feud. Evans-Pritchard writes that the feud including the role played in it by the chief, is thus a mechanism by which the political structure maintains itself in the form known to us.

Gluckman points out that a man's prestige in his own group depends on his skill as an organizer of exchanges, on the number of partners he has in several directions and his ability to deal with them; and to manage these enterprises successfully he also has to be able to manipulate his relationship with his own people in order to obtain means to exchange externally. He has to be able to direct the marriages in such a fashion that the group acquires in-laws in strategic positions. He has to be able to allocate his goods so as to put others in his debt, in order that he can mobilize resources to stage a feast. Only by showing skills in these enterprises can he become a big man and acquire prestige. Since a man's prestige in his own group depends on his relations with exchange partners, he as a big man has a great interest in the maintenance of sufficiently friendly relations with those partners who are big men in other groups. He is moved to oppose a state of all-out war. If war has broken out—over land, over theft, over vengeance for a killing—the big man needs in the end to bring about a resumption of peaceful relations, for only if there is sufficient peace for the exchanges to go on can he maintain his prestige. Therefore, there exists a mechanism which produces a peacemaker in the heart of each warring group.[6]

[6] Max Gluckman, op. cit., pp. 59–63.

In a theoretical sense disputes and their reconciliation serve as a guide to the points of strain and contradiction in a social system as well as to the structures of power and authority which are brought to bear on them. Disputes or episodes of conflict may be resolved or reconciled by means of a number of different procedural forms ranging from informal to the formal legal mode. Self-help, often violent in nature, is one kind of dispute management in which the parties handle the conflict by fighting or feuding or by other actions of offence or retribution. This often leads to the escalation of original conflict, and for this reason many societies possess other kinds of mechanism which can be used to lead conflict toward a peaceful resolution. In some cases disputes are settled by the process of ordeals or divination, and it is interesting to observe in such cases who it is who is able to manipulate or define the outcome of such procedures.

In anthropological literature divination means acquisition of information through the use of magic. There are a variety of means, from the interpretation of naturally occurring phenomena to a range of manipulative practices which are performed in order to arrive at a verdict or decision. Divination is typically employed to discover the identity of a criminal, to resolve a dispute and effect a reconciliation, or to predict the outcome of a future event. Evans-Pritchard's classic study of Azande witchcraft and divination established the tradition of structural-functionalist interpretations of religion and divinatory practices.[7] These studies focused on how oracles, divination, and the manner of interpreting their results, reflect the mechanisms of fission, fusion, reconciliation, social control, and authority within the group.

Where a third party intervenes in the reconciliation process, we may distinguish several different modes of procedure, including mediation, adjudication, and arbitration. Arbitration is a more formalized mode of mediation, in which the conflicting parties agree to submit themselves to the decision of a qualified or appointed third party. Where there is no third party, we may

[7] E.E. Evans-Pritchard, *Witchcraft, Magic and Oracles among the Azande*, Oxford: Clarendon Press, 1937.

distinguish the modes of negotiation or self-help as described above. In the anthropology of law adjudication is the intervention in a dispute of a third person (or other persons) vested with special authority within a formal legal system. We may contrast mediation, where the third party is not vested with legal authority and may be of high or low status in relation to disputing parties, and negotiation where the disputing parties or their representatives come to a direct agreement without intervention of a third party. Adjudication, or the formal legal mode of reconciliation and social control is characteristic of societies with considerable specialization of roles.

Anthropological analyses of conflict and reconciliation often focus on the manner in which situations of conflict reveal the structural alignments and divisions within the group. Differences and contradictions which are masked in everyday interaction are generally laid bare in the conflicts, where persons are subject to pressure to define their loyalties. Disputes thus reveal important features of social and cultural organization, and the mechanisms which exist for their settlement likewise indicate points of authority and cohesive power within social and political systems.

The conditions which define the presence and use of reconciliation mechanism and controlling procedures are various. Generally, anthropologists hold the view that greater density of population and the dissolution of family authority and the power that accompanies the development of a centralized state system may strengthen the adjudication procedures in place of mediation or arbitration. In recent times anthropologists have attempted a more comprehensive approach to the mechanism of reconciliation by examining the life cycles of particular conflicts. The process through which a conflict may pass may be found to be inherent in the type of conflict. Various mechanisms are employed within the same society to heal the breaches of peace. These actions range from informal arbitration to formal legal machinery to the performance of public ritual. Anthropologists believe mystical beliefs and ritual action, rather than judicial machinery, are particularly effective in dealing with disturbances arising from processes inherent in the life cycle of groups.

PROCESS OF RECONCILIATION

The process of reconciliation has been described in some detail by Bernard Cohn[8] in his study of anthropology of disputes in north India. As anthropologists shifted their attention from the study of primitive, isolated, pre-literate societies to that of social units which are part of great civilizations, they encountered a new range of problems which required description and analysis. Cohn in this study takes up the process of reconciliation in a local region in north India and the effects that the establishment of British rule had on the indigenous dispute settlement process. One of the formal organizations of dispute settlement was the formally constituted caste councils, the membership of which was based on a regional division of various lineage segments. The principal basis of dispute settlement in such councils in the past had been arbitration and the balancing of power so well analysed by students of African political organizations.[9] The system of arbitration and power balance was reinforced by the expectation that internal strife in the dominant caste would be used by the surrounding groups to destroy the suzerainty of the lineage over its little kingdom. In the case of a dominant caste like the Rajputs, the thakurs also derived important status in their role as settlers of disputes and as judges from their claims to be kings in the traditional social order.

If a dispute cannot be settled easily then the contending parties can summon a meeting of the council to hear and settle the dispute. This meeting can be either formal or informal. An informal meeting generally includes the leaders of the council, heads of the households and any interested person. In a formal meeting outside leaders are also called upon for advisory opinions. As they are not directly involved they can be less circumspect. Every one who attends the meeting is aware of the

---

[8] Bernard S. Cohn, 'Some Notes on Law and Change in North India: Anthropological Notes on Law and Disputes in North India', in his *An Anthropologist Among the Historians and Other Essays*, New Delhi: Oxford University Press, 1990.

[9] Max Gluckman, *Custom and Conflict in Africa*, Oxford: Basil Blackwell, 1973, pp. 1–26.

facts, and knows that he/she can be affected by the chain of relations and dispute which lie behind it. The meeting, after being opened by the leader, is addressed by each side and the case stated in declamatory fashion, with no attempt at cross-examination or rebuttal. The other participants comment on the facts, they may also comment on human nature, the stress and strain of life, general morality, and so on. There is no systematic procedure to determine the facts of the situation. It is assumed that all participants are aware of facts.

Participants can make general statements about the rules of behaviour and back them up with cases and earlier decisions. Generally there is no recourse to knowledge of sacred texts, law books or current civil or criminal law. The law which is being used is the customary law. The general rule is that leaders of the respective contending units will act in some sense as mediators, because by going above the interests of the unit, the leader not only enhances his prestige, but demonstrates his ability to lead in the next larger unit and take a wider and more active part in it. In fact he would endanger his role of leader in the wider circle if he were to push the claim of his immediate followers too much. Cohn writes: 'In essence, I judge, it is the role of the leader to bridge the gaps between the rings of the social "onion", by balancing between advocate of the rights of his immediate followers and the demands of the wider social group.'[10]

One of the mechanisms of reconciliation is to settle the dispute by talking it out. The act of talking lets out the steam and takes out some of the aggression accumulated in the dispute. There are no time limit and it is not expected that the dispute will be settled within a specified number of meetings. Often people talk and discuss for hours totally irrelevant issues. There is no expectation that the discussants will 'stick to the point', and in the process often a meeting held ostensibly to hear one dispute, goes beyond the dispute and people will discuss and adjudicate another dispute, coming up as a side issue, which lies behind the antagonism. In such societies life is not segmented

---

[10] Bernard S. Cohn, *An Anthropologist Among the Historians and Other Essays*, p. 562.

so that issues can be compartmentalized easily and hence they see no point in trying to decide matters only on the basis of an immediate situation.

In a more general sense we can say that the principal task of moving towards social harmony and individual composure rather than away from them toward dissonance and vertigo, is what disposition of issues is all about. It is the mechanism of decision-making, procedures of reconciliation, that occupy the centre of attention, rather than techniques of determining what actually happened. Such adjudications are also a matter of high etiquette, of patient, precise, and unexcited going through the elaborate forms of local consensus making. What matters finally is that unanimity of mind is demonstrated, not so much in the verdict itself, which is a mere denouement, but in the public process by which it has been generated. Propriety, to be preserved, must be seen to be preserved. As mentioned before, the processes involved are mainly discussion processes, the propriety mainly discursive propriety. Unanimity, or at least the appearance of it, is to be gained by talking through, in hard cases over and over again in grand variety of contexts, in a set and settled manner.

The reconciliation process here is truly a flow of admonitory proverbs, moral slogans, stereotyped speeches, recitations from didactic literature, fixed metaphors of vice and virtue, all delivered in a manner designed at once to soothe and persuade. Geertz quotes a passage, in which a mother instructs her son on how to behave when he is admitted to the various local councils:

> ... O my dear son
> if you are sent for by the council, you must answer;
> if invited you must come.
> If it happens you are sent for,
> invited to attend a council feast,
> eat sufficiently before going,
> and drink something too;
> for at a feast or banquet
> eating and drinking have a strict form,
> sitting and standing have their place.
> There you must use all your politeness,
> never forgetting where you are.

Be polite in everything
and remember all the rules,
even in passing betel or cigarettes.
Then when it comes to the speeches,
always be careful what you say:
sweet speech is a quality of goodness.
Always speak truthfully
observing all the forms of politeness,
taking care to understand people's feelings.
When you speak, speak humbly,
always deprecating yourself.
Be sure you behave correctly
and control all your passions.
A council member should live by his principles,
his speech should be of the *adat*
following the line of the right path
—calm as a waveless sea,
settled as a plain without wind
his knowledge firm in his heart,
ever mindful of his elders' counsel.[11]

Tradition and Reconciliation

The kind of institutions through which the pre-colonial societies attempted reconciliation are diverse and multitudinous as the rules they sought to apply, the group they sought to apply them to, and justification they sought to give for them. But the principle that men of learning did the justifying and men of power did the applying seems to have been pervasive. In India, there was a vast hierarchy of caste and inter-caste councils, 'dominant caste' mini-rajas of the so-called 'little kingdoms' who served at various levels of dispute settlement and reconciliation. In Thailand, there was a tangle of thirty sorts of ministerial courts, as juridically ill defined as the ministers themselves, advised by a consultative ministry of legal affairs manned, in this supposedly Buddhist country, by a dozen Brahmins. In Indonesia, there were

[11] Clifford Geertz, *Local Knowledge: Further Essays in Interpretive Anthropology*, London: Fontana, 1993, p. 212.

hundreds of legal experts of varying kinds and competence under the immediate eye of the resident lord. However, everywhere the procedural norm was that the adjudicative process and reconciliation should follow the rules of *dharma*.

In a schematic and simplified manner we can say that irrespective of the particular institutional shape of the process, the central evidentiary question to which it addressed itself pertained neither to the occasions of acts nor to their consequences, but to their type. That is, they were questions of *dharma* and *adharma* brought down to a judicial level, a matter of determining where in the local version of the grand taxonomy of dutiful behaviours a particular behaviour fell. The essence of the traditional process of reconciliation was based not so much on the sifting through evidence of particular disputes, but rather on the aptness of the final judgements as to the total value of human existence.

The reconciliation mechanism in such societies is based on some notion of 'law', not in the formal sense of the term, but in the sense of local knowledge; local not just as to place, time, class, and variety of issues, but as to accent—vernacular characterizations of what happens to vernacular imaginings of what can. Geertz calls this legal sensibility, by which he means this complex of characterizations and imaginings, stories about events cast in imagery about principles.[12] Srinivas points out that two terms that were heard frequently in the villagers' folk about disputes in Rampura were *nyaya* (according to law or rule, right, just, fair, moral) and *anyaya* (opposite of *nyaya*).[13] It was not simply the arguments or positions expressed by disputant's which were viewed as *nyaya* or *anyaya* but also the decisions of the arbitrators. The notion of *nyaya* is linked to morality and local practices and expresses the local, knowledge-based sensitivity to the subtler points of customary law and procedure.

In such a context law is local knowledge and not placeless principle which is constructive of social life. In the past this social life was characterized in terms of accumulation of prestige

[12] Cited in Clifford Geertz, *The Interpretation of Culture*, London: Fontana, 1993, pp. 336–7.

[13] M.N. Srinivas, *The Remembered Village*, Bombay: Oxford University Press, 1976, p. 314.

than in terms of territory. The disagreements among various chiefdoms were rarely concerned with border problems but with delicate question of mutual status and prestige. Korn relates an anecdote about South Celebes, which makes this point with the grave irony of traditional wit. The Dutch, who wanted, for the usual administrative reasons, to get the boundary between two petty princedoms straight once for all, called the princes concerned and asked them where indeed the borders lay. Both agreed that the border of princedom *A* lay at the furthest point from which a man could see the swamps, while the border of princedom *B* lay at the furthest point from which a man could still see the sea. Had they, then, never been fought over the land in between, from which one could see neither swamp nor sea? 'Mijnheer', one of the old princes replied, 'we had better reason to fight with one another than these shabby hills'.

Even in contemporary times, the forms of legal sensibility, of which the reconciliation process was only a minor part, persist, in the Third World, because even if it has become modernized, it has not become placeless. In every Third World country, the tension between the established notion of what justice (*dharma*, *adat*) is and how it is implemented and the imported notions is more reflective of the forms and pressures of modern life, and animates whatever there is of the judicial process. For instance, in the Indian context *dharma* is understood not only as the code of conduct for an individual or a group but also as an all-embracing system in which just relations are preserved between people and nature, between different social groups and also between people and gods. *Dharma* is both a moment in the system as well as the transcendental value of the system. Within the context of *dharma*, law would not be a set of rules to be applied to all in a mechanistic fashion by a superior authority but rather would embody a recognition that groups and individuals have a right to discover their own modes of being and to devise the rules that are to govern their existence. Various terms have been invented to characterize the process, like 'legal pluralism', 'legal syncretism', and so on, but the central issue posed by the legal pluralism of the modern world that largely escapes the classroom formulation is, namely, that how ought we to understand the office of the law now, and hence the process of reconciliation, when the varieties of 'law' are so wildly intermingled?

Legal sensibility in other words draws its sustenance from the culturally given norms and practices of reconciliation. The modernist notion and practices of law often have an uneasy relationship with the 'local knowledge' based legal sensibility, and even when the varieties of law are intermingled, they acquire a specific character, depending on the social and cultural formation of that society. While the modern law is based on a detailed categorization of rules, offences, punishments, etc., the legal sensibility is more unfocused, it is a normative order with a very broad parameters. This is also a reflection of distinct worldviews, spatial organization of people and customary practices.

In one sense one can understand the instrumentality of legal sensibility as a counter-hegemonic strategy used by communities to protect their limited and conditional autonomy; in another sense this overarching sensibility governs peoples judgement about the reconciliation procedures of modern state systems. In many of the states such semi-autonomous local jurisdictions and reconciliation processes have constituted, *de facto*, part of the apparatus of governance since the colonial period. In this sense, the incorporation of local difference into the institutionality of the state is not a new phenomenon: state power has long depended on complex negotiation with local interests (indigenous and non-indigenous), which have in turn co-opted others by extending often highly coercive clientelist networks down to village level.

However, it must be admitted that this conditional incorporation often was not premised on the basis of extending citizenship to the majority of the population. In contrast the underlying logic of incorporation of 'local knowledge', local indigenous authorities and legal practices into the national politico-legal systems has been to democratize the nation-state and construct pluralist practices of citizenship which include indigenous people within state and society on the basis of equality and respect for cultural diversity. In many of the post-colonial states a substantial section of the population continues to perceive modern state law and its institutions as arbitrary, distant, ineffective, and often unjust on the grounds of prevalent normative order. In many cases the judicial inefficiency, impunity and corruption prevent the full exercise of rights or the enforcement of obligations, creating a situation which has been termed as 'low intensity citizenship'.

The highly deficient legal system and consequently its mechanism of reconciliation, along with the general culture of impunity provide the context for constructing a more pluricultural rule of law, which is able to strengthen the local mechanism of conflict resolution and the recuperation of what is being termed as 'legal sensibilty', as a part of an overall strategy to reinforce the 'other' identities, to achieve a more efficacious judicial system and to promote greater justice. In the context of efforts to build a more culturally appropriate and responsive rule of law, what then becomes necessary is to make use of submerged signifiers, meaning and practices of previous periods as a starting point for rethinking justice, reconciliation and democracy.

The Mental Borders in South Asia

Sanjay Chaturvedi

INTRODUCTION

The *idea* of a border, and the mass production of borders, started only with modernity, together with the making of nation-states in Europe. The very idea of 'Europe' as a free association of discursively and territorially defined units developed in parallel with the emergence of borders. The Treaty of Westphalia (1648) codified the coexistence of Catholicism and Protestantism in strict terms of territorial borders. From the patchwork of historical regions of the eighteenth and nineteenth century, nation-states were developed in the nineteenth and twentieth centuries. While the European borders were redrawn many times, the very principle of a border as the ultimate marker of national sovereignty remained firmly in place, along with the idea of Europe constructed around a negative conception of unity and community (Morley and Robins 1995: 23).

The rise of a sovereign territorial state in Europe and its export to (as well as import by) the rest of the world also coincided with the technological development of cartography. This implied that a state could have a line around it—a geographically specific border. As such, geographic boundaries came to define and delimit the spatial extent of state sovereignty, through which the agents of control were able to effectively exercise their power over a given area and its constituent inhabitants (Johnston 1995). However, the extent and efficacy of sovereign authority depended not only on the 'effective' control over physical-human landscapes but also mental landscapes; that is, infusing local, personal experiences with the 'national'. Accordingly, cartography came to imply more than the technical and scientific mapping of the country concerned. It actually meant, 'the social and political production of nationality itself' through representational practices that in various ways attempted to inscribe something called 'Great Britain' or 'India', for example, and 'endow that entity with a content, a history, a meaning, and trajectory' (Krishna 1997: 82).

For two hundred years at least, political thought, institutions, and practices, as well as legal codes and economic theories, travelled from the shores of Europe and North America towards the south and east (Badie 2000:8). While the Western principle of territoriality endowed borders with institutional value and tangible quality, nationalism became a specific, strategic form of territoriality and an expression of the struggle for control over land and socio-spatial consciousness. In the case of British conquest of South Asia in the hundred years after 1750, military and civilian officials of the East India Company undertook a massive intellectual campaign to transform a land of incomprehensible spectacle into an empire of knowledge. Territorial annexation of over 60 per cent of the territory of the Indian subcontinent from 1757 to 1857 by the English East India Company (Fisher 1993) was followed by the annexation of 'Indian' in imperial knowledge systems and expropriation of Indian civilization by the British Crown. As Matthew H. Edney (1997) has ably shown, the British represented 'their' India because they mapped the India that they perceived and that they governed. Over the course of the nineteenth century, the British mapping of India further consolidated 'India' in its modern image. According to Edney,

The geographical rhetoric of British India was so effective that India had become a real entity for both British imperialists and the Indian nationalists alike. Both groups held 'India' to be to a single, coherent, self-referential geographical entity coincident with the bounds of the South Asian sub-continent and the extent of the British power but which nonetheless predated British hegemony... *the triumph of the British empire from the imperial perspective was its replacement of the multitude of political and cultural components of India with a single all-India State coincident with a cartographically defined geographical whole* (ibid.: 15). (emphasis supplied)

Once the British made themselves the intellectual masters of the Indian landscape, equipped with all the certainty and correctness granted by the Enlightenment epistemology, they placed categories such as caste and tribe at the heart of the Indian social system, along with the idea of two opposed and self-contained religious communities of the 'Hindus' and the 'Muslims' (Pandey 1990: 23-65). It was the centrality of religious communities, along with that of caste, which for the British marked out India's distinctive status as a fundamentally different land and peoples. Despite its inconsistencies and subordination to the needs of the colonial rule, the British ethnographic enterprise had far-reaching consequences. For, these very categories informed the ways in which the British, and in time the Indians themselves conceived of the basic structure of their society (Metcalf 1995: 114). The communal duality would set the stage for future conflicts on the subcontinent.

The British imperial rule was paid a handsome tribute by Mahatma Gandhi who, in the early 1930s, conceded that, 'the Indian nation was a creation of the empire-builders' (Sen Gupta 1997: 299). With independent India inheriting the colonial nation, much in the British ideology of 'difference' also survived and flourished, leaving its mark above all in the conception of a society informed by a passionate commitment to community, defined essentially in religious terms, and of the public arena as a site where those communities engaged in relentless pursuit of power. The amorphous structure of Indian civilization with its remarkable capacity to accommodate a multiplicity of social and linguistic identities, sometimes in a cluster of regional politics and on other occasions in a somewhat fragile pan-Indian polity, was also replaced by a uniquely colonial construct of the centralized state. This centralized state had an administrative bureaucracy, and a standing army in particular, and an attendant ideological trappings of 'ordered unity', 'indivisible sovereignty' and the like (Kumar 1997). The historical circumstances of partition ensured further that the apparatus left behind by the colonial state would not be dismantled, but actually reinforced.

The partition of the subcontinent was in considerable measure due to the inability to accommodate the politics of difference. The British on the eve of their departure divided the subcontinent on the basis of religion and a new 'nation-state' of Pakistan was carved out on the basis of the 'two-nation' theory, implying that the Hindus and the Muslims could never coexist peacefully. The British Empire departed, leaving behind not only a new set of boundaries and borders but also old problems. To quote Paula Banerjee (1998b: 181),

Partition, which was supposed to resolve all territorial issues rationally, turned out to be an edifice of complete irrationality. The governments in the region largely emulated their colonial predecessors not only in methods of governing but also in rationalizing territorial issues. The new boundary lines created political compulsions of their own resulting in remorseless hunt for their spatial claim which would serve the political demands of sovereignty. The Great Game was not over, it was only converted into a number of smaller games waiting to erupt at any given moment. The terrain where the game was played remained disputed. The great actors disappeared from the stage, but the acted upon remained confronting new specificities with outmoded methods.

The geopolitical implications of the partition went far beyond a geographical bifurcation of territory, causing colossal loss of life, property and large-scale migration on both the sides of a highly artificial boundary, drawn in great haste by Sir Radcliffe (Tai Yong 1997). According to Urvashi Butalia (1998: 271),

Partition is a simple division, a separation, but surely what happened in 1947 was much more than that... Not only were people separated overnight, homes became strange places, strange places now had to be claimed as home, a line was drawn to mark a border, and boundaries began to find reflection in people's lives and minds.... You had to partition your mind, and close off all those areas that did not fit the political division around you.

At the same time, the partition also set in motion a tension between 'identity logic' and 'territorial logic' on the one hand, and sowed the seeds of hate and hostility between the two nationalizing states committed to the Western idea of a defined 'national' territory. The Western principle of territoriality, which insisted on appropriating all intermediary allegiances, by defining citizenship as the direct subjection of the individual to the political centre, however, was completely at odds with an entirely fundamentally different meaning that the communal cultures—in the sense of pertaining to various communities on the subcontinent—conferred on space and place. It has even been argued that, 'partition was not so much the dark side of independence as it was of nation-formation. Designating millions as the "Other", denying them their human rights, forcing them to move, and then forgetting them were all part of this process' (Brar 1999: 64).

It is against such a backdrop that this chapter purports to examine how spatial socialization—a process through which individual actors and collectivities are socialized as members of specific, territorially bounded spatial entities—has been used as an instrument or medium of social distinction, domination and control by what Bertrand Badie (2000) calls 'the imported state(s)' in South Asia; a mode of organizing political power within a closed territory, which was born in Western Europe and subsequently exported to the rest of the world, and adopted by the political elite of the colonial and post-colonial societies. How are territory and territoriality being transformed, and with what degree of success, into national practices and meanings? One wonders how South Asian states continue to play a crucial role in the popular politics of place making and in creating naturalized links between people and places. How do the South Asian borders become territorial reifications of otherness, the construction of which occurs in socio-cultural space(s)? Since education is one of the major institutional forms of ideological reproduction in the modern state, the paper draws concrete examples from Pakistan and India to show how spatial representations are in effect socially constructed.

CRITICAL GEOPOLITICS: CONSTRUCTING AND
SUSTAINING THE 'OTHER' IN PSYCHIC SPACE(S)

Critical geopolitics is a relentless intellectual interrogation of the politics of geographical knowledge in both national and international politics (Dalby and O' Tuathail 1996: 451–6).

According to O' Tuathail (1994: 527), 'Critical geopolitics ... is a question not an answer, an approach not a theory, which opens up the messy problematic of geography/global politics to rigorous problematization and investigation.' It is of crucial importance to explore how geopolitical reasoning is integrated into boundary-producing discourses to perpetuate, sustain and justify social and political practices of dominance (see Dalby 1991). And how the boundary producing discourses are rooted in the 'power/knowledge' nexus, helping to sustain and legitimate certain interests, perspectives and interpretations.

To begin with, a critical geopolitics of borders assumes multiplicity of 'borderlands'—including the *psychological borderlands*, which are disseminated across borders and into every body that inhabits the world, whether these bodies reside near geographic borders or not (Johnson and Michaelsen 1997: 1). In other words, the idea of the 'border' or 'borderlands' is expanded to include even psychic space, about which one can thematize problems of boundary or limit. In order to comprehend the connection between the *psychological borderlands*, everyday life and the construction of socio-spatial groupings in South Asia, we need to focus, first and foremost, on the idea of *spatial socialization*: 'the process through which individual actors and collectivities are socialised as members of specific territorially bounded spatial entities and through which they more or less actively internalise collective territorial identities and shared traditions' (Paasi 1996: 8). This leads us examine (a) how socio-spatial groupings are constructed through socially constituted linguistic and semiotic constructions by the intellectuals and institutions of statecraft, and (b) how the Other is created as an external enemy against which 'we' and 'our' identity are mobilized.

Discourse, as Foucault, (Mills 1997: 17) has pointed out, is not a group of signs or a stretch of text, but 'practices that systematically form the objects of which they speak'. In this sense, 'a discourse is something which produces something which exists in and of itself and which can be analysed in isolation' (Mills 1997: 17). Whereas in terms of thinking about discourse as having effects, it is important to consider the factors of truth, power and knowledge, since it is because of these elements that discourse has *effects*. According to Foucault, each society has its regime of truth, its general politics of truth; that is the types of discourse it harbours and causes to function as true ... truth, therefore, is something which societies have to work to produce, rather than something which appears in a transcendental way ... discourses do not exist in vacuum but are in constant conflict with other discourses and other social practices which inform them over questions of truth and authority (cited in ibid. 18–19).

Hence discourses are also 'plays of power' which generate and exert various codes, rules and procedures to impose a specific understanding through the construction of knowledge within the overarching framework of these codes, rules and procedures. Furthermore, the rules that govern practices are often implicit; and seldom explicitly articulated. Constructed socially and in specific contexts, these rules are understood subconsciously or taken for granted by practitioners. Hence it is equally important to critically examine the institutional origins and commitments of these discourses and how they carry implications of power.

Constructing the 'Other': Perceptual Blockage and Enemy Mythology in Post-Colonial South Asia

As far as the role of spatiality in the construction of otherness is concerned, various scholars (including geographers) have attempted to analyse both theoretically and empirically the construction of borders, both physical and symbolic, between the Self and the Other. According to Carr (1986: 146–8), a social community is formed wherever a narrative account of a 'We' exists. Such an account or story is often articulated or formulated, may be by one or more of the group's members on behalf of the We—using the We as the subject of action and experience and of the narration itself. Carr points out that much of the communal rhetoric which projects a group as We is putative and persuasive rather than expressive of a genuine unity or an already accepted sense of communal activity. Nevertheless, the story must be shared by people if it is to be constitutive of a group's existence and activity. In most cases, the 'story-telling' aims at creating a community where none existed before. And the 'main' stories may have rival versions or versions based on different premises.

While the role of language and discourse retains its importance for political geographers interested in the politics of place-making (after all, no local worlds could possibly exist without words and other symbols), there is no denying the fact that the idea of a 'place' explicitly comes into being in the discourse of its inhabitants and particularly in the rhetoric it promotes. Certain communities may choose to define themselves as an experience rather than as a place, but the idea of demarcation and delimitation—or spatialization—is almost invariably present in all social practices. Anderson's *Imagined Communities* (1991) demonstrates that discourses represent or signify not just boundaries but various communities as coherent sociospatial units. In short, the spatial dimension is implicit in the construction of otherness, since the other typically lives elsewhere, 'there' (Walker 1993).

The construction of a 'national-self' has not been a clear-cut task for the 'ethnic-kin' states of Asia, as they continue to struggle with the seemingly eternal problem of achieving 'national solidarity' and the construction of territorial identities in the face of a serious mismatch between territorial boundaries and ethnic boundaries. First and foremost, as critical geo-historical and geo-political perspectives on the establishment, demarcation and control of the 'national' boundaries/borders in South Asia suggest, the British imperial practices of constructing and mapping borders as well as the colonial 'frontier' mentality have been accepted uncritically by the political elite in these countries in order to secure and disengage the 'national self' from the 'alien'.

Second, in the context of South Asia's mega diversity, 'national identity' can at best be treated as one of many, often coexisting and overlapping identities—religious, tribal, linguistic, caste, class, gender, etc. Whereas, the post-colonial states continue to maintain that all individuals should belong to one nation and have a national identity and state citizenship and that the bordered state sovereignties are the fulfilment of a historical destiny. This view has become pivotal in not only defining the world-views of South Asian states but also human identities. The states retain a decisive role in the production and reproduction of these manifestations of territoriality, particularly through spatial socialization and territorialization of meaning, which occur in numerous ways through education, politics, administration and governance. This territorialization takes place through physical and symbolic violence, and states everywhere in South Asia continue to control, marginalize or destroy various aspects of centrifugal otherness, such as instances of ethnic solidarity or indigenous movements.

South Asian States in general continue to suffer from what Sankaran Krishna (1994: 508) has termed as 'cartographic anxiety'; the anxiety surrounding questions of national identity and survival. Krishna argues that cartographic anxiety is a facet of larger post-colonial anxiety syndromes manifested by a society that perceives itself as suspended forever in the space between the 'former colony' and 'not-yet-nation'. 'This suspended state can be seen in the discursive production of India as a bounded sovereign entity and the deployment of this in everyday politics and in the country's violent borders'. The critical question then becomes: is there anything *post* about the post-colonial at all? According to Krishna,

If we examine the degree of anxiety revealed by the state over matters of cartographic representation, the inordinate attention devoted to notions of security and purity, the disciplinary practices that define *Indian* and *non-Indian, patriot* and *traitor, insider* and *outsider, mainstream* and *marginal,* and the *physical* and *epistemic* violence that produces the border—the answer to this question is negative. (ibid.)

A thought-provoking and scholarly account of how 'the two worlds of "cartographic anxiety" and "ironic unconcern"—one of the top, another of below—make up the twilight zone in which the border exists' in most parts of continental South Asia is found in Ranabir Samaddar's seminal work, *The Marginal Nation: Transborder Migration from Bangladesh to West Bengal* (1999). He draws our attention to the contrast between these *two* world-views: *one* reflecting the 'anxiety' of the post-colonial nationalizing state(s) in South Asia and *another* reflecting the 'unconcerned everyday life on the border' of the communities living in 'broken' villages across the artificial national boundaries.

Once the physical preservation of the national borders is held as synonymous with the very existence/survival of the state of the Indian union, the perceived indispensability of 'secure' or 'inviolable' borders for national unity diverts attention from the continued violence that produces and sustains the border (Krishna 1994: 511). A classic example of how borders can lead to a senseless costly 'war' is to be found over the frozen wastes of the Siachen Glacier. Such 'wars' (Siachen, and more recently over Kargil) illustrate that battlefields, especially those located near the border areas, are often significant sites of territorialized memory, and these may occupy a pivotal position in national iconography.

However, the manner in which territorial power and control manifest themselves not only in the border landscape but also in places, practices and discourses in which violence, the possibility for violence or memories of violence are implicitly or explicitly present, is also significant. Typical examples of how the memories of the partition are kept alive in everyday life include such elements as national armies, memorials to the Unknown Soldier, military parades, boot-stamping rituals on the border checkposts, etc. Border landscapes and border guard systems are thus only one manifestation of boundaries. Needless to say perhaps, such discourses and representations erode both the official and popular will to cooperate across 'hostile' borders.

Anxieties are also mounting in India over 'illegal' Bangladeshi immigrants or 'infiltrators', alleged to be more than ten millions in the country, half of whom are in West Bengal. It is feared that,

it may affect a demographic change in Indian areas around Bangladesh so much so that they may one day cease to be Indian territory. The idea of such demographic aggression against India has been there since 1958, but it has been put into practice with intensity after the emergence of Bangladesh. (Maheshwari 1998: 1)

According to Samaddar (1999: 63), 'States in South Asia have gone mad over migration, refugees, exiles and migrants. The State system is being subverted at will along India-Bangladesh border, Bhutan-India-Nepal border, Indo-Pak border in Kashmir, Indo-Burma border and Burma-Bangladesh border.' Samaddar makes a further insightful comment on the manner in which nation-states inevitably end up treating refugees and migrants. 'A nation... cannot and will not guarantee rights of migrants and refugees because it is the very process of nation-formation... which produces them' (ibid.: 43). It is precisely in such a context that another point assumes significance. The important question is not where a boundary is, but how, by what practices and in the face of what resistance, this boundary was imposed and ritualized. And this instantly raises the question of how the 'Other' is created as an external entity by the South Asian states, against which 'we' and 'our' identity are to be mobilized.

In the case of the elite-dominated social-political systems of India and Pakistan, we find dualistic structures of good/evil, us/them, strange/familiar operating at various levels (Yasmeen and Dixit 1995: 10–12), and the 'Other' side is generally viewed as the 'enemy across the border' intent upon posing a threat to the political stability and territorial integrity of the country. A large majority of the Pakistani elite seems to be of the view that India speaks with one voice when issues related to Pakistan are at stake. More often than not, it is the viewpoint of the hawkish elements within and outside the establishment which is taken to represent the official and the popular opinion on Pakistan in India. On the other hand, most Indians appear generally convinced that all Pakistanis think alike on issues related to India. Both sides appear convinced that, the 'Other' is manipulative, arrogant and expansionist, and the language used for such representations is often filled with terms that vilify and dehumanize the enemy; transforming individuals into something less than human.

As pointed out by Alan C. Tidwell (1998: 127), 'an enemy is, in some way, an opponent, but also much more. An enemy is a value-laden, emotionally charged entity, one that is the recipient of specific negative value connotations and meanings'. According to a study related to a discussion of the Indian and Pakistani views of the 'Other', based on interviews with a number of senior Indian and Pakistani civil and military officials, businessmen, academics and journalists (Yasmeen and Dixit 1995: 10–11), the dominant view of India among the Pakistani elite is one of an expansionist, arrogant and hegemonic state that neither accepted the idea/basis of partition nor has it reconciled to the existence of Pakistan as a sovereign nation-state. Therefore, India is accused of having a Machiavellian design to destroy Pakistan and reintegrate it with the larger India or at least subjugate Pakistan and relegate it to a subordinate status. Certain sections of the Pakistani elite also believe that India is using political and cultural subversion, in addition to military means, to weaken Pakistan. The study (ibid.: 10–11) further points out,

> The dominant view of Pakistan within the Indian elite is one of a theocratic, religiously fanatic and militaristic state that has not accepted its 'South Asian' identity. It is also seen as denying its cultural links with the Indian civilization. Pakistan's failures in democracy and the military's ascendance in the system is seen as contributing to these attributes. Pakistan is also viewed as suffering from a paranoia that India has not accepted the reality of partition and is determined to undo the Islamic state. At the same time, it is accorded a sense of vengeance which motivates Pakistan to undermine the secular basis of Indian polity by meddling in Kashmir, Punjab, and India's financial nerve centre, Bombay.

The images of the 'Other' do not remain confined to political elite, they are transmitted to the masses through education and media. As Joanne Sharp (2000: 333) points out,

> it is through institutions such as the media and education that people are drawn into the political process as subjects of various political discourses. The media and education explain the linkages between their audiences and what is being explained in order to provide a context for interpretation.

Although the historical role of mass education in the development of nationalism remains a matter of debate among scholars, most of them acknowledge its critical role in the construction and reproduction of both the (imagined) national community and the visions of the 'Other'.

ENMIFICATION THROUGH EDUCATION:
WHAT IS TAUGHT IN PAKISTAN AND INDIA?

The process of creating enemies, or what Tidwell (1998: 126) describes as 'enmification', injects emotional power into a conflict, and the medium of education is often (mis)used for the purpose. A critical look at the content of Pakistani discourse of 'national' self-portrayal, which includes the images of the 'Other', reveals that both pre-state as well as post-partition histories have been used in the first instance as an ideological force. In this sense, history becomes both a regulator of individual behaviour and a medium for creating and maintaining ties/links between members of the group. Another end-product of the communication of a 'history' appears to be control. In this instance, history acts as a rather blunt instrument to keep group members in line, and acts as a boundary between group and non-group.

Since the partition, attempts have been made by certain ruling regimes in Pakistan and India to re-write their respective countrys' pasts to suit their present political ideologies (see Behera 1998). In Pakistan, for example, it was General Zia-ul-Haq who was quick to realize the 'usefulness' of imparting knowledge of history through a 'national curriculum'. In 1981 he decided that henceforth Pakistani education was to be totally revised and history rewritten according to his vision of Pakistan. The history textbooks were now to demonstrate that the struggle for Pakistan was not simply victorious struggle for a Muslim homeland (Hoodbhoy 2000). Instead, it was a movement for an Islamic state, to be run strictly in accordance with Islamic law. The heroes of the Pakistan movement—Jinnah, Iqbal, Syed Ahmed Khan—were to be hailed as Islamic heroes, and the non-Islamic history of the subcontinent was to be ignored to the extent possible. No surprise, therefore, there is little mention of the Ashoka Empire. For the Pakistani textbooks, the history of Pakistan starts with Mohammad Bin Qasim's arrival on the subcontinent, the defeat of Raja Dahir, and the successful campaign of various Muslim rulers (Rabbani and Syed 1992: 11–12). Even the discussion of the Mogul Empire favours 'tolerant, large hearted and accommodating' Emperor Aurangzeb over Emperor Akbar, who had married Hindu women and introduced Din-e-Akbari. Indian textbooks do not ignore the Islamic traditions of the region but the manner in which they present information is hardly value free.

An eminent Pakistani physicist and educationist, Pervez Hoodbhoy (2000: 3) has cited a few excerpts from curriculum document for classes K-V in Pakistan, which are quite revealing. At the completion of Class-V, the child should be able to: (a) 'acknowledge and identity forces that may be working against Pakistan'; (b) 'demonstrate by actions a belief in the fear of Allah'; (c) 'understand Hindu-Muslim differences and the resultant need for Pakistan'; (d) 'India's evil designs against Pakistan'; (e) 'be safe from rumour mongers who spread false news'; (f) 'visit police stations'; (g) 'collect pictures of policemen, soldiers, and national guards'; (h) 'demonstrate respect for leaders of Pakistan'. To quote Hoodbhoy (ibid.: 4),

Consider the impact of the national curriculum [prepared by the Curriculum Wing of the Federal Ministry of Education, Government of Pakistan] objectives on a 12 year-old child in his last year of primary school. Instead of a future that is joyous, and a peaceful country that offers hope to all, he is told that life is about battling invisible enemies. Fear is ever-present because beneath every stone lurks a venomous snake and Pakistan is under siege of sinister forces which the child must learn to acknowledge, identify, and fight to death. What mental space can remain for this child's innocence when he or she must learn to make speeches on jihad and martyrdom? And what scope exists for being tolerant and accepting beliefs other than your own?

What kind of people does the national curriculum seek to install as role models? They are not scholars and poets or scientists, nor people like Abdus Sattar Edhi or other who have struggled for the rights of others. Instead they are policemen, national guards, and soldiers. The child must collect their pictures, revere them, perhaps kiss them. His visits to the police stations—where rapes, tortures, and deaths in custody occur so routinely as to be unremarkable—is expected to imbue him with the spirit of humanitarianism and patriotism. Is a greater perversion of human values really possible?

If Hoodbhoy is right (which undoubtedly he is) in saying that a society's educational system is like a cultural DNA, and contains within it the 'detailed blueprint determining what that society is destined to become tomorrow' then, the observations made by K. K. Aziz (1993), a noted Pakistani historian, are equally worrying. Aziz has shown how history in Pakistani schools and colleges has been reduced to the status of national mythology and further (ab)used as a vehicle for political indoctrination, and for constructing and nurturing anti-India (anti-Hindu) mindset. For various reasons, the textbooks set out to create among the students a hatred for India and the Hindus, both in the historical context and as part of current politics. The slanted descriptions of Hindu religion and culture project Hindus as 'unclean' and 'inferior'. The students are told that it was Muslim rule over the Hindus that put an end to all 'bad' Hindu religious beliefs and practices and thus eliminated classical Hinduism from India. Also, the Indian National Congress was purely a Hindu body and the communal riots accompanying and following the Partition of 1947 were initiated exclusively by the Hindus and Sikhs, and that the Muslims were at no place and time aggressors but merely helpless victims (ibid.: 193–4).

Attempts have also been made in India to 'nationalize the past. As pointed out by Partha Chatterjee (1993), nationalist history, as it started to be written in the nineteenth century, only mentioned Muslims as *the* cause of the corruption and decadence of Hindu society. The Muslims had subjugated the Hindu nation, and it was only after the British had abolished Muslim rule that the regeneration of the nation became possible. Muslims were portrayed as outsiders, foreigners, aggressive murderers, plunderers, destroyers of India's Hindu culture. If the Hindus were weak it was because of both their tolerance and corrupt practices. Yet they constantly resisted the Muslim oppression. To quote Chatterjee (1993: 113),

The idea of the singularity of national history has inevitably led to a single source of Indian tradition, viz. Ancient Hindu civilization. Islam here is either the history of foreign conquest or a domesticated element of everyday popular life. The classical heritage of Islam remains external to Indian history.

Whereas Partha S. Ghosh, in a recent study (1999), has discussed at some length the issues related to revision of school texts, and how 'the Indian state, after independence, would mould its programme to teach history, or social sciences in general, at schools in tune with the ethos on which the nationalist struggle was constructed' (1999: 238). Given that the long and protracted struggle for independence (which was directed against the Imperial Other) itself had diverse undercurrents, to define its 'ethos' in clear-cut terms was never an easy task. Moreover, even though 'the Congress had championed the cause of a composite Indian nationalism negating both communalism and the two nation theory, still both within the party as well as outside there were powerful Hindu nationalist forces' (ibid.).

Unlike Pakistan, where the one and only route-map is provided by the Curriculum Wing of the Federal Ministry of Education, Government of Pakistan, education in India has been included in the concurrent list in the Constitution. In view of the mega cultural and historical diversity of India as well as the need for an emotional integration of the disparate communal and linguistic groups, such a policy was considered as most appropriate. While the Centre would partially take care of higher education, the responsibility for school education is to be, by and large, assigned to states. However, as pointed out by Partha S. Ghosh (ibid.: 240),

distortion of history in school texts is not a phenomenon peculiar to the BJP. In the 1950s and 1960s, when the Bharatiya Jana Sangh (BJS) was nowhere in sight of power even in strongholds such as MP and Rajastan, let alone the centre, there were complaints of distortions of history. Textbooks in circulation in the Hindi-speaking states as well as Gujrat and Maharashtra were heavily loaded in favour of India's Hindu past and against Muslim rule.

Given that education has already become an important medium in the governance of the national spaces, the business of writing and rewriting 'national histories' will continue to generate all kinds of controversies. Irrespective of whether the 'national history' gets written from the vantage point of the 'centre' or 'right' of 'left' it ought to be borne in mind that, 'a sane educational system does not train students in hate. Whatever the justification for it or the compulsions of patriotism, hatred corrupts the mind, more so [as] it is still tender, and retards its healthy growth' (Aziz 1993: 195).

CONCLUSION

Peace in South Asia remains hostage to the state-centric politics of place making. Far more than empirical manifestations of state sovereignty, South Asian borders are historical constructions, with the meanings attached to them perpetually changing along with the developments taking place in the dominant geopolitical discourses in these countries. Sustained by the politics of difference and exclusion, boundary therefore becomes a text that has to be continuously written and rewritten by the 'imported state' before it can be imposed, defined and defended. In a discursive sense, therefore, South Asian borders are highly politicised manifestations of socio-spatial consciousness of both the elite and the masses.

In South Asia (where communities live in relatively closed environments, 'trapped by the lottery of their birth') tendencies related to what Ranabir Samaddar (1999) calls 'reasons of state', nationalism and ethno-regionalism linked with the patterns of migration, flows of displaced people and refugees, are creating new boundaries. Borders in South Asia operate not only in the vicinity of the international line itself, but wherever national-ideological systems confront one another. Accordingly, ethnic, cultural, linguistic, and historical borders increasingly occur in other spatial contexts and remain important components of human activity at all levels—from the individual and family to the nation-state.

With the help of a few examples, primarily from India and Pakistan, the chapter has shown how boundaries are used as social constructs by the ruling elite in South Asia to separate groups as well as territories. How the process of 'Othering' is reinforced through self-sorting, purification of space and group cultural-religious self-definition. How the perceptions of internal and external sources of threat are inter-linked, and feed on each other. How both internal and external threats are being used to raise basic existential issues facing India and Pakistan as states, and the peoples ('Indians' and 'Pakistanis') as its basic social constructs. How 'India' and 'Pakistan' become dangerous and silent places beyond familiar boundaries in each other's geopolitical imaginations. And how stereotyping in textbooks supports inclusion and exclusion between national groups and therefore favours nationalism in education.

The prospects of peace in South Asia depend to a large extent on a relentless pursuit of what O' Tuathail (1996: 256) has describes as a 'Critical geopolitics'.

A critical geopolitics is one of the many cultures of resistance to Geography as imperial truth, state-capitalized knowledge, and military weapon. It is a small part of a much larger rainbow struggle to decolonize our inherited geographical imagination so that other geographings and other worlds might be possible (ibid).

This author is of the view that the people of South Asia can and should overcome the apparent incapacity to constitute oneself as oneself without excluding the 'Other'—*and* the apparent inability to exclude the other without devaluing and, ultimately, hating him.

REFERENCES

Anderson, B. (1991) *Imagined Communities*, London: Verso.
Aziz, K. K. (1993) *The Murder of History: A Critique of History Textbooks Used in Pakistan*, Lahore: Vanguard.
Badie, B. (2000) *The Imported State: The Westernization of the Political Order*, Stanford: Standford University Press.
Banerjee, Paula (1998a), 'To re-instate historians in the history of border'. Paper presented at a seminar on 'Asian geopolitics: borders and transborder flows' at New Delhi, 23 and 24 March 1998, organized by Maulana Abul Kalam Azad Institute of Asian Studies, Calcutta.
Banerjee, Paula (1998b) 'Borders as Unsettled Markers in South Asia: A Case Study of the Sino-Indian Border' *International Studies* 35(2): 179–91.
Behera, N. C. (1998) 'Perpetuating the divide: political abuses of history in South Asia', *Indian Journal of Secularism*, 1(4): 53–71.
Brar, B. (1999) 'Partition, Fiction, History: Redeeming Divided Lives', *Studies in Humanities and Social Sciences* VI(2): 63–76.

Butalia, U. (1998) *The Other Side of Silence: Voices from the Partition of India*, New Delhi: Viking-Penguin.
Carr, D. (1986) *Time, Narrative, and History*, Bloomington, Indianapolis: Indiana University Press.
Chatterjee, P. (1993) *The Nation and Its Fragments: Colonial and Postcolonial Histories*, Princeton: Princeton University Press.
Dalby, S. (1991) 'Critical Geopolitics: Discourse, Difference and Dissent', *Society and Space*, 9(3): 261–83.
Dalby, S. and G.O. Tuathail (1996) 'Editorial Introduction. The Critical Geopolitics Constellation: Problematizing Fusions of Geographical Knowledge and Power', *Political Geography* 15(6/7): 451–6.
Edney, M.H. (1997) *Mapping An Empire: The Geographical Construction of British India, 1765–1843*, Chicago: University of Chicago Press.
Fisher, M.H. (1993) *The Politics of the British Annexation of India 1757–1857*, New Delhi: Oxford University Press.
Foucault, M. (1972) *The Archeology of Knowledge*, tr. A.M. Sherdian Smith, London: Tavistock (first published 1969).
Ghosh, P.S. (1999) *BJP and the Evolution of Hindu Nationalism: From Periphery to Centre*, Manohar: New Delhi.
Hoodbhoy, P. (2000) 'The Menace of Education: What are They Teaching in Pakistani Schools Today?' *The News* (Lahore), 11 June.
Johnston, R.J. (1995) 'Territoriality and the State', in G.B. Benko, and U. Strohmayer (eds.), *Geography, History and Social Sciences* (Dordrecht: Kluwer): 213–25.
Johnson, D.E. and S. Michaelsen (1997) 'Border Secrets: An Introduction', in S. Michaelsen and D.E. Johnson (eds.), *Border Theory: The Limits of Cultural Politics*, Minneapolis: University of Minnesota Press: 1–39.
Krishna, S. (1994) 'Cartographic Anxiety: Mapping the Body Politic in India', *Alternatives* 19: 507–21.
—— (1997) 'Cartographic Anxiety: Mapping the Body Politic in India', in J. Agnew (ed.), *Political Geography: A Reader*, London: Arnold: 81–93.
Kumar, R. (1997) 'State Formation in India: Retrospect and Prospect', in M. Doornbos and S. Kaviraj (eds.), *Dynamics of State Formation: India and Europe Compared*, New Delhi: Sage.
Maheshwari, A. (1998) 'The Face Behind the Mask', *The Hindustan Times* (*Sunday Magazine*), New Delhi, 8 August.
Metcalf, T. R. (1995), *Ideologies of the Raj*, Cambridge: Cambridge University Press.
Michaelsen, S. and D.E. Johnson (eds.) (1997) *Border Theory: The Limits of Cultural Politics*, Minneapolis: University of Minnesota Press.
Mills, S. (1997), *Discourse*, London: Routledge.

Morley, D. and K. Robins (1995) *Spaces of Identity: Global Media, Electronic Landscapes and Cultural Boundaries*, London: Routledge.

O' Tuathail (1994) '(Dis)placing Geopolitics: Writing on the Maps of Global Politics', *Environment and Planning D: Society and Space* 12(5): 525–46.

—— (1996) *Critical Geopolitics: The Politics of Writing Global Space*, London, Routledge.

Pandey, G. (1990) *The Construction of Communalism in Colonial North India*, Delhi: Oxford University Press.

Paasi, A. (1996) *Territories, Boundaries and Consciousness: The Changing Geographies of the Finnish-Russian Border* (Chichester: John Wiley & Sons).

Rabbani, M.I. and M.A. Syed (1992) *An Introduction to Pakistan Studies*, Lahore: The Caravan Book House.

Samaddar, R. (1999) *The Marginal Nation: Transborder Migration from Bangladesh to West Bengal*, New Delhi: Sage.

Sen Gupta, B. (1997) 'India in the Twenty-First Century', *Inter-national Affairs* 73(2): 297–314.

Sharp, J. (2000) 'Refiguring Geopolitics: The Reader's Digest and Popular Geographies of Danger at the End of the Cold War' in K. Dodds and D. Atkinson (eds.), *Geopolitical Traditions: A Century of Geopolitical Thought*, London: Routledge: 332–52.

Tai Yong, T. (1997) 'Sir Cyrill Goes to India: Partition, Boundary-Making and Disruptions in the Punjab' *International Journal of Punjab Studies* 4(1): 1–19.

Tidwell, A.C. (1998) *Conflict Resolved: A Critical Assessment of Conflict Resolution*, London: Pinter Press.

Walker, R. (1993) *Inside/Outside: International Relations as Political Theory*, Cambridge: Cambridge University Press.

Yasmeen, S. and A. Dixit, (1995) *Confidence Building Measures in South Asia*, Occasional Paper No. 24, The Henry L. Stimson Centre, Washington DC.

Interrogating Stereotypes: Women Making Peace

Rita Manchanda

Where are the women in conflict? They are mothers grieving for sons dead and missing. They are widows or half widows struggling to survive in female-headed households bringing up orphaned children and the aged. They are the refugees displaced from homes. They are the raped and murdered in wars. Essentially, women in conflict are visible as the overwhelming victims of war. Civilian casualties, the vast majority of which are women and children, account for 90 per cent of all deaths in the conflicts of the 1990s. Women and girls make up 80 per cent of the refugees. Disempowered in peacetime, women in time of conflict—a time of decision by arms—are even more disadvantaged in asserting their right and the right of their children to entitlements. The image of robust men and sickly women and children in refugee camps is symptomatic of the truism that women are the worst sufferers in war. It stands to reason that women have the greatest stake in peace. And where are the women in peacemaking? Women are invisible when it comes to making the big decisions of peace as of war.

History has little or no space to record women's experience of war, as if it was undifferentiated from that of men; it carries no chronicle of women's resistance and peacemaking effort, as if it made no difference. Women are the chorus at peace rallies, the front line of the humanitarian story, but they are not on the dais, they do not determine the agenda. In the end, they become invisible. Their activism is not taken seriously and no need is felt to have them at the negotiating table to talk peace. The binary in the stereotype is that men negotiate the peace and women build it informally at the local level around the 'ethics of care' as life givers and nurturers.

This sentimentalist assumption is being challenged as women's multifaceted experience of war is being made visible by largely feminist scholarship which demonstrates women's capacity to emerge as powerful agents of social transformation in conflict and peacemaking. Violent conflict blurs the divide between the private sphere of family and the public sphere of men and politics, and even calls into question the divide, as women enter into negotiations of power for the survival of their families and communities. Women's activism in conflict is rooted in their everyday role of keeping the family together. In conflict, women's everyday activity as reproducers and nurturers gets highly politicised because it ensures community survival. Its corollary is the specific targeting of women and family as a task of war to destroy the community.

Part of the difficulty of making women's activism in peace building visible and therefore mainstreaming gender in the political activity of peace agreements and the actual planning for a society's reconstruction, is that women themselves see their activity as non-political and an extension of their domestic concerns, that is, as 'stretched roles'. Moreover, women's visibility is further obscured by the fact that their language of support and resistance flows from their cultural experience, especially of being disempowered. The creative anarchy, the non-violence and non-hierarchical characteristics which mark women's innovative actions for peace, challenge traditional notions of what political action should and can be about.[1] Women avoid the classical rally and speech type variety. As we shall explore below, women's strategy of protest often uses the symbol of motherhood both for moral authority and political mobilisation.

The Mothers' Front strategy of protest is articulated through the process of taking the private act of mourning into public

---

[1] Dan Smith, 'Women, War and Peace', in *Towards a Women's Agenda for a Culture of Peace*, ed. Ingeborg Breines et al., Paris: UNESCO Publishing, 1999, 69–70.

space. In Sri Lanka, in the aftermath of the suppression of the Marxist-nationalist JVP in 1989–90, the Mothers Front drew upon a culturally specific tactic of ritualistic public cursing—the traditional weapon of the disempowered—to challenge the government over the fate of the disappearences of 40,000 people.[2] In Kenya, similarly, ritualistic cursing combined with stripping of the women was used to disarm state repression.

Women's peace activism is often sporadic and most visible when politics are less structured. Indeed the key challenge is how to enhance and consolidate what are a myriad of spontaneous and fledgling actions without distorting the authenticity of the evolving processes. Because women's peace activism is grounded in the informal space of politics, it gets undervalued and as post-conflict politics moves into formal space, it gets marginalized. Increasingly, women peace activists are emphasizing the importance of women making the transition from informal space to the formal space of political structures. From building peace and reconciliation at the grassroots level, women are entering into negotiations with formal politics to seek a place at the negotiating table. Whether a women's peace agenda or praxis will survive that integration into formal politics, is an open question.

This paper explores four broad themes, (a) the linkage between women and peace and the psycho-socialization of femininities and masculinities in armed conflict; (b) women's notion of peace and political violence; (c) women's cultural language of support and resistance and the ambivalent politics of motherhood; and (d) mainstreaming gender in the political activity of peace building. Given women's multiple responses to war and that gender is intersected by class, race, ethnicity and religion, ultimately, the basic question concerns 'whether women constitute a group for organising in any unified fashion around issues of war and peace?'[3]

Inevitably, a gender-sensitive analysis of conflict and peace over-

[2] Malathi de Alwis, 'Motherhood as a Space of Protest', in *Appropriating Gender*, ed. Aparna Basu, New York: Routledge, 1998, pp. 184–201.
[3] Jennifer Turpin 'Many Faces: Women Confronting War', in *The Women War Reader*, ed. Lois A Lorentzen and Jennifer Turpin, New York: University Press, 1998, p. 14.

determines the category of gender. Moreover, it tends to reinforce as essentialist the dichotomous categories of feminine and masculine underlying patriarchy, rather than moving towards a solution within these socialised dichotomies. In its defense, it should be said that the 'over determination' is necessary to make women's historical invisibility visible. The paper essays to examine the basic assumption of the women and peace relationship, that women, being historically disempowered, bring different values to the peace process. Therefore, on the assumption that women do make a difference, that their politics of peace are different, women need to find a place at the negotiating table if a democratic and sustainable 'positive peace' is to be built.[4]

WOMEN AND PEACE

In the first phase of the Chechnya conflict, media reports detailed how mothers went to the front to take back home their soldier sons, away from the fighting. The *'motherist'* narrative reaffirms the conservative logic of the biological connection between women and peace and men and war, but it is a logic which ends up implicitly affirming the structural inequality between men and women. Moreover, the *motherist* or testosterone logic flies in the face of empirical evidence demonstrating that there is nothing essentialist or inherently peaceful about women. Women make up a third of the combatants in the Maoist insurgency in Nepal or in the conflict in Somalia Rwandan women and LTTE women have been complicit in the ethnic massacres of women and children. However, it is a fact that men predominate across the spectrum of violence.[5] Perhaps it is more useful to think not of women's commitment to peace but of the profound depths of violence in masculine culture.

It is the psychosocial construction of femininities and masculinities in patriarchal societies, that connects women to peace.

---

[4] Brock-Unte, *Feminist Perspectives on Peace and Peace Education*, New York: Pergamon Press, 1989.
[5] R.W. Connell, 'Arms and the Man', Paper for UNESCO meeting on Male Roles and Masculinities in the Perspective of a Culture of Peace, Oslo, September 1997.

The cultural argument spotlights women's socialisation as primary child rearers which privileges values such as the ethics of care, and rewards cooperation, and not competition and conflict, privileged in the socialisation of men in patriarchy. It also reinforces women's subordinate position in a patriarchal society. Taking Brock-Unte's definition of patriarchy as 'a form of social organisation based on the force based ranking of the male half of humanity over the female half' (1989, p. 48), patriarchy has to do with power over people, mostly power to control women and nature. War is armed patriarchy. War magnifies the already existing inequality of peacetime.

Militarisation relies on patriarchal patterns and patriarchy relies on militarization. Structurally women are excluded from decision-making on security and till recently, politics. Culturally militaries need men and women to behave like binaries, i.e. women need men to protect them and men go to war to protect women. The false consciousness of 'protecting women', was exposed during an Africa regional meet on child soldiers in Mozambique. Defending the conscription of children, government officials—all men—said, 'What will happen when all of us are dead, somebody has to protect the women'. The NGOs—all women—replied, 'Women will protect themselves'. The issue is not only how to tackle conflict but how to avoid it. If a child at fourteen is fighting, who's to say at twenty-four he won't want to go back to fighting and look for an excuse to do so.

The exclusion of women from political activity makes for less of a stake or investment in political order or the issues on which conflict turns. It may be less important for women to display appropriate political attitudes of standing up for one's country at the expense of peace and fairness. 'If there is a female propensity for peace, it may be due to the male propensity to exclude women from power', argues Dan Smith.[6]

Cynthia Cockburn, a feminist researcher and peace activist maintains that 'if women have a distinctive angle in peace, it is not due to women being "nurturing". It seems more to do with knowing oppression when we see it.' Knowing what it is to be

---

[6] See also Betty Reardon, 'Women or Weapons: The Militarist Sexist Symbiosis', in *Towards a Women's Agenda for a Culture of Peace*, Paris: UNESCO, pp. 143–50.

excluded and inferiorized as women, makes them work for an inclusive and just society.[7] Peace politics are crucial for everyone in unequal relations. A radicalization of the women and peace connection is the eco-feminist argument. All oppression exists on a continuum and women's oppression constitutes the original oppression. A feminist peace politics therefore is connected to the struggle against racial, ethnic and class oppression. Feminism and peace share an important conceptual connection, both are critical of and committed to the elimination of coercive power over privilege systems of domination as a basis of interaction between groups and individuals.[8] The question of women and peace and the meaning of peace for women cannot be separated from the broader question of unequal relationships between women and men in all spheres of life and the family. Women are more likely to see a continuum of violence, because they experience the connected forms of domestic and political violence that stretches from the home, to the street to the battlefield.

The two competing discourses, on women and peace, 'essentialist' and 'egalitarian' mark the debate among researchers. The danger is that essentialising the peacefulness of women, reinforces women's powerlessness relative to men and undermines the overriding goal of working for an egalitarian partnership between women and men. Nonetheless, both the difference versus equality arguments make a contribution to understanding the role of women in peacemaking.

In the ultimate analysis, amidst the ambiguities of peace as a women's issue because of biology or culture, is the argument that peace is a women's issue because of reasons of justice. As we shall explore below, women are for a 'just peace' and a 'positive peace' as opposed to a mere absence of war. Women's peace movements have been a major influence on current trends towards redefinition of security. They have been among the first to argue that real human security lies in protection against harm of all kinds, of a healthy environment capable of sustaining all

[7] Cynthia Cockburn, 'Gender, armed conflict and political violence', Background paper, The World Bank, Washington DC, June 1999.

[8] Karen Warren and Duane L. Cady, 'Feminism and Peace: Seeing Connections', in *Hypatia*, vol. 9, no. 2, 1994.

life and of respect for the human dignity of all. Women's experience of providing for day-to-day human security and their more comprehensive and integrated perspectives on what constitutes security is essential to the redefinition of security.

Understanding women and peace is to understand the impact of militarization and the violence of armed conflict on women. Women are the worst sufferers of the political violence which renders them stateless refugees on the death of their male kin; of economic violence associated with militarisation and of cultural violence flowing from the production of 'protest masculinities' and 'protest femininities' and the physical violence of dislocation, rape and murder.

What is the impact of economic violence for women? Even before conflict, militarization entails a diversion of scarce resources from the social sectors of greatest concern to women. The disruption of armed conflict makes the socially assigned responsibility of women to feed and care for the children and the aged, all the more difficult. While the men join the militias or withdraw, it is the women who remain in the home, unless forced to flee. Conflict produces women-headed households in a patriarchal society where women are structurally and socially disadvantaged, e.g. in terms of property ownership.

Cultural violence against women gets magnified in conflict which in promoting macho values legitimizes misogyny. Rape is not an accident of war. 'Protest masculinities'[9] emerge in contexts of ethnic oppression and poverty as in apartheid South Africa. In the case of the Palestinian conflict, 'The violence used against the Palestinian men has made them violent at home in the work place and in their free time', said the Palestinian MP Dalal Salmeh. Men compensate for their loss of power by hitting at women. Moreover, with women seen as symbolic and physical markers of community identity, there is the pressure to embrace identity constructs which undermine women's autonomy of being, as in the veiling of Palestinian women after the Intifada uprising or in Kashmir after the outbreak of insurgency. It falls off as the conflict intensity eases.

[9] For an elaboration of the term 'protest masculinities' see Connell, op. cit., p. 7.

There is need, however, to guard against sentimentalising women and peace politics. Women have been known to actively support violent and sectarian organizations and have been guilty in perpetuating the 'them' and 'us' divide at the heart of conflict. Mothers' have risen to oppose a conflict that kills their sons, but equally they have raised sons to be soldiers to be sacrificed in the name of nationalism. And yet in the end, as Thandi Modise, an MP from South Africa said, 'for women, it doesn't matter which side you are on, on both sides children get maimed and killed and women get raped'. Indeed the logic of 'some mother's son', is a compelling one that makes it difficult for women to choose sides and enables them to reach out across the ethnic divide. This is particularly reinforced when the violence is perceived as illegitimate, that is, violence for violence sake. But the neutral space is a contested one with competing ideologies at play of nationalism, community, class, race and gender.

Gendered Notion of Peace Politics?

Is there a women's notion of peace politics? While feminist theorists make bold to say so, women peace activists are much more tentative. I quote from Carmel Roulston, a peace researcher and activist from Northern Ireland who argues, 'women have been to the fore in a kind of politics which has helped to limit the impact of conflict on the fabric of society'.[10] It has laid the foundation for a future where the two warring groups 'can learn to accommodate each other and to express their difference without aggression'.[11]

A 'feminist' culture of peace, which fundamentally critiques unequal structures of domination and which is built on learning to live with difference without aggression, is clearly much more than an absence of conflict or an absence of fear of direct physical violence which Brock-Unte calls a 'negative peace'. A

---

[10] 'Women, Violent Conflict and Peace Building: Global Perspectives', International Conference Organized by International Alert, London, 5–7 May 1999, p. 35.
[11] Ibid.

WOMEN AND PEACE: THE MEANING OF PEACE FOR WOMEN

	Absence of personal, physical and direct violence	Absence of indirect violence shortening life span	Absence of indirect violence reducing the quality of life
UNORGANIZED	(1) Absence of wife battering, rapes, child abuse, street killings	(3) Absence of inequalities in micro-structures leading to unequal life chances	(5) Absence of repression in micro-structures leading to less freedom of choice and fulfilment
ORGANIZED	(2) Absence of war	(4) Absence of economic structures built up within a country or between countries so that the life chances of some are reduced. Also the effect of damage on nature by pollution, radiation, etc.	(6) Absence of repression in a country of free speech, the right to organize, etc.

Source: Bright Brock-Unte, *Feminist Perspective on Peace and Peace Education*, New York: Pergamon Press, 1989, p. 47.

'positive peace', she argues, includes absence of structural inequalities in micro structures leading to unequal chances in life and an absence of economic structures built up within a country or between countries so that the life chances of some are reduced and the environment irretrievably degraded. It is characterized by freedom of repression of intellectual thought and speech.

Associated with peace, then is the notion of a 'just peace'. At a recent conference on Women and Conflict in London in May 1999 some sixty women articulated a rainbow vision of peace, stressing social justice, women's rights, economic rights, co-existence, tolerance, participatory democracy and non-violent dialogue to sort out differences. Women like Branka Rajna from Bosnia asked 'what was peace for the ostensible *victors* who had not been displaced, raped or widowed, if it meant unemployment, bankrupt social funds, no housing and a media full of hate and aggression'. What did security mean, asked Thandi Modise, if 'at night, I cannot walk down a street in Johannesburg? What does economic security mean when I am not sure what will happen to my home when I am away at work'. Issues of poverty, development and globalization, these women argued, had everything to do with a real peace, because it has everything to do with violence—economic violence, political violence, cultural violence and physical violence. The assumption is—the implications of war for women are different from men and therefore their notion of peace too is gendered.

It is a notion of peace and security from the perspective of the disempowered and marginalized, security as seen from below. Traditionally, a workable peace has been defined by national security considerations in the language of defence and foreign policy establishments. But security, a state-centric military concept, has been obliged by the expanding human rights and civil society discourse and women's peace agenda to engage with soft-belly notions of participatory democracy, social justice, development and poverty removal. Basically, peace is not real and sustainable without social justice for the oppressed, especially women. Peace is much more than demobilisation of society, it has to do with the demilitarisation of unequal power relations.

Before we rush in to answer the fundamental question on whether women constitute a group for organizing, around issues of war and peace, there is need to take heed of the empirical experience of one of the celebrated success stories of women's solidarity on a peace and women's rights charter. During a conference 'The Aftermath' in Johannesburg in July 1999, Thandi Modise raised the problem of party loyalties which can divide the fragile solidarity of women. In South Africa just before the 1994 elections, the *Inkatha* and the Freedom Party Women's League and the ANC Women's League were coming together on a peace agenda. But this was suspended because of elections. Women retreated and there was more violence and rape, she said. It spotlighted the difficulties of women qua women overcoming competing political, race class and ethnic divisions. Gender turns out to be not necessarily the most significant category. What is needed, argued Modise, is to achieve 'a definition of peace which is common to us all'.

Inherent in a gendered notion of peace, is a distinct 'women's way of doing things', that privileges consensus and accommodation. Women go into a negotiation not accepting to win but to compromise. We shall elaborate below on whether there is a gendered praxis of peace negotiation and peace building.

FROM ICON TO AGENT—MAKING VISIBLE WOMEN'S LANGUAGE OF RESISTANCE

The dominant image of women in war is that of the grieving mother—*Mater Dolorosa*. The image is necessary to sustain that other myth, man as warrior. It also reflects the reality, as Cynthia Enloe analyses, 'when a community's politicised sense of its own identity becomes threaded through with pressures for its men to take up arms and for its women to loyally support brothers, husbands, sons and lovers to become soldiers'.[12] Equally, some women and some men have resisted these pressures. Indeed, as women's narratives of war experience get recorded, the icon of the woman as a grieving and self-sacrificing mother gives way to women's variegated agency in conflict. Women experience conflict not as a homogeneous experience. It is contextual and marked by shifting constructions of the legitimacy and illegitimacy of violence. Women's response strategies are also shifting. Beyond victimhood in conflict is women's agency. Women have negotiated conflict situations by becoming citizens, combatants, prostitutes, war munitions workers, producers of soldiers and war resisters.

For women, war in a sense is what happens after the bombs, after the fighting, when their men go underground or retreat from public space. Women are left to step outside the private

---

[12] Cynthia Enloe, *The Morning After: Sexual Politics at the End of the Cold War*, Berkeley, Los Angeles: University of California Press, 1993, p. 250.

sphere of family and enter into negotiations of power with the 'other', the 'enemy', the administering authority. For the women caught in the Maoist insurgency in Nepal, it is a world without their men and thus a shift in gender roles which legitimises taking up a man's task of wielding the plough or standing for local government elections. For the Chakma women in Bangladesh, the market-place became the public site for ethnic contest as women pursued their everyday chores of negotiating survival. For the Kashmiri women, it is an entry into public space to oppose arrests and negotiate the release of sons and husbands or to demand justice for the 'missing'. For Tamil women refugees in Sri Lanka's internally displaced camps, it is overcoming the disadvantaged status of the widow or *half widow* and experimenting with a vulnerable but liberatory role made possible by the societal upheaval of a conflict situation. For the Naga women in India's conflict-scarred north-east, the moral authority of motherhood combined with the tradition of the availability and legitimacy of informal space for women's activism for peace, enables them to step across the conflictual ethnic divide and appeal to warring side for a ceasefire and negotiation to settle differences through non-violent ways.

Women's activism in war grows out of their everyday experience as home makers and nurturers, and is often perceived by them as an extension of their primary domestic responsibility as child rearers, as keeping the family together. In their negotiation of survival for their families and their communities, women's 'stretched roles' become highly politicised. And as mentioned above, women themselves do not see their activities as political. Even their language of resistance is rooted in the cultural space of women who have been historically disempowered.

Non-violence is one of the defining themes of women's type of action. It informs the way people relate to each other, absence of hierarchy, and authority, thus making for a degree of disorganization and fractiousness which is almost anarchic but capable of being very creative and innovative. It is not strong in the rally and speech variety of political activism. Indeed peace activists who are men have remarked on the visible activism of women in peace demonstrations—they come and go away'.

It may be because their activism is of a different nature. It is spontaneous, sporadic and a myriad of fledgling actions. The video film *Carry Greenham Home* captured the innovative energy of the peace camp and anarchic activities like the intrusion into the military base dressed as Easter bunnies or the famous dance on top of the missile silo.

In many non-Western societies, there are traditions rooted in the moral authority of the mother, which empowers women to stop a conflict by coming in between, metaphorically by throwing a shawl. Its social legitimacy rests on the unequal relationship between men and women which is basic to patriarchy. The conflict in 1990 between Azerbaijan and Armenia was halted through such an action. In Russia in the 1996 phase of the Chechnyan war mothers marching to the Front were stopped to prevent them from doing any such thing. In other societies where the traditional cultural mores have not been obscured, ritualistic cursing is used, as in Sri Lanka and Kenya, or in the collective public stripping of mothers to shame the men into stopping the violating of the land in the Philippines or stopping conflict in Kenya. Women's peace activism challenges fixed notions of political activism.

Much of women peace activism centres around mourning. For example, the refusal to mourn was forged into a weapon of protest by a widow whose 'innocent' husband was killed by the police in an anti-Maoist action in Nepal. She wears the social markers of a *suhagan* (a married woman) as a symbol of quiet resistance. The reverse is when there is a proscription against mourning for an LTTE cadre killed in the Sri Lankan conflict. A mother, forbidden to grieve, secretly gives a photograph of her son to a priest, and asks him to pray for his soul. In the case of the Mother's Front, Women in Black or the 'Wall of Tears', the women take their private sorrow and exhibit it in a public place.

The emergence of the Mothers' Front in various forms from Argentina, Sri Lanka, Nagaland and Kashmir in India, Russia to Israel, is grounded in the traditional mothering role of women. It is precisely as women that they have the informal space to appeal to the powerful and the power to move them to compassion and shame. In the Mother's Front these women act as women in public space thus transforming their passion of loss into political action.[13] For women are meant to accept their suffering in war and protest only against the enemy. The Four Mothers in Lebanon, the Association of the Parents of the Missing in Kashmir or the Madres des Plaza de Mayo, Argentina, are publicly protesting against the state's human rights violations at a time when all protest has gone underground. It is a politicization of the 'motherist' role of women.

However as Lepa Mladjenovic of Women in Black from Serbia, warned, there is a grave risk of sentimentalising mothers as anti-war agents. Strategies which turn on biological roles— motherist logic—carry the risk of being overturned by 'fatherist' logic. In former Yugoslavia, in 1991 women from Croatia, Serbia and Bosnia came out against war and demanded that the lives of their sons be spared. The army chiefs responded with a father language convincing mothers that there were army and state secrets beyond the reach of mothers language. Most of the mothers ended up being used to support duty in defence of the nation, the motherland. Indeed motherhood and nationalism is very closely entwined in the ideological construct of the state. Mladjjenovic argues that 'unless women who are in the role of mothers develop a clear political position, the sole fact of being mothers is not enough to resist the state's logic of war'.[14]

That 'clear political vision' is necessary if initiatives like the Mothers Fronts, which emerge as the front line of political mobilisation around human rights, do not get co-opted and subverted for narrow opposition political party, agendas. In the case of the Mothers Front in southern Sri Lanka, their devastating success made the main opposition party, the SLFP, adopt the Mothers who were used and marginalized. There is also the other risk as discernible in Argentina, where the mothers movement split in the process of transiting to more formal and multiple

---

[13] Sara Ruddick, 'Woman and Peace: A Feminist Construction', in *The Women War Reader*, pp. 213–26.

[14] Lorraine Bayardo de Volo, 'Drafting Motherhood: Maternal Imagery and Organisation in the United States and Nicaragua', in *The Women War Reader*, pp. 240–53.

agenda politics and in a sense losing the authenticity of its original radical creative energy.

Fundamentally, for women to emerge as peace makers it is vital that the Mater Dolorosa of war, or Virginia Woolf's 'outsider' in the war enterprise, engage politically, to oppose war and promote non-violent ways of resolving difference. Women peace activists are stressing, that if women whose resistance is highly visible in informal political space during conflict are not to be marginalized and their resistance undervalued in post-conflict structures of formal politics, there is need for women to make the transition into formal poliitcs. It is a trusim that women's activism is most visible when politics are less heirarchically structured. The challenge is to tap and strengthen the myriad and spontaneous actions of women for peace and facilitate access to resources which will enable them to negotiate the formal structures of power.

MAKING A DIFFERENCE: MAINSTREAMING GENDER IN PEACE PROCESSES

When decisions of war or peace are made, women's peace activism becomes invisible and their presence is not deemed necessary in negotiating the peace or determining post-conflict policies. Women are highly visible when it comes to building street level peace accords, peace villages, bi-cameral citizen committees or promoting a culture of tolerance at the local community level, but they are rarely to be found at the negotiating table, especially at the national level. At the negotiating table, civil society groups mobilized around peace tend to get marginalized and within that women's peace activism, particularly, gets undervalued.

Therefore, it is not surprising that in the negotiations for the Bangladesh—Chittagong Hill Tracts. Peace accord in 1998, no presence or weightage was given to the Hill Women's Federation. Civil society groups, and in the nineties the HWF, had been in the forefront of the political and humanitarian struggle for the rights of the hill tribes. At the negotiating table were the representatives of the armed group. The peace accord sidesteps the question of human rights violations or the land question.

Already the accord is beset with difficulties and has generated an *anti-accordists coalition*. The anti-accordist faction of the HWF has forged a common platform around a much broader 'just peace' agenda. The formal involvement of women and civil society groups in the peace process is likely to be the key element in building a sustainable peace.

Increasingly, women activists are questioning their exclusion from the negotiating table. Women are busy healing and reconciling at the local village level through informal, sporadic initiatives but they have been powerless to shape the 'big' questions which can again plunge their communities into destructive conflict and render meaningless their local level activism. Part of the problem is that women's experience of negotiating conflict and maintaining survival is not regarded as a significant resource, either nationally or internationally. International peace keepers come in and presume there is nothing to dialogue about with the women who throughout the conflict have been maintaining survival and community.

The lessons of the recent history of war and more war in Bosnia, Northern Ireland, Rwanda Burundi and Sri Lanka evoked in women's narratives of conflict, poignantly emphasize the imperative for women to move beyond the humanitarian front of the war story and claim a seat at the negotiating table. Women need to be present to discuss issues of genocide, impunity and security for all, if a 'just' and enduring peace, reconstruction and reconciliation is to be built. It is not enough for women to be for life; they must be amid politics. The luxury of Virginia Woolf's 'outsider' position in the *Three Guineas* is just not tenable in promoting a peace politics.

Recognizing the urgent need for women to move beyond the humanitarian front of the story and engage with politics, women and peace activists are organizing to facilitate women's entry into formal politics. Women dominate the peace movement in numbers as for example in the Philippines but they are primarily in the background, staffing secretarial positions or support roles. The difficulties and the determination of women to make themselves politically heard is evocatively described in the experience of the women's collective in Burundi to secure a voice at the Arusha peace talks. The women's collective comprising

30 organizations had grown in strength and legitimacy through its humanitarian work in the mixed Tutsi and Hutu neighbourhoods. The women had also lobbied the international community to lift sanctions as it was the women and children in the refugee camps who were the hardest hit. However, when the peace talks began, women's insistence to be present was ridiculed. 'Normally, women do not ask for political power, but at stake was the fight against genocide and exclusion', explained Concille Nibigira of the women's collective. Eventually, Concille's was the lone woman at the table—her voice silent. Since the first round of peace talks, the collective has been able to negotiate the presence of six women at the table, but only as observers.

At the negotiating table sat the 'representatives' of political parties (or rebel groups?). Who did the women represent? The women had no mandate. So they organized meetings in the villages to discuss the agenda for the Arusha. 'The women who sit at the Arusha talks, now have a mandate', said Concille, 'because we have listened to the women from the countryside'. The crucial element was that women had to create solidarity among themselves. 'If we join forces, then our voices will be heard and we will conquer a real peace for our country', said Concille, undaunted by the fact that so far their struggle had got them only observer status.

Women and peace activists, recognize that if there is to be a mainstreaming of gender in peace politics, women have to be amid politics. In the Northern Ireland conflict, when the peace agenda was threatened, women decided to form a political party to get into the legislature to keep the peace process on course. Women needed to be in national politics to bring in legislation protective of the rights of the weak and marginalized, the majority of which are women. Poor women have to be economically empowered if they are to focus on peace building.

'The issue of equal participation by women, is not simply an issue of gender equality, human rights and democracy but could represent the decisive factor in maintaining peaceful development in a conflict prone area', said Lul Seymoun, an Eritrean peace activist in exile in Europe. Women are not usually parties to the conflict and therefore, it is claimed, are more impartial and patient, listening to both sides. Women with their historical experience of being disempowered, bring negotiating skills of compassion reconciliation and accommodation. Women's social acculturation is not oriented towards competitive hierarchies and winning and they tend to go into negotiations, ready to compromise.

In Northern Ireland, one time when the talks broke down on the big issues and the men walked out, the women were left. For them the soft issues on which commonalities could be discussed were also important. The dialogue was kept going and the men came back to discuss a comprehensive peace.

We are still at the germinal stage of determining whether there is a specific gender-based theory and praxis of peace. As women's narratives of conflict, survival and peace building become visible, feminist scholarship has begun to claim a specific feminist peace agenda and peace praxis. This essay, in seeking to explore women's undervalued agency for negotiating conflict and building peace, too, runs the risk of over determining the role of gender as a category. But women's narratives of the war and peace story, does support the assumption that women have the capacity to emerge as a powerful constituency for peace.

ACKNOWLEDGEMENTS

I am enormously indebted to the contribution of the women who presented their war narratives at the 'Women and Conflict' in London in May 1999 and to Meredith Turshen 'Women in the Aftermath of War and Armed Conflict: A Report of a Conference', Johannesburg, July 1999.

II. REGIONS

Regionalization as a Peace Instrument: Western Europe

Helmut Reifeld

> Grenzpfähle steckst Du, um ein Gebiet zu messen.
> Doch daß Du sie nur steckst, das sollst Du nicht vergessen.
> Der grade Gegensatz setzt grad' die Wahrheit schief,
> Weil stets in Wahrheit eins in's andere sich verlief.
> —*Friedrich Rückert, 1788-1866*[1]

'Regions' can be regarded as the oldest geo-political units in Europe. The terms 'regionalism' or 'regionalization', however, are of recent origin. Even though the words are new, the inherent problems are chronic and date back many centuries. In Europe the term region traditionally applies to small geographically distinct units, like Bavaria, Burgundy, Catalunia or Wales, which normally have common ethnical or cultural characteristics. In the case of Germany, it is not always possible to distinguish between regions and federal states. As far as the European Union is concerned we can today distinguish between:

—federalized states, e.g. Germany, Belgium or Austria;
—regionalized states, e.g. Italy and Spain;
—decentralized states, e.g. Netherlands, Portugal and to some extent France and Great Britain;
—unitary states, e.g. Denmark, Greece, Ireland and Luxembourg.

---

[1] Borders you place, an area to define.
Forget not that only implanted by you they are.
The straight contrast it is, truth that bends,
Because in truth, into the other one blends.
    (translation by Tess Herzog)

The political patchwork of European regions has to be understood as the outcome of centuries-old problems. During the course of the second millennium all forms of political associations or dissociations among these multifarious regions were witnessed. Due to dynastic politics or warfare, the borders of the former European empires as well as the early nation-states have constantly been subject to change while those of the regions remained very often the same. First, before tackling the role of the regions in Western Europe at the end of the twentieth century a few examples of border conflicts around Germany might serve to illustrate the background against which the legitimate interests of regions within the European Union are increasingly viewed as a peace instrument. Second, the two most important ideas that had a profound impact on the strengthening of the political level below the nation-state have to be described. To this day the principles of federalism and subsidiarity are of great influence whenever demands in favour of regional self-determination are brought forward. Third, the regional policy of the European Union must be looked into as a contemporary answer to regional problems and demands.

BORDER CONFLICTS AROUND GERMANY:
A HISTORICAL EXAMPLE

Whenever historians discuss German territory they call it the 'German question'. This question exists because most of Germany's borders cannot be taken for granted nor seen as a natural given. The entire millennium that is now coming to a close was full of border conflicts surrounding what is called Germany today. It is, indeed, almost a millennium ago that the term 'German Empire' (*Imperium Germania*) was officially used for the first time. After the re-structuring of the old *Imperium Francorum* in the so-called Renovatio Imperii of Emperor Otto III in AD 997 the newly created eastern part was called Imperium Germania. From 1157 onwards this was called 'holy' and in 1442 the term Germania was replaced by: 'of German nation' (*Nationis Germaniae*). Until 1806 the term used was the 'Holy Roman Empire of German Nation (*Sacrum Imperium*

Romanum Nationis Germaniae), incorporating many different regions and peoples.

The Federation of the Rhine, which was formed in 1806 and then the German Federation which came into being after the Congress of Vienna in 1815 were decisive attempts to establish unity: the bureaucracy was centralized, the various administrations of the multifarious estates were dissolved and freedom of trade as well as of religion were proclaimed. At the same time, this German Federation consisted of 39 states and incorporated 35 local rulers. Moreover, the king of Great Britain ruled in Hanover, the king of Denmark in Holstein and the king of Holland in Luxembourg, although all these areas belonged to the German Federation. One of the core questions during the German Revolution of 1848 was whether a 'new' Germany should be proclaimed as a large federal structure including Austria or as a small nation-state, dominated by Prussia and without Austria. After three wars (against Denmark, Austria and France) had taken place and were subsequently won by Prussia, the newly united German Empire was founded in 1871 and it lasted for 74 years, until 1945.

After the end of World War II, the victorious allies not only had limited, but also quite different, plans for the future of Germany. Therefore, it was hardly possible to impose or even to implement any common occupational policy. When the two German republics, the former German Democratic Republic and the Federal Republic of Germany, were founded in 1949, both these states had already become elements of the 'Cold War' and on both sides the former enemies emerged as new allies. While in the Federal Republic some of the older federal states had survived and others were newly created, the former federal states on the territory of the GDR were abolished in 1952 and re-created in 1990, when the two Germanys re-united.

Most of the historical German borders were based on influence, some on convention, others on force. The two oldest borders which exist up to now are those with Holland and Switzerland, which date back to 1648. All other borders have to be discussed individually. The following examples illustrate how little legitimacy can be claimed for some parts of Germany's borders by let's call it tradition:

1. In the north there is the small state of Schleswig. In 1386 this was united with the state of Holstein. When Holstein became part of the German Federation in 1815, Schleswig was not included because a great part of the population was of Danish origin. The first war was fought between 1848–50 and another one in 1864 after which Schleswig fell to Prussia. After the Second World War it was given back to Denmark following the Treaty of Versailles and in 1937 reintegrated into Prussia. In 1946 the British created the federal state of Schleswig-Holstein and integrated this with the Federal Republic of Germany.
2. In the east the most controversial territory is Silesia. Originally it was mainly a German-speaking East Prussian province. After the Thirty Years War (1618–48), a part of it became autonomous, a part fell to Austria and another part to Poland. After Frederic the Great of Prussia had fought two wars over it, it was re-integrated into Prussia in 1742 and rapidly developed as an excellent example of Prussian administration. By virtue of the Treaty of Versailles it was split-up again. The so-called Hultschiner Ländchen area was given to the CSSR, and other parts went to Poland. In 1939 it was completely occupied by the Third Reich again, and in March 1945 Stalin transformed it into the Polish 'Voivod' provinces. This was sanctioned four months later at the Potsdam Conference by the USA and Great Britain.
3. Perhaps the most complicated territory in the west is that of Elsass. The domination here had shifted constantly, from Celtic to Roman, then Alemanian, but mainly Lorrainian. Between the fourteenth and the sixteenth century the territory was split-up completely, so that when it was formally put under the French Crown by the Westphalian Peace Treaty of 1648, many parts and institutions remained German. Only after the French Revolution was it fully integrated into France under Napoleon. It did not return to Germany at the Congress of Vienna in 1815. After Bismarck had won the war against France and proclaimed the German Reich in Versailles in 1871, the Elsass became, without question, an important part of the newly formed Reich. This was again revised in Versailles in 1919, although the majority of the population

was German-speaking and of German descent. After the defeat of France in 1940 it again fell under German supremacy only to become a French Department again in 1945.

These dates and facts hardly explain anything by themselves and each of them can be taken up as a subject for discussion. They might serve, however, as an illustration of the fluctuating instability of borders particularly in central Europe. This is not the place to discuss the importance and influence of nationalism, imperialism or even totalitarianism because we do not want to inquire into the origins of any of these border conflicts. But it might help to understand some of the background to the problems for which different forms of regionalism and regionalizations were expected to offer new solutions.

Federalism and Subsidiarity

In order to situate the idea of regionalization as a peace instrument within European history one has to go back at least to the early nineteenth century. After the experience of the French Revolution and faced with the problems of the Industrial Revolution intense political controversies took place in all European countries. One of the key questions was whether the political structure of the modern nation-states should have a bottom-up or top to bottom approach. Wherever Napoleon Bonaparte left his mark, a strong centralistic approach to political problems could be traced. In contrast to this, a alternative trend can be traced as well: one that insists on the linkage between most political questions and the smaller political units which are mostly affected by them and, therefore, are supposed to understand these problems best. These smaller units could be the federal states, counties, the municipalities or even the villages. The two guiding principles of this second approach to political thinking are federalism and subsidiarity. In order to understand regionalism in Europe these two inter-related principles have to be considered.

Apart from its linkage to the principle of subsidiarity, federalism can be understood as legitimate in itself and justifiable in substance. Seen in a broader perspective it obviously shows many different facets. The phenomenon of federalism is probably older than all its different written concepts. Its political appearance changed not only with time and place but especially under different social conditions. Common to all forms of federalism is the endeavour to safeguard the smaller political unit against the bigger one without depriving the former of the latter's indispensible help and support. Federalism supports the greater political unit deliberately because it is convinced of its political necessity while centralism requires the submission of smaller political units.

The principle of federalism attempts to overcome the mass formation of people in many different social and ethnic groups and is able to provide structural and formal political help in this respect. In doing so, it provides at the same time a dynamic element in the political life of any given community. There is no *a priori* or fixed form for the principle of federalism because it is only fixed in its principal goals while it remains flexible in its ways to achieve them. It requires a strong framework together with a dynamic methodology. But it should not maintain elements which are contradictory to the constant and unpredictable changes that take place in any living state, economy or society.

It is not only in the sphere of great politics that the principle of federalism is legitimized. It generally defies the bigger and stronger political unit in the interest of the smaller and weaker one. Wherever the existence of local organizations, regional cooperations or vital provincial interests are threatened, federalism has a role to play. Wherever ethnical groups are supposed to give up their own way of living, wherever individual possessions are requested in the interest of the community and wherever local creativity as well as individual freedom are questioned politically, federalism has its specific role to play.

From the history of federalism in Germany, it is apparent that federalist structures have supplied both the tools and the procedures used in achieving national political unity. After the Reformation the multifarious small political structures in Central Europe were strengthened by the religious Peace Treaty of Augsburg in 1555. The principle of this epoch-making treaty was comprised in the phrase, 'cuius regio, eius religio', that is, he who rules over a certain region decides about its people's religion. Apart from this historical background, federalism as a structure of domestic organization may be justified on ethnic and geographical grounds as well. It may be justified on ethnic grounds whenever a population of a country consists of different ethnic groups settled in relatively sharply defined areas, and provided these groups can be made to join the collective and form a state if allowance for their ethnic differences is made in a federalist structure. Federalism may also be justified on geographical grounds whenever the territory of a state is so large that no central government could possibly be capable of acting swiftly and in conformity with regional peculiarities.

One of the existential problems of any democratic order is the legitimacy it requires from its citizens. The measure of consent of these citizens to fundamental elements of democracy, their preparedness to engage in politics, and their ability to identify with the democratic system in principle are problems that are vital to the survival of the system. The more chances a democracy affords both institutionally and procedur-ally to arrive at a consensus, to show commitment, and to identify personally with democracy, the greater are the chances of achieving functionality, stability, and permanency. Compared to the unitarian system, the federative system enhances these chances considerably. And the citizens of a federal state enjoy more opportunities for democratic participation than those in a unitarian state, particularly if there is a refined structure of independent communal self-administration.

There are good reasons for arguing that a federative democracy will conform better than a democracy with a unitarian organization to the principle that power is received in trust, that government must be accountable and supervised, and that citizens must be involved in the process of government. While it is true that a federative order is not an indispensable condition of democracy, it comes closer to the democratic ideal than any unitarian order. Due to the vertical separation of powers in a federal state, political decisions on technical matters and appointments may be arrived at in a process that is more transparent, more considered, more balanced, and consequently more controllable.

The principle of federalism was established with the intent of preventing greater political structures ruling out or even destroying the smaller ones. Political decisions that can be taken care of and can find response from the villages, towns, or perhaps even 'regions' should be left to them. Daily problems, which these smaller units are able to solve themselves, should not be solved for them by the higher echelons. The autonomy and self-respect of these smaller units are regarded as of higher value than their uniformity and equality within the nation-state. Towards the end of the nineteenth century and particularly after the First World War the idea of building up a federalized Europe and of constantly diminishing the strength of the traditional nation-states acquired increasing popularity.

Much of the intellectual support for this movement is based on the positive reception of Johann Gottfried Herder's (1744–1803) political philosophy. Herder's writings were very much in favour of the cultural and political integrity of the European regions in general. For him all the achievements and potentials emanating out of these regions had to be regarded as precious and as a value in themselves. His entry points were the different groups of people with common linguistic and cultural characteristics. What started as an interest in popular songs and rites soon developed a political and even 'national' perspective. Herder viewed the cultural pluralism and the diversity of many small nations as enriching the 'humanity' of the world in general. Later on some nationalist thinkers reinterpreted Herder's sociopolitical philosophy negatively in order to justify the individual strength of one nation-state against the other.

In France the plea for a federalization of Europe was taken up by Victor Hugo and later by the foreign minister Aristide Briand. There was, however, a decisive difference. What Briand had in mind was the creation of a European confederation of nation-states, similar to what later on Charles de Gaulle was willing to give his consent to. Others, like the Dutch Henrik Brugmanns or the Catalan Jordi Pujol, wanted to federalize from top to bottom and thus create what they called an 'integral federalism' on the European level, with the effect of completely undermining the existing nation-states. Between the two world wars these ideas expressed the few positive approaches to the political problems of that time. After the deaths of Aristide Briand (1932) and Gustav Stresemann (1929) this discussion died down for nearly a decade. It was revived by Winston Churchill before the Second World War ended as he regarded the idea of a federalized Europe as a good solution for placating quarrelsome nation-states on the Continent, thereby giving peace to Britain.

The principle of federalism is the political twin of subsidiarity. Both principles have often been related and the linkage between them can be located in the fact that the tiered structure of the governmental order reflects the two-track idea which forms one of the constitutive elements of subsidiarity. A federal governmental structure forms a pyramid of steps, safeguarding the genuine self-administration of smaller units and ensuring their connection with superior units. Thus federalism might be understood to represent—as Oswald von Nell Breuning has often put it—the implementation of the principle of subsidiarity in the life of a state. In this interpretation federalism is, in fact, the application of the principle of subsidiarity.

The principle of subsidiarity emerged as a consequence of a reappraisal of the political philosophy of Thomas of Aquinas (1225–74) during the nineteenth century. For Saint Thomas the state was like a body, and the groups formed by individual human beings (especially the family) were the limbs. It is in the best interest of the body to help and support (*subsidium afferre*) its limbs whenever this support is needed. According to Aquinas the head should also refrain from helping if the limbs are able to help themselves. Every form of self-help is regarded as more precious than the help of others. In the same sense, Abraham Lincoln has often been quoted for his remark in 1854:

The legitimate object of government is to do for a community of people whatever they need to have done but cannot do at all, or cannot so well do for themselves in their separate and individual capacities. In all that people can do individually as well for themselves, government ought not to interfere.[2]

---

[2] Quoted in Oswald von Nell-Breuning, *Baugesetze der Gesellschaft. Gegenseitige Verantwortung*, Hilfreicher Beistand: Freiburg/Brsg, 1968, p. 88.

In the course of the nineteenth century the ideas relating to subsidiarity were discussed in all those European countries where the Catholic church had sufficient influence. While the Protestant churches strongly supported the nation-state, the Catholic church was predominantly and very much against this mainstream and had —like the Social Democrats—in Bismarck's Germany even been persecuted for that. A first conceptualization of the principle of subsidiarity can be found in the encyclical *Rerum Novarum* of 1891 and then, more precisely, in the encyclical *Quadragesimo Anno* of 1931. In the latter paragraph 79 states:

—that the nature of all social action is subsidiary: it must support all the different limbs of the social body without absorbing one of them;
—that whatever an individual is able to do for himself, no other political unit is allowed to take from him;
—that whatever smaller political units (families, social or political organizations) can achieve, no bigger political unit is allowed to exploit or even to destroy;
—that whenever individual human beings or a group of individuals are not or not sufficiently able to help themselves, the bigger political units not only may but must provide their help in the interest of the political body as a whole.

The principle of subsidiarity gives full justice to society. The functioning of the social order in a democratic society depends on the stability of primary or intermediary groups. On the one hand, it guarantees them a space to live, a certain freedom of action and self-determination. On the other hand, these groups are integrated into a social order. It offers them a chance to carry out their own solutions from below. Although some regard that principle as pre-modern, for others it pays a particular respect to the complexity of modern societies and to the plurality of interests. Therefore, it gained decisive influence in the building up of the new Federal Republic of Germany after the Second World War and served as the guiding principle when the new constitution (Basic Law) was formulated in 1948, and for the building-up of a social market economy.

The principle of subsidiarity was not only of importance for the political development of West Germany, it began to get reflected more and more in other West-European countries as well. It provided a benchmark of orientation especially for the different forms of cross-border regional cooperation that had started in particular regions since the early 1970s. These forms of regionalism (as for instance in Catalunia) refer back to the original idea of integral federalism. For them the European Union resembles a multinational state in that their particular demands for self-determination are be given more attention in Brussels than on any national level. In Maastricht (February 1992) this attention was documented for the first time in a European Treaty. It was mentioned in its preamble. Article 3b states that:

In areas which do not fall within its exclusive competence, the Community shall take action, in accordance with the principle of subsidiarity, only if and insofar as the objectives of the proposed action cannot be sufficiently achieved by the member states and can therefore, by reason of the scale or effects of the proposed action, be better achieved by the Community. Any action by the Community shall not go beyond what is necessary to achieve the objectives of this Treaty.[3]

While some decision-makers in Europe look upon the reference to subsidiarity in the Treaty of Maastricht as a breakthrough for more regionalization and democratic representation, for others it is still subject to debate and they are doubtful how it will ever be implemented. In order to understand some of these controversies we have to remember that activities within and among certain regions on the one hand and the regional policy launched in Brussels, Strasbourg or elsewhere on the other are often too different to be harmonized. At the same time there is little agreement on what should characterize a region. An area with certain autonomies can be called a region, a federal state or part of it can be a region, and a nation-state itself, like Luxembourg certainly is a region or perhaps even only a part of a bigger region. What are the elements they should have in common? For

[3] Quoted in: Heinrich Albert Hoffschulte, 'Federalism as Practised in Germany: The Status and Role of Regions and Local Bodies in the Federal System', in D.D. Khanna and Gert W. Kück, ed., *Principles, Power and Politics*, New Delhi: Macmillan, 1999, p. 119.

some experts many of the existing definitions are regarded as 'soft law'.[4]

The regions within the European Union (leaving Eastern Europe and especially the Balkans aside) might be differently structured, be based on different legal grounds, and also geographically be differently shaped. Even within one state, like for instance in Spain, the existing regions are structured in a completely different way, be it legally, socially or economically. The regions of the EU concentrate on political as well as economical issues, on infrastructure building as well as on technology, and on social as well as on cultural matters. In recent years, environmental concerns have found increasing attention; especially since the late 1970s these common concerns over environmental issues have very often become the focal point of cross-border regional interests.

REGIONAL POLICY AS AN ELEMENT
OF EUROPEAN INTEGRATION

If it is correct that none of the German borders described above are controversial anymore today, much of the credit for that goes to the process of European integration. Faced with the consequences of two world wars, a strong movement for the unification of Europe marked an end to many of the border conflicts in the Old Continent by changing the meaning and the relevance of these borders. According to Jean Monnet, one of the most influential 'behind the scene' founding fathers of European unification, the primary aim was not to unite states but to bring people together. In fact, many of the people living in border regions had always cooperated with each other, no matter whether these contacts were social, cultural, commercial, or trade.

As far as the future of Germany was concerned, the ideas of European unification gained a decisive influence in the thought processes of decision makers in Western Europe. During 1946 and 1947 the growing conviction was that new sovereignty to

[4] Rudolf W. Strohmeier, 'Regionalisierung: Konstruktionselemente für ein modernes Europa', in *KAS-Auslandsinformationen* 7/1994, pp. 57–71, here p. 66.

any part of Germany could only be granted if this area was incorporated into a strong framework of European cooperation. The new Federal Republic of Germany was perhaps the first state in Europe, which gained sovereignty by integration. The reconciliation between France and Germany especially, who had been rivals for centuries, took place during the 1950s. For a start, it was based on a Community of Coal and Steel, followed by many other forms of cooperation. As it turns out today, it can be regarded as one of the greatest political achievements of European integration. The two most important names that have to be mentioned in this respect are Charles de Gaulle and Konrad Adenauer. They not only created exchange-programmes that brought millions of young people from both countries together but also initiated a process of close economic cooperation which has deepened and expanded all through the past fifty years.

Aside from this unique French-German relationship, increasing support for border regions was a key issue for all member states the moment the first of the European Treaties was signed in Rome in 1957. The idea that the process of European integration should lead to a balanced development within the incorporated countries was a general aim right from the start. Regionalism, however, did not play an important role during the 1950s and 1960s.

From the end of the 1960s onwards, increasing attention was given to the demands for a European regional policy. Although the idea of an equally balanced economic development within the European Community had been considered earlier, it had been originally hoped that a free and open market economy might help diminish regional discrepancies. As events unfolded, they led to the realization that this concept was difficult to sustain, and increased demands for limited interventions became acceptable. A coherent policy in favour of specific disadvantaged regions was regarded as an important element of the common as well as of each national political agenda from now on.[5]

Initially, these demands were specifically being pushed by Italy, which was one of the six founding states and at that time had some of the poorest regions within the community. After Great

[5] Vgl. Thomas Oppermann, *Europarecht*, Munich: C.H. Beck, 1991, pp. 324–8.

Britain, Denmark and Ireland had joined in 1973 they immediately supported the quest for a regional policy, so that a special fund for regional development was implemented in 1975. This fund was not supposed to become independent of European politics to support the separate national initiatives. It was put under the control of the European Commission and could be used for common as well as for national projects, given that these were of common interest.

The demand for a stronger regional policy was further strengthened after the so-called expansion to the south which incorporated Greece, Spain and Portugal in 1981 and 1986. Since then, Greece, South Italy, some parts of Spain, Portugal and Ireland are regarded as regions coming under the first category for the support of the community. Parts of Middle and North England as well as small parts of South France were put into the second category. Before the unification of the two Germanys the Federal Republic was expected only to donate to the regional fund. Among the countries which received this support, Italy was in the first place with a maximum limit of 29 per cent of the respective annual budget, followed by Spain with 24 per cent, Great Britain with 19 per cent, Portugal with 14 per cent, Greece with 11 per cent, France with 10 per cent and Ireland with 5 per cent. The actual figures, however, change from year to year.

From 1985 to 1992 the main thrust was on the so-called Integrated Mediterranean Programme. At this time the per capita income of, for instance, the region around Paris (Ile de France) or the federal state of Hamburg was six times higher than that of Portugal. Along with the 'Single European Act', signed in February 1986, the regional policy became a constitutionally integrated element of the European Union. It also played an important role in the integration of the former German Democratic Republic because it was agreed from the beginning that immediately after the unification the whole area of the GDR would be given top priority for regional support. The re-creation of the former federal states by the last and transitory government of the GDR[6] was not a precondition for the imple-

[6] On the re-creation of the federal states in the former GDR see, Christian Starck, 'The Constitution of the new German Länder and their origin.

mentation of the European regional policy. It was, however, very important for German-German integration. While some parts of the population in the East found it difficult to accept this step, the federal states in the West tried hard to avoid taking on too much of the financial burden, which then had to be carried by Germany at the national level and also at the European level.

Since the mid-1970s the regional policy of the European Union has gained constant momentum. Support of the policy is accepted as a common duty of all member states and is expected to strengthen the identification with the Union as a whole. Some of its critics point out that an emphasis on regionalism supports provincialism and separatism at the same time, in addition to having a negative influence on specific cases like the breaking-up of political order in the former Yugoslavia. On the whole, most people in the European Union see the main aims of its regional policy being fulfilled: it contributes to an equally balanced income for the population, it is regarded as a form of minority support and it encourages cross-border regional cooperation.

The direct cooperation between many European regions and institutions also has another important impact: it further reduces the power and the influence of the traditional nation-states. Today, regions interact and deal with one another directly. Within this vast area of more than 370 million inhabitants we now count at least 50 different regions.[7] Given the fact that many of the former borders are open by now there is a lot of direct regional cooperation, as well as competition. Some of the positive examples of direct regional cooperation deserve to be mentioned. These for instance are:

(i) 'EUREGIO' along the German-Dutch border, including 104 villages, towns and counties from either side;
(ii) 'ArgeALP' and 'ArgeALPENADRIA' which include also parts of Switzerland although it is not yet a member of the Union;

A comparative Analysis, in Gert W. Kück, Sudhir Chandra Mathur and Klaus Schindler, eds., *Federalism and Decentralisation. Centre-State Relations in India and Germany*, Delhi: Mudrit, 1998, pp. 163–212.

[7] Vgl. Peter-Christian Müller-Graff, 'Die Europäischen Regionen in der Verfassung der EG', in *Integration* 20/3, 1997, pp. 145–59.

(iii) The same is true for the community of regions around Lake Konstanz, formed by Baden-Württemberg and Bavaria from Germany, Vorarlberg from Austria and Thurgau as well as Sankt Gallen from Switzerland;
(iv) 'Sar-Lor-Lux', consisting of the German federal state of Saarland, the French region of Lorraine and the state of Luxembourg.

These forms of cooperation should not be regarded as an outcome of a regional policy introduced from above, but rather as expressions of independent and successful regional activities. On the whole, many of the aforementioned 50 regions still have to be listed as comparatively disadvantaged. To address this problem, Article 198a of the Treaty of Maastricht established a 'Committee of the Regions' (COR). The COR was set up in 1994 and serves as a model of European federalism. Right from the beginning it was linked to the ongoing debate on a 'Europe of regions'. This debate is perceived and viewed rather critically in some of the old nation-states (e. g. Great Britain) because it further undermines their influence. At the same time most of the German federal states would like to see the COR institutionalized into a 'Chamber of Regions' and thus implant a third tier into the European structure. Dietrich Pause, the first Secretary General of the COR, called it a 'living expression of subsidiarity'.[8]

The COR gives regions and cities a say for the first time in the process of European integration. It has the right to take up any issue and present it to the European institutions. It also initiates cross-border activities and, in general, has taken an open and positive stance on equal opportunities. It can, therefore, be regarded as a driving force that ensures the mainstreaming of equality within the Union. The COR influences policy-making so that the diverse needs of local communities are met. A common critique of the COR, however, should also be mentioned: in several regions there are ongoing controversies regarding the contradiction between what these regions demand for themselves

---

[8] Undated interview, put on the web-page under: www.cor.eu.int/Archive/Pause.html.

on the European level and—contrary to the spirit of subsidiarity—what they consent to at the lower levels.

The regional politics of the EU has always been structured with the aim of providing support for economically weaker regions. The modalities of these forms of assistance were implemented and applied by these regions themselves. There have always been regions which were able to push their interests more forcefully than others. In some cases political compromises had to be made. In general, regional politics as it has developed since 1975, can be regarded as a proof of European solidarity because it has been carried forward mostly by justified regional demands rather than by expectations of a *juste retour*.

CONCLUSION

The policy of the European Commission in Brussels has often been criticized for being too centralistic and, thus, lacking democratic legitimacy.[9] The principle of subsidiarity is, in this respect, seen as a counter-balance, for it not only influences the distribution of power but also affects its implementation. The strengthening of the process of regionalization is the most important impact of the principle of subsidiarity. While many regard it as a chance to bring political decisions closer to the people, others deplore the deprivation of power for the nation-states. Legally, these nation-states still have to be accepted as the constitutive elements of the European Union, while the Committee of the Regions only has the right to be consulted. As far as the question of good governance is concerned, however, it is hoped that the principle of subsidiarity will increasingly function so as to democratize the European Union's institutions.

In the context of contemporary discussions about the need for reforms, and the possible re-structuring of EU funds policy there are two guidelines to be fulfilled. On the one hand, the criteria according to which certain regions are justified in demanding

---

[9] See: Wolfram Hilz 'Bedeutung und Instrumentalisierung des Subsidiaritätsprinzips für den europäischen Integrationsprozeß', in *APuZ* B21–22/1999, pp. 28–38.

special privileges or support have to be re-defined more specifically, and on the other a new consensus might be necessary among the member states about their long-term aims as far as regional policy is concerned.[10]

The process of European integration is still unfolding, and the speed of the movement even seems to increase. Although up to now the old Continent is marked by cultural diversity and more than 40 languages are spoken, politically and economically it is developing towards a single entity. The 1992 Treaty of Maastricht is commonly regarded as an economic breakthrough. It will not be long now before a unique European currency will be fully implemented. The Treaty of Amsterdam in 1997 was a further step towards consolidation. It established new rules for the internal security system as well as for the integration of possible new member-states in the future, the most controversial among these being the case of Turkey. The Kosovo-crisis has brought all states closer together again in order to agree—more than ever before—on a common foreign policy. The common security interests tend to create a kind of 'fortress' against uncontrolled and unwanted migration particularly in east and south-east Europe, and thus contributing to a 're-territorialization' of regional interests. At the same time, some internal regional security problems still remain unsolved, be it the Basque-country, Corsica or Northern Ireland.

The European Union has proved to be a political community of common values, one of the most important being peace. A more courageous answer to some of the demands for regionalization can be regarded as an important element in its own striving for legitimacy.

---

[10] Vg. Rolf Berend, 'Die Notwendigkeit der Strukturfondsreform', in Günter Rinsche and Ingo Friedrich, eds., *Weichenstellung für das 21. Jahrhundert. Erfordernisse und Persperktiven der europäischen Integration*, Böhlau, Köln, 1998, pp. 267–74.

Regionalization as Peace Instrument: Central Asia

Devendra Kaushik

The vast area of Central Asia and Kazakhstan which spreads from the Urals to the Pamirs and from the shores of the Caspian Sea to the Altai mountains has been historically, geographically and economically a distinct regional entity with specific features. The region has had several names such as Turan, Maverannahr, DeshtiKipchak and Turkestan. Before its incorporation in the Tsarist Russian Empire the Central Asian cultural space comprised not only the above-mentioned territory but also the adjacent area of northern Iran, Afghanistan, part of western China and even the north-west portion of the Indian subcontinent. The present area of Central Asia (the five Central Asian Republics of Kazakhstan, Kyrgyzstan, Uzbekistan, Turkmenistan and Tajikistan) covers about 4 million sq. km. with a population of more than 55 million people.

A Holistic View

The region is territorywise equal to half the size of the United States and the whole of Western and Eastern Europe. The area of Central Asia proper excluding Kazakhstan comes to only about 1.3 million sq. km. Both Tsarist Russian and Soviet scholars did not include Kazakhstan in the Central Asian region. In the Russian language there exist two different names for what is commonly designated as Central Asia in the English language (Srednyaya Aziya or Middle Asia and Tsentralnaya Aziya or Central Asia). A specific feature of the Central Asian region is its strong link with Russia. Geographically speaking, Central Asia is a continuation of the Russian steppe. The Urals which do not run all the way from north to south hardly represent a natural divide.

Russia's relations with the transcaucasian and the Central Asian region, currently designated as 'Near Abroad' in the lexicon of Russian diplomacy, have a millennium old history. Beginning with the Kama Bulgars, the close interaction between the peoples of Russia and the great steppe region resulted by the end of the twelfth century in the formation of what noted Russian orientalist Lev Gumilev described as a single ethnographic space. Russian historian Robert Landa characterizes Russia's relationship with the peoples of the periphery who embraced Islam after the Arab conquest of Central Asia in the eighth century AD as a complex one of 'proximity and divergence'. Seventeen per cent of the Russian nobility in the eighteenth century could trace back its ancestral lineage to the Golden Horde. In several Russian provinces most of the aristocratic families were of Turkic descent. In the Volga Ural region the Russians, Tartars and Bashkirs developed a common culture and lifestyle.[1]

By the end of the nineteenth century following incorporation of Crimea, the transcaucasus and the Central Asian region Russia became a multi-ethnic and multi-religious country with a population of 18 million Muslims, equal to the number of Muslims in the Ottoman Empire.

Russia and Central Asia constitute a common Eurasian security and economic space. British geographer Halford Mackinder viewed the Empire of Russia as a unique institution inasmuch as it represented a remarkable 'correlation between natural environment and political organisation. unlikely to be altered by any possible social revolution'.[2]

Thus the links of Russia with Central Asia are as strong and natural as the latter's ties with Iran and Turkey. True, the people of the Central Asian Republics of Uzbekistan, Turkmenistan, Kazakhstan and Kyrgyzstan have close cultural and linguistic affinities with Turkey as the people of Tajikistan have with Iran,

---

[1] Robert Landa, 'From the History of Relations between Russia and Islam', *Russia and the Modern World* (Moscow), no. 5, 1997.

[2] Halford J. Mackinder, 'The Geographical Pivot of History', *The Geographical Journal*, 23, 1904, pp. 421–44.

and the historical ties of Iran with Central Asia are older than the latter's ties with Russia. But then there was no imperial state on the territory of present-day Russia in the pre-Christian era and Central Asia has never been part of a single state formation with either Iran or Turkey in modern times. The Russian settlers in Central Asia numbering 8–10 million far outnumber the Arab, Iranian or Turk settlers in the region. The Russian language is understood and spoken throughout the entire Central Asian region and the Central Asian elite feels more at home with it than with its own native language. Millions of mixed marriages bear testimony to the Central Asian region being an integral part of a common Eurasian cultural and ethnic space together with Russia which has been marked apart from west and south-west Asia and China by a great knot of mountains joining Kopet Dagh, Hindukush, Pamir and Tienshan. Notwithstanding the advocacy of throwing Russia out of Central Asia by Z. Brzezinsky in cooperation with China, Pakistan, Iran and Turkey, 'geopolitical realism' is seen even by some Western analysts as a powerful factor preventing the rupture of Central Asia's traditional ties with Russia.[3]

It is necessary to take a holistic view of the ongoing process of regionalization in Central Asia if it is aimed at bringing peace and stability to the region and the countries bordering it. The Central Asian states' efforts to forge a balanced relationship with their neighbours in the north as well as the south—by seeking to develop economic cooperation with their Islamic neighbours within the framework of the ECO and with Russia through the CIS while trying to consolidate their ties at the regional level by setting up the Central Asian community—can only be commended. Ties with the West as well as neighbouring states such as Turkey, Iran and China have also expanded.

Moves Towards Regional Integration

Steps towards creation of a single Central Asian economic space were in fact taken even before the disintegration of the Soviet Union. Thus Central Asian integration was discussed in 1990

[3] See A. Banuazizi and M. Wiener (eds.), *The New Geopolitics of Central Asia and its Borderlands*, London, New York, 1944.

during a Conference in Alma Aty. When the USSR collapsed in December 1991 the Central Asian leaders were uncertain about the prospects of their independence and three days after the Slavic states of Russia, Ukraine and Belarus formed the CIS, they met in Ashgabat to decide upon their course of action.

After some discussion on regional cooperation these leaders decided not to press for a Central Asian alternative to the CIS and pleaded for their inclusion in that organization.

However, in April 1992 at a summit in Bishkek, the Central Asian Republics' heads signed agreements to coordinate economic reforms and create multilateral institutions for monetary and investment cooperation. In December 1992 the Central Asian Republics joined the Economic Cooperation Organization (ECO), formed by Iran, Pakistan and Turkey and aimed at promoting economic ties and development. In early 1993 more concrete discussions were held about establishing a Central Asian economic cooperation area. Thus the way was paved for the creation of a 'common economic space' and an inter-governmental council in April 1994 among Kazakhstan and Kyrgyzstan, and for the adoption of an ambitious proposal to create a European Union type common market by the year 2000.

After the abolition of the rouble zone, Kazakhstan and Uzbekistan began their efforts for creating a single economic space. The two states concluded on 10 January 1994 negotiations on the agreement for the creation of a single economic territory. They were joined shortly thereafter by Kyrgyzstan. By a declaration in Alma Aty on 8 July 1994 the three heads of states resolved to form an inter-parliamentary work group entrusted with the task of harmonizing the legal frameworks, increase their joint efforts to protect the environment specifically in the form of additional measures for rehabilitation of the Aral Sea and coordination of their foreign policies.

The Alma Aty Declaration left several questions about details of a single economic territory unanswered and took a project specific approach by identifying 60 joint projects in important sectors of the economy and recommended the establishment of a Central Asian Bank to serve as a clearing house and development bank. The Alma Aty Declaration emphasized the open nature of the integration project making it possible for Turkmenistan, Tajikistan and other CIS states to join this organization. The three heads of state not only issued a non-binding declaration of intent but also took the concrete step of forming an Interstate Council consisting of the presidents and prime ministers of the member states. In addition to the creation of this supreme body they resolved to establish the Council of Prime Ministers that was to meet four times a year, as well as the Council of Defence Ministers and the Council of Foreign Ministers. They also decided to form an Executive Committee with headquarters at Alma Aty. The Executive Committee is expected to provide solutions for the problems of economic policy that the individual states have been unable to resolve. The Interstate Council appointed Serik Primabetov, a Kazakh, as the committee's first chairman. Kyrgyzstan and Uzbekistan were each represented by one vice-chairman.

The three Central Asian states also held discussions on trilateral military cooperation. In September 1995 their leaders expressed satisfaction at their progress towards integration and invited Turkmenistan, Tajikistan and Azerbaijan to join them. The chairman of the Inter-Governmental Council stated that the Central Asian states have recognized an 'objective' need to cooperate and integrate in order to foster economic growth, security and political stability.[4]

A CAUSE FOR GENUINE CONCERN

The need for regional cooperation for development and security in Central Asia cannot be overemphasized. The unstable situation in Central Asia represents a threat to peace. The vast oil and natural gas resources of the region have made it an object of intensified international activity and interest. There is an ongoing competition among external powers for influence in Central Asia and this competition is likely to intensify further with the projected development of oil and gas reserves in Kazakhstan, Turkmenistan and Azerbaijan which also happen to be the littoral states, along with Iran and Russia on the

[4] Paul Kubicek, 'Regionalism, Nationalism and Realpolitik in Central Asia', *Europe Asia Studies*, vol. 49, no. 4, 1997, p. 642.

Caspian Sea, known to be fabulously rich in oil. However, to designate this competition as the new 'Great Game' is to belittle the importance of the Central Asian peoples as independent actors and masters of their national destiny. India, which earlier rejected the concept of power vacuum in the Indian Ocean region in the late sixties and early seventies following the British withdrawal, does not subscribe to the new 'Great Game' thesis which is based on the so-called power vacuum in Central Asia in the wake of disintegration of the Soviet Union and the continued weakness of Russia.

The rejection of the 'Great Game' scenario, however, does not imply denial of a fierce competition for influence over the new Central Asian states. The rich mineral wealth of the region and its strategic location in the centre of the Eurasian landmass has made it a cockpit of international rivalry. According to experts the region is believed to contain 20 billion barrels of proven oil reserves and 7 trillion cubic metres of natural gas. The oil reserves in the Caspian shelf are estimated at 17 to 21 billion tons. As the world moves towards the twenty-first century a new element has entered the energy equation. Most of the Asian countries, not just Japan but all the so-called Asian tigers from the Philippines to China and the whole of South and South-East Asia need larger supplies of oil. In such conditions the Central Asian energy resources have begun to attract worldwide attention.

Geopolitical considerations are becoming crucial in determining the transport routes for oil and gas through new pipelines. Little wonder then, the area of vital US interest has been extended from the Persian Gulf in the time of President Carter to the Caspian Sea basin during the second presidential term of Bill Clinton.

Against the backdrop of this intensified global interest in the energy resources of Central Asia the current unstable situation in Central Asia is a cause for genuine concern. This situation has been further aggravated by several distortions in the state boundaries inherited from the Soviet period. The boundaries of the respective states contain large minorities of other ethnic groups of this region as well as sizeable Russian populations. The current economic situation in the Central Asian states with the probable exception of Uzbekistan is also a cause for concern as it has been showing few signs of stabilization. The potential threat of Islamic fundamentalism in central Asia need not be ignored. Given the economic hardships of the transitional period, an attempt by the opposition to mobilize the masses in the name of Islam cannot be ruled out. This threat is particularly serious in the Ferghana region of Uzbekistan, the adjacent Kyrgyz region of Osh and Tajikistan where the Islamists seized power in 1992 with the support of democrats skillfully exploiting the clan and regional rivalries. Under conditions of social tensions caused by problems of transition of a free market economy and democracy there persists a danger of easy conversion of 'folk Islam' into 'political Islam' and, through the exploitation of the latter by vested interests and internal opposition, into 'fundamentalist Islam'. The Islamist fundamentalist forces are trying to come to power in Central Asia through coercion and outside interference resulting in civil war and turbulence in Tajikistan and Afghanistan. This is having a spillover effect on the Indian state of Kashmir and the transcaucasian region of Russia. Cross-border terrorism instigated by the fundamentalists or religious extremists has become a serious threat to security in the Central Asian states and the adjoining regions of India, China and Russia.

Whether one subsribes to the 'neorealist' or 'interdependence' theories or not, the imperatives for regionalization of Central Asia are generally acceptable. The weak states of Central Asia are likely to collaborate in the face of common preponderant threats. They are bound to act rationally by collaborating at the regional level. Growing economic interdependence and awareness of common transitional problems have reduced the importance of national boundaries and created a demand for international cooperation at the regional level. The newly independent states of Central Asia cannot solve their numerous problems through unilateral action. Common problems demand a pooling of resources and creation of institutions to oversee cooperation. This naturally takes place at the regional level, for states in the same region share a variety of concerns, possess similar cultures and social structures and have greater interaction. Central Asian states share numerous common problems some of which have been mentioned earlier. Problems such as environmental degradation in the Caspian and Aral seas or water resource management demand an inter-regional response.

REGIONALIZATION: THE CENTRAL ASIAN EXPERIENCE

The Central Asian experience of regional cooperation through various forums such as the CIS, the Central Asian Economic Union subsequently renamed Central Asian Economic Community, the stillborn Eurasian proposal, and the Economic Cooperation Organization (ECO) which includes Iran, Turkey and Pakistan has been far from satisfactory. The CIS has turned out to be 'neither marriage nor divorce'. The CIS summits have only added to the already large number of unimplemented agreements and declarations running into several hundreds. Even the much talked about Customs Union of the four CIS states—Russia, Belarus, Kazakhstan and Kyrgyzstan—in which Tajikistan has also joined in 1999 has not so far made much headway with the member states still grappling with problems of streamlining the existing structures and laws.

Yet the very fact that four states of the CIS have reached an agreement to set up a Customs Union with Russia in a move towards creating a common market marks a new stage in the direction of Eurasian regional integration. Russia, it appears, is all set to cast off its earlier stance of distancing itself from its 'poor cousins' in Central Asia who were forced out of the common rouble zone in the hope of speeding up the economic reforms. Moscow has of late been compelled by the existing circumstances to encourage the integration process within the CIS. The eastward expansion of NATO, the threat posed to its territorial integrity by international terrorism supported by religious extremism after the succcess of the Taliban in Afghanistan and the dismal failure of free market reforms which it had expected to complete faster by shedding off the 'dead weight' of the Central Asian Republics dependent upon heavy central subsidies. It changed the perspective of the Kremlin on closer integration of the Central Asian states in the CIS. The new approach favoured a multi-speed integration of the CIS depending upon the willingness of the individual states.

Broadly speaking, the CIS states may be divided into three groups. The first ring of states favouring closer military and economic union includes Russia, Belarus, Kazakhstan and Kyrgyzstan. In the second group Armenia, Tajikistan, Georgia and Uzbekistan may be included. The third group consists of Azerbaijan, Moldova, Turkmenistan and Ukraine which are opposed to integration whether military or economic. The situation is somewhat fluid and the composition of these three groups keeps on changing. Thus Tajikistan has already moved on to the integrationist first group and Georgia has recently joined the third group. Uzbekistan has, of late, started taking a more favourable view of cooperation with Moscow, at least in the military sphere. This is particularly so following the attempt by religious extremists on President Karimov's life in Tashkent on 12 February 1999 and the activization of Islamist terrorist groups in Uzbek cities of Namangan, Andijan and Yangiabad. Tashkent extended a warm welcome to the acting Russian President Vladimir Putin in January 2000 and declared full support for Moscow's Chechnya war. A common defence space still more or less exists in the CIS and Russia has taken upon itself the responsibility of protecting the air space of the CIS Republics. Russian forces were guarding the international border of Tajikistan and also of Turkmenistan until recently. The Central Asian Republics, with the exception of Turkmenistan, are all signatories to a collective security treaty with Russia, signed in Tashkent in May 1992. There are indications that Uzbekistan which had declined to renew this treaty would be willing to reconsider its stand.

Kazakhstan is an enthusiastic supporter of both integration with Russia within the framework of the Eurasian Union as also of the Central Asian regional integration. President Nazarbayev finds no contradiction in such a course. The division of the republic into the Russian dominated north and the Kazakh dominated south dictates this stance of Nazarbayev. In the economic sphere Kazakhstan is closely linked with Russia. The President of Kazakhstan is not satisfied with the pace of integration followed within the framework of the CIS and looks upon the Eurasian Union proposal with Russia as the real solution for carrying out the economic reforms by forming a monetary and economic union without sacrificing state sovereignty. The Eurasian project also envisages a political union through the creation of a common Parliament along the lines of the European Union. The Eurasian Union is oriented towards Russia and seeks to join around it a number of states lying between Russia and India on a voluntary basis, with Kazakhstan playing a key role in its formation. Uzbekistan is opposed to the Eurasian proposal of the President of Kazakhstan and does not favour a closer economic union with Russia. Tashkent supports the Central Asian Economic Community with Uzbekistan playing a key role in it. Alma Aty on the other hand views the Central Asian Economic Community as but an initial step towards the formation of a Eurasian Union. It feels that stronger Central Asian regional cooperation will help Kazakhstan in withstanding the Russian pressure from the north.

The ECO has never achieved the desired impact. Rather than viewing the ECO as a genuine forum for integration, its three important members, Iran, Turkey and Pakistan, have tried to use this organization to promote their own interests in the Central Asian states. The differences between the participating countries are too great to permit them to undertake regional integration projects. Three important members of the ECO, viz., Turkey, Iran and Pakistan view the organization as an instrument to promote their interests in Central Asia rather than a serious effort towards regional integration. Iran considers ECO as a step toward setting up an Islamic Common Market as a counterweight to the West. Such an approach is not shared by Turkey. Uzbekistan President Islam Karimov looks at the ECO as a 'particularly trade and economic organization which does not permit any attempt at its politicization'. Notwithstanding the differences in the approach of the various members of the ECO, this organization has some creditable achievements especially in the field of transport and communications. The completion of the Tejen Sarraks Meshed Bandar Abbos railway line has linked Central Asia with the Persian Gulf. India, Iran and Turkmenistan concluded a tripartite transit agreement for utilization of this route. By joining the Meshed-Tehran rail link, Beijing has now been connected to Tehran and Istambul through Urumchi, Alma Aty and Tashkent. According to experts the transasiatic railway line will be carrying a load of 7 to 8 million tons per year. Agreements signed by Uzbekistan, Azerbaijan, Turkmenistan and Georgia have also opened the transcaucasus rail route to Europe which will enable the landlocked Central Asian region to join the global trade and economic mainstream.

Uzbekistan and Turkmenistan have also signed agreements for construction of a gas pipeline to Pakistan through Afghanistan. Work has already begun on the pipeline from Turkmenistan to Iran. Agreement on the construction of an oil pipeline from Azerbaijan to the Turkish port of Ceyhan on the Mediterranean through Georgia has also been concluded last year. The ECO has however not so far succeeded in making any worthwhile diversion in the direction of Central Asian trade. Nor has it resulted in bringing a sizeable investment in the region from Pakistan, Iran and Turkey.

The Central Asian Economic Union which has been renamed as the Central Asian Economic Community in 1998 and joined by Tajikistan has made some modest progress in the direction of regional cooperation by identifying about 40 joint projects and establishing a Central Asian Development Bank to execute them. Out of these 40 projects the focus is currently on 12 important and viable ones. In the field of water resource management notable success has been achieved by setting up the Syr Daria Consortium to direct the allocation of water in this river and construction of reservoirs and dams in Kyrgyzstan, Uzbekistan and Tajikistan. This has encouraged the taking up of the task of a similar agreement on the Amu Daria water.

Central Asian regional cooperation has suffered on account of the clash of leadership ambitions between President Islam Karimov of Uzbekistan and President Nazarbayev of Kazakhstan. According to a news item published in the Kyrgyz press, President Karimov did not attend the Cholpan Ata summit in July 1998 in Kyrgyzstan as he was not happy with the 'political wedding' of the children of the Kyrgyz and Kazakh Presidents.[5]

Despite the functioning of the Inter-State Council of Presidents of four Central Asian states, the Central Asian Republics

[5] *Slovo Kyrgyzstana*, 21 July 1998.

have largely relied on bilateral agreements. Turkmenistan, which pursues a course of positive neutrality, has steered itself clear of the multilateral framework under both the CIS and the Central Asian Economic Community. It has, however, been participating in the efforts to save the Aral Sea. Caution has thus been the hallmark of Central Asian regionalization. It was aptly summed up in an observation made by President Akaev of Kyrgyzstan: 'Running ahead can result in no less harm than being left behind.'[6]

A statement by the chairman of the Council of Federation of Russia, E. Stroev, also struck a similar note. Stroev commended the Russian approach of gradual movement from one form of integration to another. 'This process has to be evolutionary as it entails synchronization of behaviour of market reforms, achievement of parity of prices and setting up of financial and industrial groups'. President Nazarbayev of Kazakhstan was perhaps not off the mark when he stated that it was too soon to talk of any confederation among Central Asian states since 'each is preoccupied with resolution of its own vital problems and the process of establishing authentic statehood has only just begun'.[7]

The Central Asian summit held in Bishkek in June 1999 recommended the adoption of effective measures for creating a free trade zone which would function as a mechanism of the stage-by-stage formation of a single economic space in the region by AD 2000. The summit emphasized the need to first create conditions for effective multilateral trade and economic cooperation by means of preliminary agreements on measures for regulating bilateral and multilateral relations. This was to be done in particular in the spheres of mutually advantageous and effective utilization of regional transport and communications, water, fuel power and investment resources; creation of favourable conditions for reciprocal and joint investments; free passage of goods, capital and manpower; guarantee of ecological safety and attraction of investments for the member states of the

[6] Ibid., 30 January 1996.
[7] Heribert Dieter, 'Regional Integration in Central Asia: Current Economic Position and Prospects', *Central Asian Survey*, vol. 15, 1996, p. 314.

community; and further development of production cooperation on the basis of long-term programmes for developing the main sectors of the economy.[8]

Prospects of Central Asian Regional Integration

The prospects of future development of regional cooperation in Central Asia are viewed with optimism by its participants, particularly by President Islam Karimov of Uzbekistan who has provided a conceptual framework for Central Asian union under the slogan 'Our Common Home Turkestan'. However, foreign specialists do not believe in the realistic nature of the union. Thus Ross Munro of the Philadelphia Institute of Foreign Policy in his interview with Radio Liberty (25 September 1996) rules out the possibility of uniting the Central Asian countries inasmuch as each of the Central Asian republics pursues its own interests and the leaders of none of these republics are willing to delegate their powers to any supranational organ unless there is some grave political or economic crisis. Boris Rumer of the Harvard University Centre for Study of the Former Soviet Union does not find any compelling factor for economic union of the Central Asian states in view of the absence of economic prerequisites such as export specialization of the Middle Eastern countries, or interest in each others markets and their union as in Western Europe, or the existence of investible resources as in the North American economic bloc (NAFTA). According to Rumer, the creation of the Central Bank of Central Asia with a ridiculously low capital fund (US $ 9 million) was only meant to have a demonstrative effect. The Harvard University scholar views a political union of Central Asian Republics as a more probable instrument to oppose the imperial legacy of Moscow and to counteract the Tajikization of the region.[9]

This sceptical approach towards the economic union of the Central Asian republics is not confined to Western specialists

---

[8] Summary of World Broadcasts, Part II, SU/3574 G/1, 30 June 1999.
[9] N.I. Komissina, 'Uzbekistan i Politika Regionalnalnoi Integratsii v Tsentralnoi Azii', E.M. Kozhokin (ed.), *Uzbekistan: Obretenie Novogo Oblika*, Tom. 2, Moscow, 1998, p. 217.

and is also shared by some of their Russian counterparts. N. Shmelov of the Russian Academy of Sciences has doubts about any effective regional cooperation in Central Asia at the economic level. The common market in Central Asia has still a long way to go as the volume of intra-regional trade is 2.5 times less than the trade with Russia. Despite some reorientation in the direction of foreign trade since 1991, trade with Russia still contributes up to 50 per cent of their commodity turnover whereas their level of intra-regional trade accounts for only 10 per cent which is quite low in comparison with the 60 to 70 per cent level of trade among the members of the European Community.[10]

In the opinion of L. Lutsenko, Chief Specialist of the Economy Ministry of Kyrgyzstan, the Central Asian market is being formed slowly but the prospects of economic integration between Kazakhstan and Kyrgyzstan are higher than the integration of these two states with Uzbekistan, whose interests lie mainly outside Central Asia.[11]

Specialists in the Economy Ministry of Kazakhstan are of the view that the Central Asian Economic Community would continue to grow as it draws sustenance from the prolonged existence of interdependence based on territorial division of labour formed during the Soviet period. The pressure of external developments like the situation in Afghanistan would also contribute to this.[12]

Thus, given the circumstances noted above, the four states of Central Asia, with the sole exception of Turkmenistan, have come together to form the Central Asian Economic Community. Whether or not the community progresses beyond the declaratory character would depend upon the relations between the two large Central Asian States of Kazakhstan and Uzbekistan. Both of them have leadership ambitions in Central Asia. Uzbekistan's claim to leadership is based on its large population and its position as the anchor state in Central Asia during the Soviet period. Kazakhstan stakes its claim on its territorial primacy and

[10] Paul Kubicek, op. cit.
[11] *Aziya Ekonomika i Zhizn*, no. 32, 1996, p. 3.
[12] *Delovaya Nedelya*, 26 December 1997.

geographical location as a connecting link between Europe and Asia. Modest progress has been registered in the direction of regional integration in Central Asia within the framework of the Central Asian Economic Community. The Central Bank of Central Asia has started functioning with its headquarters in Alma Aty and a sister branch in Tashkent. It is financing some enterprises of regional importance in Bishkek, Alma Aty and Tashkent. In August 1997, a concrete agreement was reached among the Central Asian states—Uzbekistan, Kazakhstan and Kyrgyzstan—on the regulation of tariff for rail transport. Agreement has also been reached for the construction of a road linking Andijan in Uzbekistan to Kashgar in China via Irkeshtam in Kyrgyzstan. Work has been completed on a long-term agreement on the use of the Naryn and Syr Daria cascades of hydro-electric stations. All the five Central Asian states have worked out a scheme for development of thermal power resources in Central Asia. Agreements are ready for signature on the establishment of a common market for electrical energy for Central Asia and on proportionate financing for repair and maintenance of water reservoirs of regional importance. Since 1996 trade restrictions have been removed between Kyrgyzstan and Kazakhstan and since 1997 between Uzbekistan and Kyrgyzstan and Kazakhstan on a bilateral basis. Uzbekistan, however, is reluctant to remove customs check for fear of smuggling of narcotics and arms.

In 1997, the Kyrgyz Parliament adopted a resolution on interstate water utilization by Uzbekistan, Kazakhstan and Tajikistan of the water resources of Kyrgyzstan. The Kyrgyz Parliament demanded a sum of 4 million U.S. dollars which it had spent on repair and maintenance of water reservoirs on its territory. The problem has been resolved by an agreement that states that Kyrgyzstan would be compensated by supply of natural gas from Uzbekistan and petroleum from Kazakhstan for the use of its water resources.

In 1995, the four Central Asian states decided to form a Central Asian Battalion as a joint force for peace keeping operations. Central Asian leaders have not lost hope about the participation of Turkmenistan notwithstanding the pursuit of a policy of positive neutrality by the latter. At the time of the Ashgabat summit of the five Central Asian states in January 1998 an attempt was made to persuade the Turkmen President to join the Central Asian Union. President Niyazov was reported to have shown some interest when he asked for a copy of the charter of the Central Asian Economic Community on the eve of this summit.[13]

Azerbaijan, Ukraine and Georgia are also reported to have shown interest in joining the Central Asian Economic Community as observers. Russia has already joined this organization as an observer and the European Union is helping the cause of promoting regional cooperation in Central Asia by organizing seminars and conferences on the subject.

The limited successes attained by the ongoing regional integration process in no way minimize the vital role that belongs to it in promoting peace and stability in this region which has acquired prominence because of its growing geo-political and geo-economic importance. The creation of ethnically homogeneous states out of the present-day Central Asian Republics, which have ethnically overlapping settlements, is hardly possible without large-scale bloodshed. Hence, regional integration is the only way out to prevent the development of a Yugoslavia-like situation. The threat to peace in Central Asia is really grave in view of a protracted civil war in Tajikistan and the bloody conflict in Afghanistan, which shares borders with the three Central Asian Republics of Tajikistan, Uzbekistan and Turkmenistan. The prospects for development of regional integration in Central Asia are not so bleak as believed in certain circles. The Central Asian successor states of the USSR have a vast pool of human and natural resources which can be utilized for the modern-ization of their economies. They have much in common to facilitate cooperative efforts. Their integration is well grounded in their common historical and cultural heritage. Successful regional integration is also a pre-condition for any attempt at their integration into the world market. Since Central Asia has no direct access to the ocean, increased exchange of goods and

---

[13] *Nezavisimaya Gazetta*, 20 December 1997.
[14] Herbert Dieter, op. cit., pp. 370-1.

services is of necessity tied to building a common infrastructure within Central Asia.[14]

The success of regional integration will depend on the positive interplay of forces active at three levels, viz., internal developments in Russia, relations between Russia and the Central Asian states, and relations between the various elite groups therein. One thing is clear: regional integration in Central Asia is not likely to succeed if it is pushed in the direction of anti-Russian sentiment. Only a holistic view of regional integration based on a balanced safeguarding of the interests of Russia and the Central Asian states can help develop regional co-operation as well as serve the interest of peace and stability in the Eurasian region and the adjoining states in West, South-west and South Asia.

The New Search for a Durable Solution for Refugees: South Asia

Jagatmani Acharya and Tapan K. Bose

Millions of people throughout the world are being forced to move against their will. While some are uprooted as a result of deliberate government policy, a much larger proportion are displaced by unbearable conditions of insecurity and poverty. The newspapers and the electronic media are full of headlines that tell us that increasingly the European and North American countries are 'slamming' their doors on these fleeing people. This is indicative of a disturbing global trend of forced movements of populations, known variously as 'refugees', 'displaced persons', 'expellees', 'returnees', 'asylum seekers' or 'economic migrants' and of the reluctance of governments to provide them shelter and protection. In the first half of the twentieth century involuntary migrations were concentrated in Europe. Since the 1950s the vast majority of forced migrations have taken place within and from the developing countries of the 'south'. The forced migrations in Europe before and during the two world wars and subsequent territorial realignments produced a series of mass displacements. These upheavals led to the emergence of a network of international organizations and covenants to deal with the problem of forced migration. The office of the United Nations High Commissioner for Refugees (UNHCR) was set up in 1950 with the primary responsibility of protecting refugees all over the world.

Belying all hopes of an era of peace and prosperity, the end of the Cold War triggered massive civil unrest in many countries of the former socialist block. Civil war and ethnic cleansing in the Balkans and Central Asian countries, famines in Africa and economic crises in parts of Asia and the Pacific region increased the number of displaced persons from 17 million in 1991 to 27 million in 1995.[1] On 1 January 1999, as per the UNHCR estimates, the world total of refugees and asylum seekers stood at 21.5 million. Additionally there were about 30 million internally displaced person's (IDPs), a bulk of whom were waiting to cross the international borders in search of safety and security.

The uprooted of the world share a number of common characteristics. The majority are poor and live in circumstances that offer them a narrow range of choices in life. Many are members of minority communities. Asia is the largest refugee-hosting continent with about 41 per cent of the total refugees. According to official estimates, the four countries of South Asia, Bangladesh, India, Nepal and Pakistan together host about 2 million refugees. However, non-official sources claim that the actual number of the persons who are in refugee-like situations in South Asia is much higher than the official estimates.

Large percentages of displaced persons of this region are not regarded as refugees by the host governments of South Asia. They are usually treated as undesirable aliens or illegal immigrants. There are no national laws which define or distinguish refugees from others who cross the borders. The governments have also not signed or ratified the 1951 UN Convention Concerning the Status of Refugees and its 1967 Protocol, the only available UN mechanism for the protection and rehabilitation of refugees. The purpose of this paper is to take a hard look at states and forced migrations, review hôw the international community has responded to them and suggest how these responses might be made more effective.

'NATION-STATES', 'REJECTED PEOPLE'
AND FORCED MIGRATION

There is a close link between the ideology of 'nation-states' and forced population movements. The 'nation-states' had politicized identities. The theory of popular sovereignty established the politics of majoritarianism, which led to marginalization,

[1] UNHCR, 1998, Geneva.

and rejection of large numbers of people who were forced to migrate from their traditional habitat. Throughout history people have moved from one place to another in search of better living conditions and greater economic opportunities. Before the rise of the 'nation-state', ethnic, cultural, linguistic or religious demands were not linked to a polity's claim over a territory. As the history of the Austro-Hungarian Empire shows, in empires or territorial states which had control over large tracts of landmasses inhabited by people belonging to divergent national and ethnic identities, identities and control were in such a convoluted relation among each other that identities of people *per se*, whether ethnic or national, did not make much of a difference to their political status. The democratic revolutions in Europe broke up the old empires. New states were formed. These became the nation-states. The nation-state was the opposite of the empire. The nation-states implied that its territory belonged to the population which inhabited it, and to no one else. In other words, the ideology of the nation-state claimed that the 'authority' of the state or 'sovereignty' belonged to the people who inhabited the landmass and not to any other outside agency or ruler. At the beginning of the twentieth century it seemed impossible that the nationalities' problem of the Austro-Hungarian Empire, in which populations belonged to different nationalities and ethnicities, would ever be unscrambled in a territorial fashion. But to a large degree that is what actually happened.

With the rise of the nation-state in Europe began the process of sorting out the territorial rights of communities. Yet these nation-states often encompassed people belonging to different communities/identities. These contradictions were to be resolved through the guarantee of equal rights as citizens to all individuals, irrespective of ethnicity or nationality. Political equality for all inhabitants or citizens was to be achieved through the liberal institutions of constitutional government, freely elected assemblies, the rule of law and respect for citizens' rights. The challenge to liberal values was inherent in the logic of the nation-state, in which the ethnic homogeneity of the political community was a precondition for laying a claim over a landmass. Within the nation-states, particularly those which had gained independence from empires, tensions with the newly 'nationalised' populations continued. Hannah Arendt in her *Origins of Totalitarianism*, observes,

... the secret conflict between state and nation came to light at the very birth of the modern nation state, when the French revolution combined the declaration of the Rights of Man with the demand for national sovereignty. The same essential rights were at once claimed as the inalienable heritage of all human beings and as the specific heritage of specific nations, the same nation was at once declared to be subject to laws, which supposedly would flow from the Rights of Man and sovereign that is bound by no universal law and acknowledging nothing superior to itself. The practical outcome of this contradiction was that from then on human rights were protected and enforced only as national rights and the very institution of a state, whose supreme task was to protect and guarantee man his rights as man, as citizen and national, lost its legal, rational appearance and could be interpreted by romantics as the nebulous representative of a 'national soul' which through the very fact of its existence was supposed to be beyond or above law. National sovereignty, accordingly, lost its original connotation of freedom of the people and was being surrounded by a pseudo-mystical aura of lawless arbitrariness.[2]

The crisis accentuated during the economic crisis of late nineteenth century, causing mass migration of the poor across the oceans and international frontiers, from rural areas to cities, from one region of the same state to another. Under the combined pressure of the economic crisis and mass migration, the values and institutions of liberalism collapsed giving rise to the political ideology of nationalism. Racism formed the core of this 'nationalism of pure race' and mass xenophobia in the new political order of the nineteenth century.

Minorities and Refugees

As we have seen, persecution and suppression of minorities and cross-border population flow are linked phenomena. As the history of the early twentieth century tells us, it was not just the

[2] Hannah Arendt, *The Origins of Totalitarianism*, Harcourt Brace, Jovanovich, New York, 1968, pp. 230–1.

Fascists or the Nazis but even the liberal democracies embraced the ideology of nationalism and barred their frontiers to others. The states embarked on the enterprise of building a homogeneous national identity. In consequence, the diversity of identities existing within these nation-states came under pressure. Attempts to preserve these identities—ethnic, religious and linguistic—were looked upon with suspicion. The rise of territorial nation-states in Europe, the colonial conquest of Asia, Africa and Latin America and the process of post-colonial state formation finally led to the creation of 'minorities', the 'rejected people' and the 'stateless' as a universal phenomenon in modern times.

The period of decolonization, in the sixties and seventies, saw the emergence of new nation-states in Asia, Africa and Latin America, areas with ethnic, religious and linguistic diversities. As these new 'nation-states' embarked on the task of 'nation building' the process of 'minoritization' and rejection began all over again in these parts of the world. This generated new flows of populations across the borders of the countries in the global South.

During the four decades long Cold War, human rights was considered a marginal political issue by the UN. In consequence minority rights had remained a fringe issue. Not surprising that despite the decade-long effort by the UN Sub-commission on Minorities, the draft 'UN Declaration on Persons Belonging to National or Ethnic, Linguistic and Religious Minorities' had made little progress till the mid-nineties. Similarly, the Council of Europe or the OSCE were unable to create regional mechanisms for the protection of minorities in Europe.

The collapse of the communist states in Central and Eastern Europe in 1989 and the consequent eruption of violent ethnic conflicts involving minorities in Europe changed the attitude of Western states to some extent. By 1993, the war in former Yugoslavia—Croatia, Bosnia and Serbia with its Vojvodena and Kosovo—had taken toll of several thousand lives and displaced nearly two million persons in Europe. As violence erupted in the Caucasus and Moldova, and the danger of conflicts within the emerging new states of the former Soviet Union loomed large, the European states tried to establish new standards for treatment of minorities as a conflict prevention measure. The Conference of Security and Cooperation in Europe, which in 1994 was renamed as OSCE and the Council of Europe took the lead. Mechanisms were devised for the protection of minorities in Central and Eastern Europe. A framework convention was adopted by the European states for the protection of minorities. However, some of the European governments continue to oppose the application of these new measures to secure minority rights in their own states. Obviously the mind-set of some of the European states which had prevented the Council of Europe from taking up the issues of violation of minority rights in Austria, Italy, France and United Kingdom has not changed.

States 'Recognize' Refugees

Traditionally, any person who has been forced to flee his or her home for fear of life or lack of subsistence is regarded as a refugee. However, in international law, which is based on the principle of respect for the sovereignty of states, only those who have lost the protection of their home states and as a result have crossed international borders to seek refuge in another country are accepted as refugees, as these were stateless people. And, as the Rights of Man could only be protected by a state, these people had to find protection in another state. Faced with the problem of a vast number of such stateless, displaced and uprooted persons after the First World War, the Western nations created international instruments for the protection, return as well as resettlement of these persons in other countries. Between 1922 and 1926 under the auspices of the League of Nations, several treaties were concluded to recognize the displaced people as refugees.

As these treaties created certain obligations on the contracting states, it was necessary to define the term refugee. A League of Nations treaty of 1926 had defined refugees as a category or groups of persons who were (a) outside their country of origin and (b) without the protection of the government of their home state.[3] In 1938 the definition was restricted to only such persons who had left their countries of origin due to fear of persecution. The 1938 instrument excluded those who had left their home-

---

[3] League of Nations, *Treaty Series No. 2204*, 12 May 1926.

land for purely personal reasons. It was also decided to exclude the victims of natural disasters, as the governments of their home states did not forcibly expel them. While the disaster victims required humanitarian aid, those who had lost the protection of their home state required protection, asylum and rehabilitation and hence these were the only people to be regarded as refugees under the international treaties.

The Second World War generated about 45 million refugees, mostly in Europe. The International Refugee Organization (IRO) was created to seek an early return of the refugees and the displaced persons to their countries of origin. The United Nations took up the task of rehabilitation of the refugees in a serious manner. In 1950 the Office of the UN High Commissioner for Refugees was created by the UN General Assembly, which replaced the IRO. In 1951, the United Nations Convention Relating to the Status of Refugees was adopted. The UN Protocol Relating to the Status of Refugees was adopted by the General Assembly in 1967. In the same year the General Assembly also adopted a Declaration on Territorial Asylum.

Migrants and Refugees Today

During the twenties and the thirties of the twentieth century—the period of mass movement of refugees across Europe—the international community, particularly the League of Nations, took a category or a group approach to the definition of refugees. In the Cold War period, when there was no mass movement of refugees across Europe, the attitude of the Western nations towards refugees witnessed a change, influenced largely by the politics of the Cold War. The emphasis shifted from the group to the individual. As a consequence, a more individualistic and narrower definition was adopted by the 1967 UN Protocol.[4] The 1967 UN Protocol of the UN Convention Regarding the Status of Refugees defined the refugee as any person,

... who owing to well founded fear of being persecuted for reasons of race, religion, nationality or political opinion is outside the country of his nationality and is unable or, owing to such fears or for reasons other than personal convenience, is unwilling to avail

---

[4] Goodwin-Gill, *The Refugee in International Law*, Oxford, 1997.

himself of the protection of that country; or who, not having a nationality and being outside the country of his former habitual residence, is unable or, owning to such fear or for reasons other than personal convenience, is unwilling to return to it.

This definition is being questioned today by social scientists and human rights activists. They argue that this definition is state-centric and runs contrary to the very notion of universality and indivisibility of human rights. They argue that this definition puts emphasis on the so-called cause of migration but not on the conditions in which these people are forced to live and their vulnerability to gross abuse of human rights. The states and the international bodies, in order to dismiss a large percentage of the victims, are also using this definition to call forced migration as 'voluntary'. It is argued that voluntary migrants cross international borders attracted by the pull of better economic opportunities and that, unlike political refugees, are not pushed out by the states through widespread human rights abuses or by racial and communal riots. Cross-border social, religious and ethnic linkages, especially in situations where the same community enjoys majority status in one country and that of an oppressed minority in another, also encourage migration. Migration is therefore, essentially a voluntary action. As a result, the states argue that migrants cannot be treated at a par with those refugees who are persecuted in their home states for reasons of religion, race or political opinion.

However, studies have shown that an overwhelming majority of displaced persons in the Third World, who are generally classified as immigrants by host governments and international agencies, belong to the minorities and economically backward sections of society. For example, between 1950 and 1990 about 21 million people were displaced in India by projects like big dams, mines, industries and wildlife reserves. Of these, nearly 40 per cent were tribal/indigenous peoples who constitute a meagre 7 per cent of India's population.[5] As these persons did not cross any international border they remained displaced within India.

---

[5] Walter Fernandes, *Development, Displacement and Rehabilitation in Tribal Areas of Eastern India*, New Delhi: Indian Social Institute, 1994.

The New Search for a Durable Solution | 145

In the mid-sixties more than a hundred thousand Chakma tribal people were displaced by the Kaptai dam built in the Chittagong Hill Tracts of the then East Pakistan, now Bangladesh. Nearly 52,000 people displaced by the dam belonging to the Chakma and Hajong tribes had crossed over to India. In the Mirpur district of Pakistan-controlled Kashmir, about 30,000 persons were rendered homeless by the Mangla Dam constructed around the same time, with World Bank assistance, by the Pakistan government. Most of these displaced persons from Mirpur ended up swelling the ranks of Pakistani immigrants to UK. Under these circumstances the usefulness of the distinction between voluntary and involuntary migrants remains doubtful.

Need for Reconceptualization

Clearly there is an urgent need to reconceptualize the definition of refugees in the context of universality of human rights. It is not being argued here that those who have been forced to flee their land because of political persecution and direct threat to their lives should be equated with those who have been forced to move due to loss of livelihood, man-made disasters and natural calamities. At the same time we can no longer ignore the fact that certain policies of governments have impoverished vast masses of their peoples, particularly those belonging to minority communities and economically backward sections. Studies have shown that some of the development projects implemented with international support have had an adverse impact on the livelihood of people within a country, and at times across the borders, uprooting them from their homes. They have become the rejected peoples and unwanted migrants.

Academics and NGOs today prefer to use such terms as environmental refugees and refugees of development projects to distinguish between certain types of displaced persons and voluntary migrants. The international community needs to apply its mind to the problem of this type of forced displacement. As a recent United Nation Environment Programme (UNEP) report has predicted, that day is not far off when wars would be fought between communities and states over basic resources like water. The existing definition of refugees, displaced persons and migrants is rather narrow and one-dimensional. It has to be considered also if the received distinctions between the forced/willed and political/economic regarding the refugee/migration definition hold true today. These need to be reviewed and reformulated in order to accommodate the existing reality. New and effective international instruments and national laws need to be created to protect the rights of these hapless millions who have no legal existence in most countries of the world today. The current definition of refugees focuses on examining the causes that create refugees; for example, fear of persecution due to political belief, religion, race and ethnicity. However, it is the situation of statelessness, abuse and disenfranchisement that creates the need for legal protection. Thus, when defining refugees the emphasis should shift from the factors that created the refugees to defining the circumstances that refugees must live in, i.e. as stateless and vulnerable to abuse. New and effective international instruments and national laws need to be created to protect the rights of these millions who have no legal existence in most countries of the world today.

Africa and South America expand Definition of Refugees

In this regard it may not be out of place to mention that in regional instruments adopted by the states in Africa and South America a wider meaning has been given to the concept of refugee. For example, the Organization of African Unity (OAU) Convention Governing the Specific Aspects of Refugee Problem in Africa (1969), while retaining the definition of refugees contained in the 1951 UN Convention, expanded it by adding that the term refugee shall also apply to every person or persons who, owing to external aggression, occupation, foreign domination or events seriously disturbing public order in either part or the whole of his/their country of origin or nationality is/are compelled to leave his/their place of habitual residence.

The Cartagena Declaration on refugees adopted by the Central American Governments in 1984 further expanded the definition of refugees to include persons who have fled their country because their lives, safety or freedom have been threatened by generalized violence, foreign aggression, internal conflicts, massive violation of human rights or other circumstances which have seriously disturbed public order.

The Crisis in the International Refugee Regime

The international refugee regime has never been under such strain as in the 1990s. The rising number of forced repatriations in the 1990s carried out by powerful Western governments, and the 'imposed' repatriation of refugees by UNHCR to areas where the safety of the returnees cannot be ensured, raises several questions. Several critical questions emerge. Can the core protection provision of the international refugee regime endure? Should the UNHCR remain the guarantor of the international refugee regime or be an apologist of the Western powers who control its purse strings? Is the principle of global responsibility for refugees any longer valid? The apologists of the non-entrée regime claim that the massive increase in refugee flows in the eighties and nineties from the less industrialized countries in the 'south' to the industrialized states in the 'north' created an 'asylum crisis'. As a result of this crisis the northern states comprising Western Europe and North America abandoned their relatively 'liberal' asylum policies of the Cold War period and initiated steps to restrict entry of potential asylum seekers, first individually and then collectively. There is talk of 'difference' between the European refugees of the earlier decade and the essentially non-European refugees of the current decade. Some of the European and North American scholars who subscribed to this 'theory of difference' argued that while the European refugees between 1920-60 satisfied the individualist criteria of the 1951 Convention of political persecution, the bulk of the Third World refugees did not. It was said that a majority of the non-European asylum seekers were thinly disguised economic migrants rather than political refugees. This 'unprecedented explosion' in the arrival of non-European asylum-seekers in the West in the eighties, which caused the 'asylum crisis', was also attributed to the revolution in transport technology.

The 'non-entrée' regime

Having propounded the theory of 'difference', the Northern states made it the basis for new types of restrictive regulations intended to prevent or deter Third World refugees from seeking refuge in Western Europe and North America. The European Union took the lead and a legal framework of Cupertino was created through the Dublin and Schenghen Conventions. Some of the important features of these restrictive regulations which have come to be known as the 'non-entrée' regime were:

1. Visa restrictions on citizens of known refugee-producing countries.
2. Carrier sanctions against airlines and ships which transported refugees or potential asylum-seekers without 'proper papers'.
3. Re-admission agreements with states of origin.
4. Application of the principles of 'safe third country' and 'safe country of origin' which allowed speedy expulsion of asylum seekers, often without even a hearing.

The Direction of Refugee Flows

This numbers game—massive flow from the South to the North—has successfully diverted the attention from the fact that the real asylum crisis was never in the post-war West or the post-Cold War 'north', but in the less industrialized countries of Africa, Asia, Latin America which constitute the 'south'. During the period of de-colonization in the 1960s and 1970s, the newly emerged post-colonial states of the Third World had to provide shelter to millions of people uprooted by liberation wars, revolutions, coups and counter-coups. It should be noted that during the last three decades the largest flow of refugees has been from one country in the 'south' to another. These poor Third World countries provide refuge to about 74 per cent of the world's refugees.

In mid-1980s, when West European states started constructing the non-entrée regime, the bulk of the world's refugees were being housed and protected by the poor Third World Countries. In 1995, out of a world total of 14.4 million refugees (recognised by the UNHCR under the 1951 Convention), only about three million were housed in Western Europe, Canada and USA.

The 'Root Cause' Theory

The international refugee regime until recently was concerned with the consequences rather than the 'root cause' of the flight of refugees. The 1951 Convention does not contain any specific reference to the responsibilities of the country of origin. However, the so-called third refugee crisis of the twentieth century, which was heralded by the collapse of the Soviet system and the consequent rise of ethnicity-driven nationalist movements in the former socialist states, seemed to frighten the victors of the Cold War. The very introduction of open market mechanisms, the preferred engines of economic growth and, the IMF-dictated 'structural adjustments' in the economies of these countries, led to the collapse of the food security, land security, water security and job security of vast numbers of already impoverished people. There is growing evidence of the critical link between the policies of economic globalization and the 'ethnic' conflicts. Recent studies have revealed that the genocides in former Yugoslavia and Rwanda were sparked by the 'structural adjustments' introduced in the economies of these countries on the recommendations of the international financial institutions. In the case of Rwanda, the crash in the global price of coffee was an added factor.

Unable or unwilling to deal with the core social, economic and political factors responsible for such massive displacement, the Western states took refuge in the security perspective. Post-Cold War refugee flows were seen as constituting threats to international peace and security. This categorization brought the refugee issue into the framework of Chapter VII of the UN Charter. During the 1990s, the UN Security Council adopted several resolutions empowering military intervention by US and other forces in northern Iraq (1991), former Yugoslavia (the first in 1992 and then several in 1993), Somalia (1992) and Rwanda (1994). The objective of these resolutions was to create the so-called safe havens for the refugees in the countries of origin or within the area of conflict. It is true that the safe havens provided a limited amount of safety to many refugees. However, the shortcomings of this policy of protecting threatened people in their own state have also become clear.

REFUGEES IN SOUTH ASIA

In the communal holocaust that followed the partition of the Indian subcontinent into India and Pakistan in 1947, about 1.3 million persons were killed and about 15 million were forcibly displaced. While about 8 million Hindus and Sikhs were forced to leave their homes in Pakistan and migrate to India, nearly seven million Muslims were uprooted from their homes in India and forced to migrate to Pakistan. These persons were accepted as citizens and rehabilitated by the states of India and Pakistan.

After Burma's independence in 1948, about 5,00,000 persons of Indian origin were forced to leave Burma under the programme of Burmanization. These people had lived in Burma for generations. Most of them returned to India in penurious conditions during the fifties and the sixties. Sri Lanka, after becoming independent, created approximately 9,00,000 stateless persons by refusing to grant them citizenship. These were the Tamil plantation workers who were taken to the island by the British in the early nineteenth century. The government of Sri Lanka wanted India to take them back. After several rounds of bilateral negotiations between 1964 and 1987, India agreed to accept about 3,40,000 Tamil plantation workers from Sri Lanka.

The liberation war of Bangladesh in 1970–1 had sent about 10 million refugees to India. Most of them went back to Bangladesh after its liberation. However the liberation of Bangladesh left about 3,00,000 stranded Pakistanis in Dhaka. They are mainly Bihari Muslims who had migrated from India to the erstwhile East Pakistan in 1947. During the period between 1948 and 1961, according to the reports of the Indian Home Ministry, about 3.1 million persons, mainly Hindus, migrated from erstwhile East Pakistan (present-day Bangladesh) to India. Bangladeshi migration is a hot political issue in India. In the north-east of India in the eighties there were widespread political agitations demanding the expulsion of foreigners, mainly the Bangladeshi Muslims. Local political parties and the ethnic elite were afraid that the rising number of Bangladeshis would finally tilt the demographic balance against them. In other words they would lose their power base. The fear was not totally unfounded as can be seen in the case of one of the north-eastern state, Tripura. Within a period of thirty years since India's Independence, Tripura's demographic balance was changed by the Bengali Hindu settlers from East Pakistan/Bangladesh. The Indigenous/tribal people of Tripura became a minority in their own homeland. The Indian government and the national political parties ignored the objections raised by the indigenous/tribal people of Tripura against such large-scale migration into their land. Nobody was willing to evict the Bengali Hindus back into East Pakistan. When Tripura's indigenous peoples protest movement re-emerged in the form of an armed insurgency, riots spread over the entire state, and the Indian government had to send security forces and the army to crush them.

The Muslim migrants from erstwhile East Pakistan and present-day Bangladesh have become the target of an expulsion campaign launched by the radical Hindu nationalist parties of India. They claim that about 20 million Bangladeshis have illegally entered India after 1971. The Indian Home Ministry has however chosen to remain silent on the figures relating to Bangladeshi migrants in India (*vide* Annual Report of Indian Home Ministry, 1995–6).

Since 1991 nearly 97,500 Bhutanese of Nepali ethnic origin in southern Bhutan have been taking refuge in Nepal. They have been stripped of their citizenship and pushed out of Bhutan by its Royal Government following the implementation of the programme of Bhutanization. Bhutan refuses to take them back while Nepal has refused to rehabilitate them.

In short, the birth of the post-colonial states in South Asia led to the expulsion of a large number of people. The state system, as it stands today in the region, is perched precariously, having been the source of creation of minorities, stateless populations and the cause of the continuing exodus of victims of various kinds of violence.

Absence of a Protective Legal Framework

None of the countries of South Asia has signed the 1951 UN Convention on Refugees or the 1967 Protocol. There are no national laws, which define and regulate the status of refugees in the countries of South Asia. In most of the countries of the region, the powers to grant residential permits have been relegated to administrators at district and sub-district levels. They grant and revoke these certificates at their discretion. The refugees have no legal protection against summary expulsions as they are treated as illegal immigrants and not as refugees fleeing persecution. As a result, the UNHCR has not been able to provide effective and meaningful protection to most refugees in the region. Even international humanitarian agencies are often not allowed to assist the refugees meaningfully in most of these countries.

In South Asia, in Sri Lanka alone more than a million people have been rendered homeless within their own country by the 18-year old ethnic conflict. In India nearly 250,000 Kashmiri Hindus and Muslims have become internally displaced. Under its expanded mandate, the UNHCR has accepted these 'internally displaced persons' or 'persons in refugee like situations' as 'persons of concern'. The enormity of the situation can be sensed from the latest estimates: there are 16 million IDPs in Africa, about 7 million in Asia and another 10 million in Europe and South America. Out of these the UNHCR assists an estimated 5 million in various regions.

However, as the internally displaced are under the control of their national governments and as their rights are often abused by the law enforcement agencies of their own governments, it is unlikely that the UNHCR will be able to effectively extend its protection mandate to the internally displaced. There is a justified concern that the UNHCR's involvement with national governments in providing humanitarian aid to the internally displaced will compromise the organization's ability to fulfil its protection mandate. The Bosnia-Herzegovina experience has underlined the danger of balancing the so-called right to remain with concerns of safety of the IDPs.

The New Search for a Durable Solution | 153

REFUGEE POLICY OF GOVERNMENTS:
NEED FOR A LEGAL FRAMEWORK

South Asia is witness to massive movements of displaced persons and refugees from one country to another. An estimated 30 million have crossed borders as displaced persons or refugees since 1947. This includeds the followers of various religious faiths, members of ethnic or cultural groups and nationalities. Governments in the region have responded to such emergencies with a spirit of accommodation, providing the asylum-seekers with every possible help and assistance. Although the SAARC countries are not signatories to the UN Convention on Refugees and its Protocol, these countries have perhaps offered more humane treatment to victims of forced migrations, at least in terms of not closing their borders and throwing people out, than many developed countries of the world who have now adopted very strict entry procedures.

Generous as they are, the South Asian states follow different policies towards the refugees or asylum seekers from within the region. While a state might welcome some groups of asylum seekers it may not be very receptive or kind to others. These policies have been dictated by the politics of kinship and interstate relations. Experience shows that there is no consistency in admissions, grant of asylum, education, employment, rehabilitation and repatriation. Every influx of refugees receives a different package depending on political motivations and ethnic and religious linkages. As the states look upon cross-border migration as a bilateral issue, the refugee issue has also not been taken up at the regional level by the states. In the absence of laws concerning treatment of asylum seekers/refugees, the response to refugee influxes have remained ad hoc. Many of these problems can be avoided through the enactment of legal norms on status and rights of asylum seekers or refugees.

NEED FOR HARMONIZED NATIONAL LAWS

The legal framework for the protection of refugees requires provision to be made for their protection during their refugee status; it needs to find solutions for their problems; to enable them to return to their home country; and to provide protection to the returnees in their home countries; At the same time it should not be forgotten that protection of human rights has to remain a global responsibility. The protection mechanism for refugees cannot be strengthened in the Third World through regional agreements and national laws when the richer nations of the 'north' are abdicating their responsibilities.

Refugees, asylum seekers and illegal migrants are no longer hidden from the public eye or tucked away inside refugee camps. These people are visible everywhere. In the big and small cities of South Asia they work in peoples homes, factories and shops. They provide many essential services to the inhabitants of these cities. In rural areas they also work as farm labour. They provide cheap labour and make very little demands on their employers. From time to time the some of these illegal immigrants are rounded up by the police and are thrown into makeshift detention centres. The sporadic attempts by states to deport these persons have made little difference to the cross-border flows. Erection of barbed wire fences along the borders and increasing the number of border check-posts have been counter productive as the borders of the post-colonial south Asian states are too long and too porous. It is the failure of the states of South Asia to guarantee the human rights of its citizens, which is at the root of these massive cross-border flows. The states of South Asia are more concerned about their 'national security', and defence of their territorial integrity. They have diverted large proportions of their scarce resources to arm their military at the cost of the security of food, shelter, jobs and health care of the people.

The presence of vast numbers of such 'illegal people' is also adversely effecting the society and polity of the states of the region. Their 'illegal' status makes them vulnerable to the machinations of the corrupt and unscrupulous elements of the host countries. It further depresses the already low wage rates for unskilled and semiskilled jobs. It increases corruption. These 'illegal' people, in desperate attempts to 'legalise' their presence in the host country, buy false citizenship documents from corrupt officials. Unethical elements in some of the political parties of these countries in search of captive 'vote banks' often pressurise officials to 'regularise' these 'illegal' migrants. It is obvious that it is not the 'illegal' immigrants, whether 'forced' or 'voluntary', who suffer under the present system. Such action is also affecting the societies of the host countries and undermining the democratic foundations of their polities. One of the major difficulties created by the absence of a legal framework for refugees and asylum seekers is that there is no method of separating the really vulnerable who need the protection of a host state from the ordinary job seekers.

South Asian human rights groups and activists have been demanding the creation of a legal framework for protection of refugees and asylum seekers. They have been asking the governments to fulfil their obligations under international covenants by bringing the national laws at a par with the provisions of International Human Rights Law. Although the governments have not changed their position, the advantages and disadvantages of ratifying the 1951 UN Convention regarding the Status of Refugees and its 1967 Protocol are now being openly debated by civil society groups in the region.

All the South Asian states are parties to various international human rights covenants like the Convention on the Elimination of all Forms of Discrimination Against Women (CEDAW), Child Rights Convention (CRC) and International Convention for Elimination of all Forms of Racial Discrimination (ICERD). They are obliged to respect and protect the rights of the women and children, racial and ethnic minorities in refugee situations. Under article 22 of the CRC, states have agreed to give refuge to children. As parties to international covenants on Civil and Political Rights (ICCPR) and on Economic, Social and Cultural Rights (ICESCR), India, Nepal and Sri Lanka are obliged to provide asylum to vulnerable persons and protect their right to life. Nepal and Sri Lanka are also bound to respect the protective provisions of the Convention against Torture, which they have ratified. Though it has been argued that the provisions of international law are not enforceable through court orders, there is a growing body of opinion among the jurists of South Asia that in the absence of a specific municipal law, the provisions of international law should prevail.

South Asian States are also signatories to the four Geneva Conventions, which oversee the observance of the provisions of

International Humanitarian Law during inter-state wars and internal wars. The Geneva Conventions require each state party to enact an enabling law to fulfil its obligations under the conventions to provide humane treatment to civilians threatened by cross-border and internal wars. Some of the common provisions of the Geneva Conventions have already come to be regarded as Customary International Law. However, unlike the Geneva Conventions, the International Human Rights Law, as embodied in the UN conventions does not contain provisions for compulsory enactment of enabling national laws by state parties. The convention states are expected to enact new laws ensuring the enjoyment of these rights by their citizens, or wherever necessary amend existing national laws to bring these in tune with the provisions of the International Human Rights law. UN Conventions have also set up monitoring mechanisms and the contracting states are obliged to submit annual reports regarding their observation of the treaty obligations. In some cases, individuals and NGOs are allowed to file complaints with the UN treaty monitoring agencies regarding violations of the International Human Rights Law by states.

The argument that states are sovereign bodies and no outside party can interfere in the internal affairs of a state can no longer be allowed to stand in the way of enjoyment of basic human rights by all people. Imperfect as it is, the international order today is moving closer to accepting the idea that human rights are not the internal affairs of a state. The failure of the states in the arena of human rights is no longer a mere source of embarrassment. It is seriously effecting the ability of the indicted states to negotiate international and bilateral trade agreements. International economic assistance is increasingly being linked to the human rights records of the receiving states. The setting up of the War Crimes Tribunal and the efforts to install an International Court of Criminal Justice have strengthened the provisions of International Human Rights Law. The provisions of Customary International Law can no longer be summarily dismissed by any state. The international community is continuing to mount pressure on the South Asian states to enact new laws or amend the existing ones to fulfil their obligations under the UN Conventions. The demand for such reforms are not only being put forward by the international community, these are also being voiced by increasing numbers of civil society organizations, human rights activists and sections of opinion makers of the countries. The adoption of national laws for refugees and asylum seekers by the states of South Asia, which incorporate the principles of international human rights law for refugees, will help ensure transparency, fairness and a humane treatment for refugees. It needs to be mentioned that, through these laws the states of South Asia will give formal expression to the existing practices and responses to the refugees. Having a national law would not only ensure the protection of refugees and uphold obligations enjoined by the Constitutions of most of the countries, it will also enable the states to discharge their international treaty obligations. It will prevent any diplomatically sensitive occurrence of discriminating in favour of or against any group of refugees. Ultimately both the states and the asylum seekers will derive benefits from such laws. The adoption of a harmonized national law on refugees by all the countries of the region is a first step towards seeking a regional solution to this problem.

Pluralist Politics under Monistic Design: Water Accords in South Asia

Dipak Gyawali

Society in Water

The road to hell, it is often said, is paved with good intentions, and acclaimed accords too can take conflict to a new dimension if features of institutional plurality are not built into them. Accords on water resources development or sharing can hide many elements of potential conflict and thus need to be examined more dispassionately. In South Asia, wherever one sees virulent pathology in the practice of irrigation or other water related ventures, the root cause is perplexing and difficult to fathom until the philosophy and practice of 'development' is heretically questioned and its social carriers critically examined. This ostensibly benign, if not noble, venture of the second half of the twentieth century has primarily benefited only the social carriers of a particular technology to the disadvantage of others at the receiving end of the technology's unintended consequences. This perceived lack of fairness invokes counter responses from other elements of society ranging from fatalist resignation to violent armed peasant uprisings. However, mainstream water managers led by the civil engineering community have failed to address this predicament that underlies the crises in South Asia's water resource management (Ahmed et al. 1999).

If one were to go back to the metaphors of an earlier cosmology, blood flow was seen as the flow of the vital life force itself. Very often, the quality of water flow in an area is said to be akin to the flow of blood in the veins of the society around it. The state of natural resources in an area reflects the state of the society dependent on those resources, and water too, like blood, captures within it the larger intricacies—the habits of the heart—that give dynamism to social life. With the flow of water is intermingled the social philosophy and mores that guide collective action. Development interventions in natural hydrological cycles are experiments that can be sagacious over the longer timeframe or myopic but very clever in the short run with serious long-term consequences. Water resource management has been a long-term proposition and societies have been organized around pluralistic patterns that match the diversity of hydro-ecology as well as human groupings. How well, or how badly, they do it is often a reflection of how healthy they are as a society.

An approach of seeing society reflected in water and its use helps in appreciating the complexities of many of the endemic conflicts in South Asia. A name that has been given to the multifaceted interlinkage between physical and social systems is Himalaya-Ganga, the highland-lowland interactions of South Asia that are extraordinary in their intricacy (Gyawali and Dixit 1994). Can these complexities be 'managed'? Or does one 'cope' with them within limits, taking advantage of water where possible and avoiding its fury when it is wiser to do so? What kind of institutional pluralism allows a less ambitious 'coping', and what kinds of pitfalls lie in the more ambitious 'managing'? This question also begs the answer whether a society is pluralist and democratic in substance or claims to be so only in form. While the various official agreements between countries of South Asia would give the impression that the nation states of SAARC have taken a step towards conflict resolution and new development possibilities, a closer look would indicate that these accords which come from the 'management' paradigm filter out many of the elements of uncertainty and thus hide within them other features of conflict that could emerge down the road.

The following sections look at some of the water accords of South Asia—between countries and within countries—from a critical, often heretical, perspective. Using some of their insights, the final section attempts to elucidate how a more pluralist design of accords may lessen chances of conflict or impasse.

Quiet Flows the Indus?

It was at a diplomatic watering hole in Kathmandu that a Pakistani diplomat, while discussing the Tanakpur imbroglio in Nepal, mentioned to this writer that an unspoken reason for the Kashmir conflict in 1948 was the deep-seated fear in West Punjab that allowing India to control the headwaters of the Indus would be tantamount to a disaster. This 'revelation' kept returning like a bad penny until laid to rest in print in a special issue of *Water Nepal* where, while cataloguing ninety-three unanswered research questions on the Himalaya-Ganga, it was asked (Dixit and Gyawali 1994):

> Despite a largely common heritage of language, culture, religion, and economic structures, an unrelenting race for arms supremacy reigns over South Asia. This occurs even while politicians and other dream merchants sell visions of prosperity that would be heralded by large-scale water resources development.

1. What is the saddle point in the region where massive investments in the arms race end and those equally massive in water resources begin?
2. Is the battle for control of the Siachen Glacier as a specific case, and the tension in Kashmir as a more general one, related to the unarticulated need to control the headwaters of the Indus?
3. What implication does emerging religious intolerance in the region have for equitable resource development in the basins of the Himalaya-Ganga?
4. What cooperative research role should academics and diplomats play in this context?

The ink had already dried on this writing and much water had flowed down the Bhagmati and the Jhelum when, on the banks of the Yamuna in March 1999, India's redoubtable former Foreign Secretary, J. N. Dixit, threw in a bombshell. Addressing a plenary session in a JNU seminar[1] he said that, while it was not

---

[1] A two-day conference on 'The Resolution of Interstate Conflicts in South Asia' organized by Jawaharlal Nehru University's (JNU) School of International Studies, South Asian Studies Division, 29-30 March 1999, New Delhi, in which this writer was present.

discussed in academic or journalistic circles, it was well accepted 'in our strategic studies circles' that much of the passion on Kashmir was generated because India controls the headwaters of the Indus.

Now, the Indus Treaty is cited as one of the most successful treaties of natural resource sharing in our region for the reason that, while wars have been fought in the Indus basin several times in the last fifty years between India and Pakistan, none have been fought to challenge the treaty itself. But is that really true? What the venerable Pakistani and Indian diplomats let slip was the underlying fear that gives rise to conflicts, the (mis)perceptions, (biased) hunches, etc., that seem to guide action more often than rational logic, procedural dictates and cold scientific choices. The question is: can peace be captured in the neat rational procedures of agreements or should those procedures stem from an underlying understanding that may be clumsy but addresses fears, howsoever irrational?

Below the calm of the Indus Treaty lies a dynamism that is not really cold and procedural. It is characterized by the following:

1. Indus Treaty is *not* a resource sharing treaty but a treaty that partitions the resource, just as the British Raj lands were partitioned between new inheritors, with the northern tributaries of the Indus going to Pakistan and the southern ones to India, giving each absolute sovereignty over their share.
2. Sharing requires socio-systemic involvement on a continuous basis while partition is a one-time affair that has little succeeding involvement of the parties concerned except in the case of a breakdown of the partition arrangements. In the semi-arid tropics that these waters irrigate, sharing a river's resources would entail not only sharing its placid bounties but also the uncertainties of floods and droughts, assuring that the stochastic burdens of climate and rainfall are equally shared. The Indus Treaty absolves both parties of such responsibilities as the need to sit down amicably and discuss water sharing before every *rabi* or *kharif* season based on the hydro-meteorological realities that prevail.
3. There was third party mediation between India and Paki-

stan, where the third party was stronger (or at least perceived to be stronger or more resourceful) than either of the two rivals, a third party that neither of the two could ignore nor aggravate.[2]

4. To smoothen the passage of the treaty, the rival parties were tempted with offers that went beyond the issue of rights over river waters to that of access to other resources in the future, i.e. Pakistan and India were both promised 'aid' to build other dams and conduct development activities if they behaved reasonably. The temptation was applied not to the informal sector peasants (who bear the hydro-meteorological uncertainties) but to the ruling elite and their construction industries that controlled the formal economy and its polity.

5. There are murmurs of disgruntlement over the downstream reaches (sudden floodwater releases, soil salinization, etc.). But these are neither well articulated nor are they listened to, because to do so is not within the institutional interests of the single mission construction bureaucracies that were the beneficiaries of the largesse of aid that smoothened the passage of the treaty.

Mahakali Impasse

Nepal's modern internal politics since the overthrow of the Rana regime in 1951 has, in many ways, been 'water politics', with various political groupings accusing each other of either selling out to India with accords harmful to the country's interests or being 'anti-developmentalist' by refusing to enter into such agreements with the large southern neighbour. The Kosi and the Gandak projects agreed to in the 1950s have been seen *post facto* as giving Nepal a raw deal, although few in Nepal have understood how they have given UP and Bihari peasants in India an even worse deal as the history of the last fifty years have shown (Gyawali 1998). Notwithstanding this experience, the

---

[2] This was not just the World Bank but also the entire Bretton Woods system with the then major Euro-American superpowers that the Bank represented.

Nepali state has gone ahead in 1996 with a major agreement with India on sharing the Mahakali river, which forms the western border of Nepal with India, and developing a 315 meters high, 6,480 MW Pancheswar High Dam project on this river. Ratified by the Nepali parliament with a two-thirds majority in September 1996, the treaty was envisaged to have its multi-billion dollar financing agreements completed in two years and the project itself completed in eight. Four years after ratification, even the detailed project report (DPR) has not been completed, and the Vajpayee-Koirala joint communiqué of July 2,000 has pushed its preparation to the end of 2001. It is obvious that deep conflicts lurk under the surface of this acclaimed accord, effectively making it a non-starter.

Three water resources projects in Nepal have been the subject of much controversy since the restoration of multiparty democracy in April 1990, which gives us an idea of the social forces at work in these subterranean conflicts. The first was Arun3, a 201 MW run-of-river hydroelectric power plant promoted for a decade by a World Bank-led consortium of eight donors as the cheapest and only alternative for development in Nepal's power sector. The saga of foreign aid and high cost projects began in 1973 with the 60 MW Kulekhani-1 and continued with Arun3 at US$ 5000/kW when comparative costs in China and India for similar ventures were $800 and $1200-1600 respectively. Nepali private sector had also built projects of smaller scale at a fifth of the cost of Arun3 (Gyawali 1997).

With the restoration of multi-party democracy in 1990, the space was open to Nepali activist groups, and they engaged in a spirited campaign focused not on environmental issues but on bad economics by the World Bank. The reasons for this were strategic: if the Bank could be made defensive on its own theology, there would be a chance to stop the project. Focusing on environmental ill effects would make the campaign vulnerable to the Bank's procedural defence of mitigation measures. Activism would then not be able to retain a high moral ground but would be enmeshed in procedural matters that would leave the core decision of going ahead with this expensive project intact. This first civil society activist movement in Nepal in recent years forced the Bank to withdraw its support for Arun3 in August 1995, leading the other donors to shift to other projects. As a result, there are currently six alternative projects underway, some of them funded by private money, some from the money earmarked for Arun3 while others are funded by the Nepali utility from the proceeds of a 300 per cent tariff increase that was among the Bank's conditionalities for Arun3. The six projects (which give a third more electricity at half the construction time of Arun3) are being constructed at an average cost of $2300/kW, still higher by the standards of our neighbours but half of the cost of Arun3.

The second controversial project is a trans-basin water transfer project to supply drinking water to Kathmandu, the capital city, through a 29-km tunnel across uncertain Himalayan geology in the record time of three years.[3] A construction industry-led venture, it fails to answer some fairly basic questions: given that the current supply by the state-owned water utility to the approximately 1,00,000 connections in Kathmandu Valley is 60 million litres per day even in the driest season and discounting the official figure for loss in the system to 40 per cent, that is, about 360 litres of water per day per connection (which can be assumed to be a household) is available even in the driest of seasons. The question then is: where is the shortage? Other questions relate to realistic rates of tunnelling in Himalayan geology (which has been at a maximum of about 2 km. per annum), and role of sovereign loans for the already well-off in the capital. A nascent civil society agitation looms on the horizon awaiting answers.

The third controversy was relates to the Tanakpur project built unilaterally by India on a border river that tied the Nepali executive, legislature and the judiciary into knots for several years. Initially India denied that this project on a boundary river concerned Nepal in any way. However, by 1988, it approached Nepal for 570 m of Nepali territory for building the left afflux bund that would ensure that the river did not outflank the

[3] As per the 1999 campaign promise of (subsequent) Prime Minister Krishna Prasad Bhattarai of Nepal.

barrage during high stage. This was viewed by Nepali polity as an affront, and was not assuaged by the Nepali prime minister agreeing to an 'understanding' with his counterpart in December 1991 wherein Nepal would receive ten million units of electricity from the project as well as 150 cusecs of irrigation waters. An appeal was made to the Supreme Court to enforce Article 126 of the Constitution that would require parliamentary ratification by a two-thirds majority that no party had. The deadlock could not be settled by the all-party parliamentary committee formed for the purpose and was subsequently skirted by subsuming Tanakpur within a much larger integrated Mahakali Treaty which hopes to build the world's highest rockfill dam at Pancheshwar to provide power and other benefits. This move has split the main opposition parties both of the left and right, and has left deep rift-like bruises in the ruling party as well. It has also raised a whole new set of controversies, from downstream benefits in Uttar Pradesh to hitherto hidden border disputes at Kalapani (Gyawali and Dixit 1999).

All these three projects bring forth fundamental issues of governance, from the role of governments to the role of civil society and markets, and are slated to figure prominently in Nepal's public discourse for a long time to come. The Tanakpur/ Mahakali Treaties have tied up the state machinery—the executive, the legislature as well as the Supreme Court—and split political parties asunder. Given the manner in which the treaty was rammed through Parliament, it has acquired legality without the requisite legitimacy, with its own repercussions on governance. While the Mahakali Treaty has been hailed as a success by one group, opposition groups have argued that, having failed to meet the deadlines stated in the treaty, it is now no longer valid. They have raised several contentious issues that have not been addressed so far:

1. While one clause states that Nepal and India share the waters of the border river equally, another clause (number 3 in the main treaty and item 3 in the Lohani-Mukherjee exchange of letters) essentially deprives Nepal of the equal rights she enjoys over those waters by limiting her rights to as low as

four per cent of the waters. This has essentially shackled any further implementation of the treaty.[4]
2. This treaty is only an enabling treaty that requires subsequent treaties for effectiveness. When the very first bite leaves such an after-taste, what hope is there for smooth sailing in the future? Will stalling not be a tactics to be used effectively by the weaker party to regain some of what is, with hard sight, perceived as lost ground?
3. The treaty is done as 'cart before the horse': while its two main purposes were to wriggle out of the Tanakpur imbroglio and build the Pancheswar High Dam, none of the homework that were necessary before embarking on building this highest dam in the world was done (or has been done till date). Because of this lacuna, other related problems have begun to come out of the woodworks, e.g. the Kalapani border issue at the headwaters of the Mahakali, as well as the issue of downstream benefits that India would acquire as free-rider benefits.[5]
4. It ignores completely the reality of the Himalaya-Ganga hydroecology that is amenable to a very different type of technological intervention.[6]

[4] Depending on how one interprets it. Dixit (1996) demonstrates that the treaty has at least seven interpretations where Nepal's 'equal' share can range from 4 per cent to 41 per cent.

[5] In this context, it is interesting to study the opinion of the former minister of state for water resources and the current Nepali Congress coordinator for its water resources policy in *Samanata*, vol. 2, no. 4, Magh 2056 (Jan./Feb. 2000):

Until the issue of Kalapani and the source of Mahakali is settled, it is impossible to prepare the DPR (detailed project report) of Pancheswar. If India agrees to our position on Kalapani based on documents available with us, the implementation of the Mahakali Treaty may move forward, but even then I doubt whether the DPR can solve the issue of water sharing in an agreeable manner. . . . The treaty should have been ratified by the parliament only after the DPR had been prepared and all clauses of the treaty clarified. At present the treaty is frozen in a deadlocked state.

[6] The difficulty of copying technologies adopted elsewhere is shown in the Bihar case referred to above (Gyawali 1998). The embankment technology

5. Since the treaty is based on the hydraulic engineering paradigm and is geared towards introducing a type of technology, it is neither attuned to the physical or the socio-economic realities nor is it very sympathetic to alternatives. Associated with the Mahakali Treaty is the still un-ratified Power Trade Agreement between Nepal and India that has not looked at the political implications of a monopsonistic energy market in India (Gyawali 1999a). The net result may be social dislocation without development.[7]

WATER AND OTHER SOUTH ASIAN UNRESTS

Such issues of concern are not only between countries: the fight for control over water can also be as contentious between administrative delineations within a country. In the current battle for a separate statehood for Uttarakhand, lowland Uttar Pradesh (U.P.) seems unwilling to allow this new hill state to be carved out from its erstwhile self, or to share control over the Ganga and the Yamuna. While the Indian Constitution declares water and electricity to be state subjects, among the many amendments suggested by Lucknow to Delhi over the draft statehood bill is that the existing dams and water resources projects in the Uttarakhand area remain properties not of Uttarakhand but of Uttar Pradesh. As this goes against the spirit of the Indian Constitution, the proposed amendment may not be accepted by Delhi, but the fears of U.P. will, however, remain as will the affront that the suggestion makes to the hill *paharis*.[8] Within this underlying state of suspicion lie the seeds of a future conflict. While analysing the unarticulated concerns in water resources research, the following had been further stated in

---

is not something that is conducive to the rainfall sedimentation pattern in the Himalaya-Ganga. The rapid sedimentation of the Kulekhani reservoir in Nepal (which lost its projected 100 year life in 13 years with one major cloudburst in 1993 accounting for half the sediment) is also a case in point.

[7] In the case of Sri Lanka, the hydraulic engineering paradigm, as opposed to the ecosystems perspective, has led to the destruction of ancient tank irrigation systems. See Mendis (1999).

[8] Personal communication from Shekhar Pathak, editor of *Pahar* published from Nainital U.P., in Kathmandu, 5 February 2000.

the Himalaya-Ganga article quoted above (Gyawali and Dixit 1994):

Inflow of massive revenue from large-scale water developments have gone to one set of social carriers of development and related technologies in many parts of the Himalaya-Ganga. Disorders of other forms that threaten to tear apart the social fabric are endemic, which cut across the countries.

● Could it be that this is the cause of social unrest in South Asia, notably Chukha in Bhutan, Trisuli or Marsyangdi in Nepal, Damodar in Bihar/Bengal Jharkhand, Mahawelli in Sri Lanka, and Karnaphuli in the Chittagong Hills of Bangladesh?

Since these lines were written (rather diffidently then), constant input has been received from many different scholars in South Asia who corroborate the fears expressed in the above article. It is now openly talked about (and sometimes written) that a critical factor in escalating the simmering ethnic violence in Sri Lanka was a bad re-settlement attempt in the Mahawelli west of Batticaloa. Similarly one can ask, what percentage of the misery of the Lotsampa refugees can be traced to the largesse of Dutch Disease revenue inflow into the weak capitalist institutional structures of a feudal elite in Bhutan?[9]

The Damodar Valley Project in Bengal and the tribal reaches of Bihar have their own hidden tales about the delegitimization of the state in the eyes of the affectees from dam building. Even though the original plan of the Damodar Valley Project (and the corporation DVC that operationalized it) was founded on the concept of flood control, once the construction was underway, the money-spinning power component took over the project to the extent that 'other (multipurpose) objectives of the projects have been put on the backburner' (Thakurta 1998). This shift in objective has left the farmers angry because 'the DVC confines itself only to the urban and industrial areas. In the upper reaches of the Damodar the farmers suffered because their land was acquired for the DVC and they were displaced while in the lower areas the land gets flooded and remains submerged leading to

---

[9] Dutch Disease aspects of large investment projects such as mega dams are only recently being studied. See Gyawali (1989), Thapa (1997) as well as Dhungel (1999).

deprivation' (Dey 1998). Indeed, one aside to the case of dacoit Veerappan and his kidnapping of a silver screen idol to make topsy-turvy the politics of both Tamil Nadu and Karnataka, is that Veerappan is the grandson of a Mettur Dam oustee.[10] Such aspects of misery swept under the carpet need further research to shed light on the potential for conflict inherent in them.

The Farakka Treaty of 1996 is hailed as a major solution to a long-standing vexing issue, but already there are indications of some fraying at the ends. Bangladesh's problems with regard to the Farakka barrage issue are several:

1. Low dry season availability of water had meant the drying out ('desertification' in popular parlance) of the south-west section of the lower Ganga-Brahmaputra delta. This deprivation, according to some scholars, has contributed to the migration of environmental refugees from Bangladesh into Indian cities such as Delhi and Bombay (Swain, 1996).
2. The issue is not so much of sharing (there is too much demand and too little to share in the lean seasons) as of augmenting supplies, which involves either encroaching upon Bangladeshi sovereignty (if the Brahmaputra link canal cuts across the country, as proposed by India) or Nepali sovereignty (if through high dams an attempt is made to export seasonal lowland flood into Nepal as permanent floods that submerge Nepali villages, as proposed by both downstream riparians, Bangladesh and India).
3. Even the sharing provisions in the 1996 Farakka Treaty skirt the really difficult issue of what to do when the flow goes below 50,000 cusecs as it well might in the future if the upstream riparian states decide to kindly ignore the problems of Delhi. Water, after all in India, is a state and not a union subject, and Delhi can and does plead helplessness in this matter if it suits its interests.[11]

[10] See Editorial by Anil Agarwal, *Down To Earth*, vol. 9, no. 8, 15 September 2000, New Delhi.

[11] See the problems that Biharis in Patna have with the Farakka Treaty in Gyawali (1998) as well as (Gyawali 1999b). To Nepali complaints of the non-availability of irrigation water in the western Nepal Kosi Canal from the Kosi barrage, Delhi's reply has often been that Patna is supposed to look into it.

4. The Farakka Treaty of 1996 does not make any dent on the augmentation issue but allows one set of social carriers of construction technology to concentrate on materializing the Ganga Barrage project and the Ganga-Kovadak irrigation scheme, which now seems to have been the main guiding motive of those pushing for the treaty. If the Farakka Treaty was a really good resource sharing treaty, it would not be necessary to construct another expensive barrage on the Ganga a few kilometres downstream of the existing Farakka barrage: water could just as well be made available to southwest Bangladesh from a branch on the existing takeoffs at Farakka![12]

Bihar[13]

Bihar, which has half the area of Poland and more than twice its population, constitutes less than 14 per cent of the overall Ganga basin. It is the inland deltaic meeting ground of several violent Himalayan rivers that are characterized by heavy monsoon peak floods a thousand times higher than their dry season runoff. Such an extreme hydraulic regime of the rivers of the Himalaya-Ganga assures high sediment load that has helped build the Indo-Gangetic floodplains as well as the Bengal delta. It is a geologic process of immense scale that is only faintly and locally exacerbated by anthropogenic misdeeds. The implication of this hydro-ecological fact is that hydro-technical control technologies such as large dam reservoirs and embankments that have to be designed for extreme flood events, will need to be many times more expensive here to be effective than would be the case in the much more temperate Europe. Correspondingly, the economic

---

[12] The same construction-driven hydraulic redundancy is seen in the two Teesta barrages, one in West Bengal and the other in Bangladesh. In the current atmosphere, if Nepal wished to utilize its larger rivers such as Karnali or the Gandak for irrigation of its lowland Tarai along the 'go-it-alone' mode, it would have to build barrages similar to the Girijapur or Gandak barrages as the existing ones at the Nepal-India border would be useless for her purposes.

[13] This section is based on Bihari activist literature (mostly in Hindi) summarized in Gyawali (1998), also in Gyawali (1999b).

investments made in such technologies become that much more costlier.

The technology of embankment building to contain floodwaters of a river within demarcated channels becomes ineffective because the sediment, instead of spreading out over the flood plains, gets deposited within the embankment and raises the bed level of the river. This induces more seepage from the river during high stage into the allegedly protected area that, compounded with the water already collected from normal rainfall, remains trapped outside the embankment. It contributes to what is known as water logging where land that would have been flooded for two to fourteen days of a year remains so for as long as nine months or more.

It is within the last fifty years of Indian Independence that the marginalized north Indian state of Bihar experienced extensive development in the areas of irrigation and flood control. During the British Raj, there were serious doubts about the viability of large-scale surface irrigation schemes as well as embankments in the north Ganga plains. After Independence in 1947, the welfare objectives of the new state needed such projects for its legitimacy in the eyes of the newly liberated masses and introduced a missionary zeal in selecting this method of flood control and irrigation. In examining the history of decision-making in this period, one is struck by the institutional filters at work which, having selected the technology of embankment building for the mission at hand, chose to disregard all evidence pointing to the need for caution. It may be described as runaway technology for the furtherance of which the state and society is pressed into service. From 154 km of embankments in 1954, Bihar recorded 3,454 km by 1988, but the flood prone areas have increased in this period from 2.5 million ha to 6.46 million ha. In essence, more land has gone out of production from the Kosi project than has come under irrigation under it.

The most striking impact of fifty years of embankment building in Bihar is the entrenched corruption in its polity and the displacement of a waterlogged peasantry to the urban slums of India. The iron triangle nexus between the engineer-contractor-politicians has become the bane of its water management, and

Pluralist Politics under Monistic Design | 173

is found in many other parts of South Asia as well.[14] Because state-level water managers in India, whether in Delhi or in Patna, have made no attempt to review the impact of irrigation and embankments on the productivity and human welfare within the command area, or to initiate corrective measures, a burgeoning grassroots activist counter reaction of a very confrontationist style has taken over. Since questioning the efficacy of embankment building would question the very reason for the existence of the Department of Water Resources, the state machinery continues to look for a new construction solution in a high dam in upstream Nepal. Activists, however, question the core philosophy of the construction approach to flood control and engage in embankment demolishing. The wide rift in perspectives between these two social solidarities leaves little room for conflict resolution at present.

Sri Lanka[15]

An understanding of the resource base that is at variance with its hydro-ecology and development efforts initiated in accord with such an erroneous paradigm can be a source of conflict and breakdown of order. Mendis (1999) highlights such a case in southern Sri Lanka, a hydro-ecological region of monsoonal tropics where an ancient system of irrigation operating sustainably for more than seven centuries began to decline, *inter alia*, with the introduction of a 'hydraulic engineering perspective'. Such a perspective, which has its origins in a state-centric model of resource control with single-focused hydraulic efficiency as its goal, became dominant with the advent of colonialism.

Even though colonialism is often associated with the Dutch and the British in Sri Lanka, in terms of resource management its origins can be, and often are, indigenous if there is a high degree of alienation of national governments from their subjects. Catering to the whims of rulers for prestige projects or

---
[14] For a good description of the best art form of this form of management see Bharti (1991).
[15] This section is based on Mendis (1999).

foreign conflicts can result in a highly extractive polity where the peasantry is bled white. Swift siphoning of accumulated resources becomes the short-term goal that ignores completely the long-term need for sustaining the productive potential of land and water. The concept of 'hydraulic efficiency' caters to this need for short-term resource extraction and, in the case of Sri Lanka, made its advent in the reign of Parakrama Bahu in the twelfth century—although its most widespread promulgation was with the spread of colonialism—leading to the decline and destruction of ancient irrigation systems.

In the hydraulic engineering perspective, water is seen as inanimate but active with small village ponds as inefficient and primitive systems that need to be replaced with larger storage reservoirs that ostensibly provide better benefits on the principle of 'economy of scale'. Distribution systems are designed in well-laid grid blocks to supply water to individual farmers who are seen as individualist entrepreneurs in mechanistic-atomistic isolation from both nature and their peers. In the reaches downstream of large construction works, land is 'levelled' first so as to make it amenable for the construction of large canals. Forests have to be cleared to make way for efficient mono-cropping and may be limited to the upper catchment area to reduce silting in the reservoir.

In contrast, the ecosystems perspective views water as animate and passive, due to its role as a facilitative agent in nature's biogeochemical cycles, especially in the root zones of soils that 'live' because of water. Perfected over thousands of years, small tanks are micro-irrigation ecosystems that are essential part of a total macro-irrigation complex of man-made ecosystems. Farmers are not just Western-style economic agents of agribusiness using this system but part of a whole: the outflow from one farmer's field is the input to another farmer's plot in a web that interconnects the whole village. Small ponds are interconnected (as are villages) with larger canals and bund structures that adapt to the contours of the land and its ownership as well as to the nature of the rainfall. Forests are an intrinsic part of this perspective and they are interspersed with fields in development areas for better conservation of nutrient flows.

The hydraulic engineering perspective is based on the strategy of domination of nature while the ecosystems perspective gives rise to ecostrategies that adapt to nature either actively or passively, depending upon the strength and complexity of the social organization. Modern irrigation engineering, by being a top-down, expertise-based approach has relegated the farmer to a passive role and with it the ancient system of irrigation that he had perfected by actively adapting to nature. This hydraulic perspective took hold in modern Sri Lanka with a paper by J.S. Kennedy, director of irrigation in 1933. It was followed by the hypothesis of deputy surveyor general R.L. Brohier in 1956 wherein evolution and development of ancient irrigation systems in Sri Lanka were seen as inefficient 'little evaporating ponds'. The perspective failed to see how the village tank was the centre of village life and a major source of security against the inevitable drought.

Based on this belief system, efforts were made to construct large reservoirs that were deemed more efficient, in the process obliterating the ancient systems. Mendis documents how the modern technology of hydraulic engineering brought with it a class of social carriers whose concept of dominating nature was as alien to the traditional practices that were based on actively adapting to nature as the social carriers themselves were from the peasants for whose welfare they ostensibly practice their trade. The stories of the Lunugamvehera or Udawalawe projects in the south or the Eppawala Jayaganga in the northern dry zone tell of resource manipulation that fail to meet the stated objectives (they often fail to provide the water promised) and in the process alienate the farmers from the state itself. The burning down of the Lunugamvehera project engineer's office just after it was ceremoniously inaugurated was the first indication of the dissatisfaction rife in the area that was to express itself in a later *avatar* as the Janatha Vimukti Perumena (JVP) uprising. The social carriers of this technology, however, chose not to read the writings on the wall, an expression of the peasants whose lifestyles were being threatened: they labelled this an anti-social and anti-government act to be met with all the violence at the state's behest rather than an honest audit of the project and its claims.

Pluralizing Monistic Accords

Treaties are made between sovereign states. The difficulties that relate to them have an entropic quality to them: how sovereign is sovereign? 80 per cent? or 99.9 per cent? While there might be a compromise of sovereignty between two states, the larger issue is the degree of sovereignty of a state bureaucracy within the state. Will all within the state boundaries accept its diktats, howsoever lacking in fairness they may be? Are there no other countervailing forces that would champion the alternative? Whatever little bit is the entropic uncertainty margin between and within states, it has within it the potential for conflict unless there are inbuilt ameliorating mechanisms. What could be the nature of such an ameliorating mechanism?

One interpretive approach to studying and understanding society, which does not take the nation-state boundaries as the only container of social life, goes by the name of Cultural Theory, which maintains that, depending upon the degree of *openness* (group affinity or competition that is fettered or unfettered) and the degree of *connectedness* (grid ascription or transactions that are symmetrical or unsymmetrical), there are basically only five permutations of possible social environments. These give rise to five styles of organizing (or five solidarities) at all scales from villages to nation-states and the international arena, which make technological choices to further the interests of their respective solidarities.[16]

Hierarchy is characterized by unequal roles for unequal members and its overriding concern is *control* for which it has an armoury of different *procedural* solutions to manage conflicts, internal and external, including upgrading, transferring, re-segregating, co-opting, etc. The army, the bureaucracy and the internal structure of large corporations are examples of this institutional style.

Egalitarian communards lack internal role differentiation but are held together in bounded group loyalty and allegiance to an ethical cause. Resolution of disputes is difficult because compromises will be seen as cutting moral corners, and also because

[16] See Gyawali (1998, ibid.), which draws this concept from Douglas (1992), Thompson, Ellis and Wildavsky (1990) as well as Thompson (1996).

these groups are guided by a suspicious and *critical* rationality. Schisms are frequent and groups are held together only by *alarmist* causes that highlight threats from the outside. Social, environmental or religious fundamentalism campaigns are based on this style.

Individualism gives rise to a libertarian, social context where all boundaries are provisional and subject to *free* negotiations that have to have *substantive* benefits for the agreeing parties. Networks are based on bargaining rather than on bounded group loyalty or the sanctity of traditional procedures. This is the style of the market and its businessmen.

Fatalism of the conscripted means enduring the isolation of individualists without the freedom to organize one's own network and suffering the constraint of hierarchy without the support of loyal group affinity. Just *coping* with everyday living as best as fate allows is the only viable strategy. This is the lot of the peasant *ryots* of the Bihari plains.

The *hermit* who, unlike the fatalist, could exercise power but has voluntarily withdrawn from it, is at the centre of *autonomy* of inaction. This is a world away from all the four styles that is without competition or transaction—a retreat neither open nor connected where new action could grow out of inaction. It is in this environment of the deserts and caves, of exiles and hibernation, where future reformers are born. The three active solidarities that cognise and strategize all the time *vis-à-vis* one another are the hierarchic bureaucracies, individualist operators and egalitarian enclavists. The fatalist is an inactive solidarity that is only strategized upon by others, while the hermit's withdrawal permits no active involvement.

Looking upon water conflicts, not as India-Nepal or India-Bangladesh issues, but as one of conflicts between solidarities from the local to the global that uphold different rationalities would provide new insights. The way not to go forward is the one conventionally followed: create another 'commission' or 'authority' headed by ministers as co-chairmen, etc. The reason is that such a measure is based on procedural rationality, i.e. a state of mind that says that the essential elements, objectives, etc., are all fine and all that is needed is a fine-tuning of procedural details. Unfortunately, many of the conflicts identified above are not so much about procedures as about the very rationale or basis behind them. There are deeper issues of insecurity regarding sovereignty, uncertainties regarding the future, uncertainties in the science of land and water, etc., that find expression in activist anger down the road. These cannot be solved by procedural means: they need more substantive measures that often question the very paradigm around which procedural rationalities are built. And in South Asia, with the rise of a mass culture of production and consumption, that which is being questioned by newly emerging forces at all levels of society is the essential framework around which treaties have attempted to manage the complexities of water.

The previous understanding of international treaties was that the states were quite competent to handle any conflict conditions within their geographical boundaries, that the state was an adequate container of such problems since they were 'sovereign'. The following quote adequately expresses the inadequacy of the state as the only container of social activity:

> The focus on progress and the politics of organizing social change made the temporal dimension of social existence crucial, but left the spatial dimension in limbo. If processes were universal and deterministic, space was theoretically irrelevant. The set of spatial structures through which social scientists assumed lives were organized were the sovereign territories that collectively defined the world political map. Nearly all social scientists assumed that these political boundaries fixed the spatial parameters of other key interactions—the sociologist's society, macroeconomist's national economy, the political scientist's polity, the historian's nation. Each assumed a fundamental spatial congruence between political, social, and economic processes. In this sense, social science was very much a creature, if not a creation, of the states, taking their boundaries as crucial social containers. (Wallerstein et al. 1996)

It was enough in the past if nation-state bureaucracies reached a consensus among themselves and signed a treaty. However, a better understanding of the process now shows (see Fig. 1: International Treaty) that the state bureaucracies are but one set of actors in a clumsy process where other non-state actors weave through state boundaries and operate along national and international solidarities of their own. Without understanding the

FIGURE 1: INTERNATIONAL TREATY

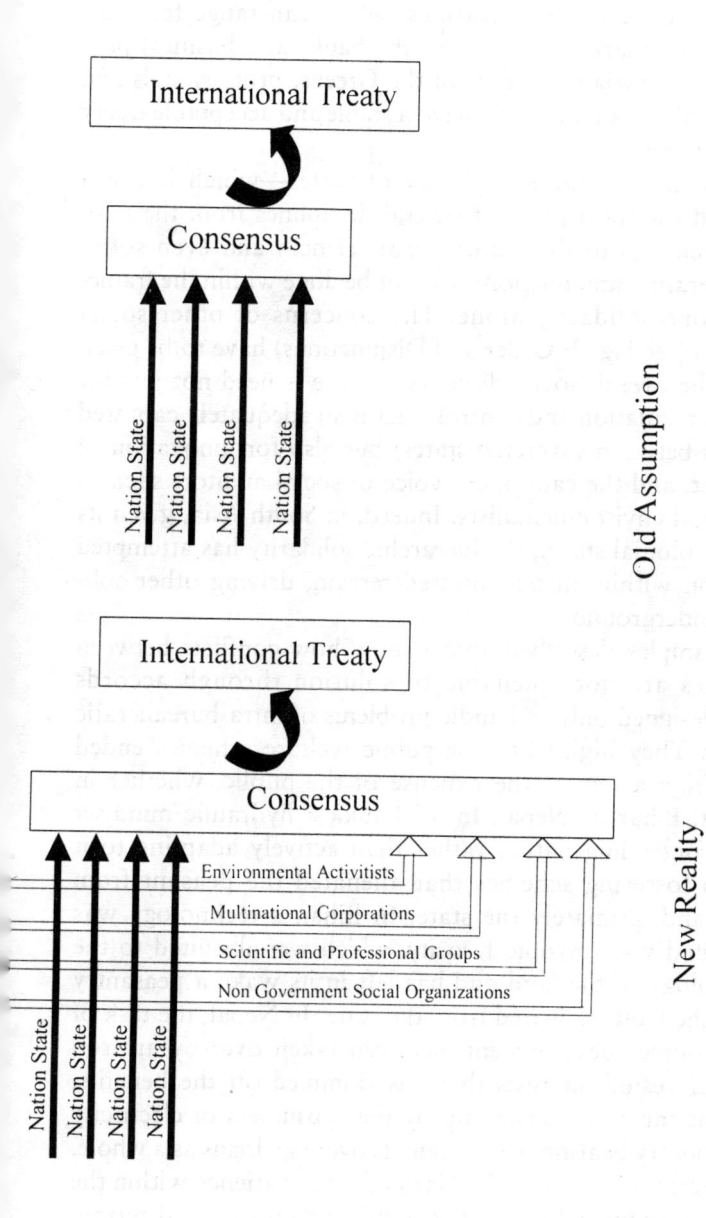

SOURCE: Based on S. Rayner and E. Malone, 1998, *Social Science Insights in Climate Change*, in Human Choice and Climate Change, Ohio: Battelle Press.

concerns of these other solidarities (which can range from the individualistic market concerns of the banks and business people to the egalitarian concerns of the Greens, professionals and academia), the chance of arriving at a stable and acceptable treaty is fairly remote.

Management of the complexity of water—which is not a subject but the focal point of several disciplines from the hard physical sciences to the softer social sciences and even softer poetry, literature and religion—cannot be done within the framework of one solidarity alone. The concerns of other social solidarities (see Fig. 2: Order and Disjunctions) have to be given space in the overall social discourse. There is need not just for hierarchic regulation and control (that is so adequately captured in treaties between sovereign states) but also for innovation of the market, and the cautionary voice of social auditors such as activists and environmentalists. Indeed, in South Asia, given its legacy of colonial states, the hierarchic solidarity has attempted to function within an uncontested terrain, driving other solidarities underground.

The examples described above show how conflicts between solidarities are not amenable to solution through accords that are designed only to handle problems of intra-bureaucratic solidarity. They highlight how public welfare schemes ended up benefiting a few at the expense of the public, whether in Sri Lanka, Bihar or Nepal. In Sri Lanka a hydraulic mind-set bent on controlling nature rather than actively adapting to it ended up fostering schemes that alienated the peasant from the land and ultimately the state. In Bihar, a technology was implemented with myopic ferocity, which was ill-suited to the hydro-ecology of the land and has left in its wake a peasantry impoverished and alienated from the state. In Nepal, the task of water resources development has been taken over by an iron triangle of vested interests that has skimmed off the benefits, leaving the tab to be picked up by the consumers of electricity and the country bearing the burden of sovereign loans as a whole. In the current debate over the Narmada, the patience within the water establishment functioning within an uncontested terrain to listen to voices of caution or alternative innovation, is very thin (Roy 1999, 2000). The Indus Treaty too is thus a specific

Order and Disjunctions

Development Input
(Foreign Aid)

Government
- Real
  - Rule of Law
  - Equitable and Just Tax
  - Transparent Exercise of Power
- Phantom
  - Rule of Individuals
  - Rent Seeking State
  - Conspiratorial Exercise of Power

Uncontested Terrain

Government runs inefficient "crony capitalism" business. Phantom Market prevails

Government monopolizes Social Service State feels threat from independent NGOs

Contested Terrain of Human Choice

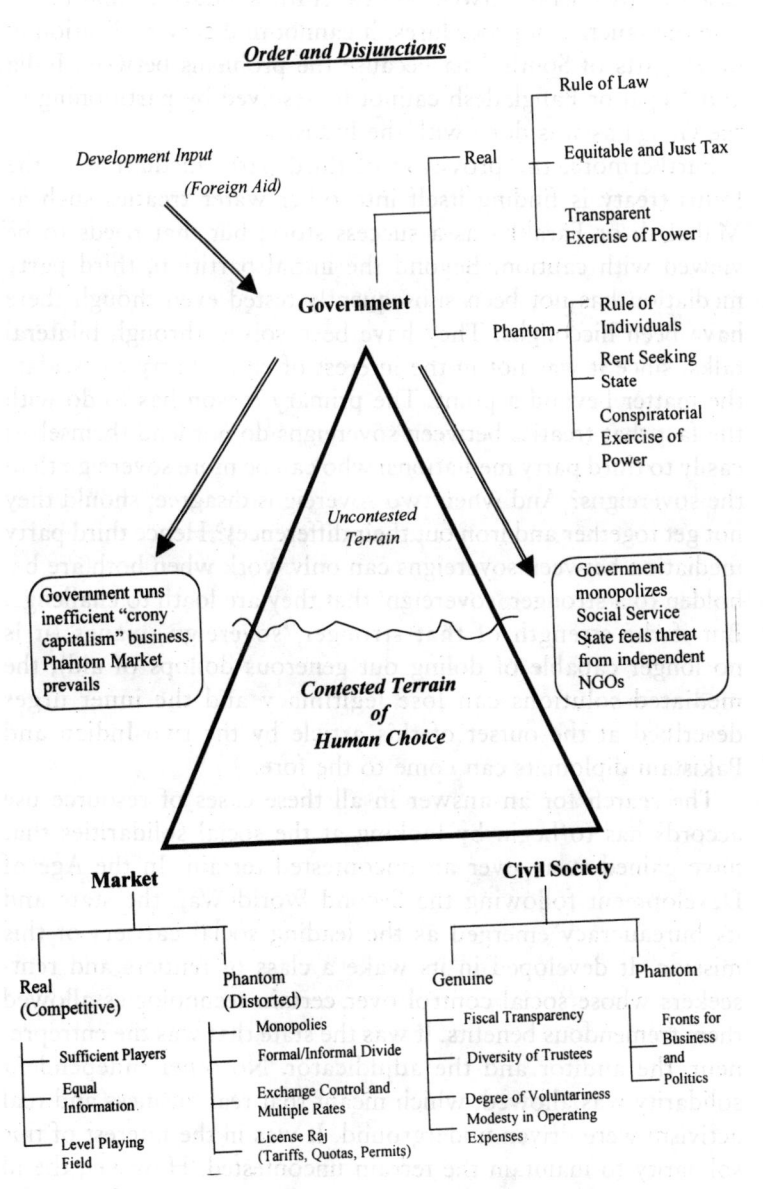

Market

Real (Competitive)
- Sufficient Players
- Equal Information
- Level Playing Field

Phantom (Distorted)
- Monopolies
- Formal/Informal Divide
- Exchange Control and Multiple Rates
- License Raj (Tariffs, Quotas, Permits)

Civil Society

Genuine
- Fiscal Transparency
- Diversity of Trustees
- Degree of Voluntariness Modesty in Operating Expenses

Phantom
- Fronts for Business and Politics

FIGURE 2: ORDER AND DISJUNCTIONS

case of agreements between bureaucratic solidarities that maintain the sanctity of procedures. It cannot find easy replication in other parts of South Asia because the problems between India and Nepal or Bangladesh cannot be resolved by partitioning of the Ganga as was done with the Indus.

Furthermore, the provision of third party mediation in the Indus treaty is finding itself into other water treaties such as Mahakali or Farakka as a success story; but that needs to be viewed with caution. Beyond the initial partition, third party mediation has not been subsequently tested even though there have been hiccoughs. They have been solved through bilateral talks, since it was not in the interest of either party to escalate the matter beyond a point. The primary reason has to do with the fact that treaties between sovereigns do not lend themselves easily to third party mediations: who can be more sovereign than the sovereigns? And when two sovereigns disagree, should they not get together and iron out their differences? Hence third party mediation between sovereigns can only work when both are beholden to a stronger 'sovereign' that they are loath to challenge. But if the strength of that stronger 'sovereign' wanes (it is no longer capable of doling out generous dollops of aid), the mediated solutions can lose legitimacy and the inner urges described at the outset of this article by the two Indian and Pakistani diplomats can come to the fore.

The search for an answer in all these cases of resource use accords has to begin by looking at the social solidarities that have gained sway over an uncontested terrain. In the Age of Development following the Second World War, the state and its bureaucracy emerged as the leading social carriers of this mission. It developed in its wake a class of rentiers and rent-seekers whose social control over certain technologies allowed them tremendous benefits. It was the state that was the entrepreneur, the auditor and the adjudicator. No other independent solidarity was allowed, which meant that real business and real activism were driven underground. It was in the interest of this solidarity to maintain the terrain uncontested. However, the ill effects of runaway technology soon began to manifest in the social polity and activism emerged anew. The restoration of democracy in South Asia has meant the emergence of 'civil society' action groups. By assuring a degree of freedom to social solidarities other than the state (such as non-profit volunteer groups as well as profit seeking investors), democracy has created a contested terrain where the forces of innovation (market), caution (volunteer activism or social auditors) and dispassionate adjudication (regulators) are all able to engage one another in creative tension.

Had the terrain not been uncontested to start with, perhaps the voices of cautionary activism and innovative entrepreneurship would have provided solutions that may have been less damaging to the environment and the body social. The cases above do demonstrate that uncontested terrains are hijacked by one set of interests at the expense of others. Hence, reform would entail creation of contestation where space is provided to all solidarities. Perhaps the difficulty lies in seeing 'governance' as synonymous with 'management', because the socio-physical complexity of the Himalaya-Ganga cannot be micromanaged. The uncertainties are too high, the complexities too intricate, and the potential for surprises all too frequent for 'management' to be the goal of good governance. Such an approach can easily lead to the hubris of monistic control such as has occurred with Nehruvian socialism or Stalinist totalitarianism. A more modest goal would be to reduce the scale and scope of surprises, which can be achieved with interventions in nature that are modest in scale, with decisions regarding the same made as close to the users as possible, and with ample scope for challenge from the innovators and those raising voices of caution.

The old way of managing water was to allow the state machinery free and unquestioning play in an uncontested terrain. It was based on the legitimacy of 'development' as a new *dharma*. With the failures of the last fifty years in water management, the new method of dealing with the complexity of water would be to 'tread with caution'.[17] With the rise of mass consumption has come mass politics that is best served with democracy, howsoever flawed and inefficient it may be. In water management, this would essentially mean preserving a clumsy, contested terrain where all three social solidarities—innovative market, cautionary civil society and adjudicatory state—are guaranteed their space that old treaties and accords do not reflect.

---

[17] See Ahmed et al. (1999) ibid.

REFERENCES

Ahmed, I., A. Dixit, and A. Nandy, 1999: 'Water, Power and People—A South Asian Manifesto on the Politics and Knowledge of Water', *Water Nepal*, vol. 7, no. 1, Kathmandu.

Bharti, I. 1991: 'Fighting the Irrigation Mafia in Bihar', *Economic and Political Weekly*, vol. XXVI, no. 38, 21 September, Bombay.

Dey, Dr. Basudeb (Burdwan), 1998: in *Proceedings of the Seminar on River Crises in South Asia*, edited by Dinesh Kumar Mishra, 21–2 June, Barh Mukti Abhiyan, Bihar, p. 78.

Dixit, A. 1996: 'Mahakali Nadi Sajha Ho, Pani Adha Ko Adha Ho' (in Nepali: Mahakali is common, water is half of half), *Mulyankan*, no. 42, Kartik-Mangsir 2053, Kathmandu.

Dixit, A and D. Gyawali 1994: 'Understanding the Himalaya-Ganga—Widening the Research Horizon and Deepening Cooperation'; *Water Nepal*, vol. 4 no. 1, Kathmandu.

Douglas, M., 1992: Risk and Blame, Routledge. London.

Dhungel, H., 1999: 'Risks and Rewards of Mega Projects—The Political Economy of Paraguayan Hydropower', *Water Nepal*, vol. 7, no. 1, Kathmandu.

Gyawali, D., 1989: Water in Nepal, Environment and Policy Institute, East West Center, Occasional Paper 8, Hawaii.

———, 1997: 'Foreign Aid and the Erosion of Local Institutions—An Autopsy of Arun3 from Inception to Abortion', in C. Thomas and P. Wilkin (ed.), *Globalization and the South*, Macmillan, London.

———, 1998: 'Patna, Delhi and Environmental Activism—Institutional Forces Behind Water Conflict in Bihar', *Water Nepal*, vol. 6 no. 1, Kathmandu.

———, 1999a: 'Nepal Bharat Bidyut Byapar Samjhauta—Nepal Na Bandhinu Nai Phaida', *Mulyankan*, Bhadra 2056 BS.

———, 1999b: 'Institutional Forces Behind Water Conflict in the Ganga Plains', *GeoJournal*, vol. 47, no. 3, October, Kluwer, Amsterdam.

Gyawali, D. and A. Dixit, 1994: 'The Himalaya-Ganga: Contending with Interlinkages in a Complex System'; *Water Nepal*, vol. 4, no. 1, Kathmandu.

———, 1999: 'Mahakali Impasse and Indo-Nepal Water Conflict', *Economic and Political Weekly*, 27 February, Bombay.

Mendis, D.L.O., 1999: 'Hydraulic Engineering versus Water and Soil Conservation Ecosystems: Lessons from the History of the Rise and Fall of Sri Lanka's Ancient Irrigation Systems', *Water Nepal*, vol. 7, no. 2, Kathmandu.

NFEJ, 1998: Pani Ko Kura (in Nepali, About Water), Nepal Forum for Environmental Journalists (NFEJ), Kathmandu, 1998.

Roy, Arundhati, 1999: *The Greater Common Good*, India Book Distributors, Bombay.
———, 2000: 'The Cost of Living', *Frontline*, vol. 17, no. 3, 5–8 Feb.
Swain, Ashok, 1996: *The Environmental Trap: The Ganges River Diversion, Bangladeshi Migration and Conflicts in India*, Report no. 41, Department of Peace and Conflict Research, Uppsala University, Sweden.
Thakurta, Chinmoy, 1998: 'Could Do Better, But For Funds', *Science and Culture*, vol. 64, nos. 5–6, May-June, Calcutta.
Thapa, P. J., 1997: 'Water-led Development in Nepal—Myths, Limitations and Rational Concerns', *Water Nepal*, vol. 5, no. 1.
Thompson, Michael, Richard Ellis and Aaron Wildavsky, 1990: *Cultural Theory*, Westview Press, Boulder.
Thompson, Michael, 1996: *Inherent Relationality*: An Anti-Dualist Approach to Institutions; Report 9608, Norwegian Center for Research in Organization and Management, Bergen.
Wallerstein, I. et al., 1996: *Open the Social Sciences: Report of the Gulbenkian Commission on the Restructuring of the Social Sciences*, Stanford University Press, Stanford, California.

III. CASES

Civil Societies in India and Pakistan and their New Peace Initiatives

Dagmar Bernstorff

Introduction

In today's world South Asia is the only trouble spot, where a nuclear war could possibly break out, causing destruction, mutilation and misery to hundreds of millions of people. The antagonism between India and Pakistan is an unresolved conflict that emerged from colonial rule and subsequent partition and independence. The contours of the discord between the two countries are well known, it is a syndrome of memories that hurt, competition that frightens, of antagonistic value-systems and lifestyles, of threat perceptions, real or imagined. During fifty years of independence both countries have had very different histories in social, political and economic development, which shaped the outlook and behaviour patterns of their people. This factor is often underestimated particularly by Indians. Pakistani elites tend to identify with the Islamic cultures of West-Asia and to negate their Indian past. Yet on the other hand they fail to understand that Muslims in India have been moulded by the Indian political and social system.

Pakistan is still struggling for its political order. Short spells of democratic government alternate with military rule; on 12 October 1999 another military coup ousted the Muslim League government headed by Nawaz Sharif and General Pervez Musharraf took over. The relationship between Islam and the state, law and society is still an unresolved problem. The question, which interpretation of Islam—strict adherence to the

Koran and the Sharia according to the Hannafi school or Reform Islam of the Egyptian or Turkish model, or nearer home an Islamic society as envisaged by the poet Mohammed Iqbal—still eludes consensus.

India's institutions have proved viable, yet there is a crisis of credibility. Moreover, for the past ten years governments had fragile majorities in Parliament, nevertheless prime ministers I.K. Gujral and A.B. Vajpayee did take some steps towards a peace process. The conflict about Kashmir and its future status may be only a manifestation of a deeper antagonism. Be that as it may, the dispute about Kashmir *is* the incendiary issue and both Governments perceive internal compulsions for not compromising on their positions, compulsions which may not be real.

We will not be discussing the two governments and their hard-headed, seemingly irrational and often irresponsible styles of functioning in the paper, but societies, civil societies. We do not have reliable data on how the people of India and Pakistan really perceive the relations between their two countries. It seems to be a generational question and one of closeness or distance to Kashmir. Is it only a problem of the Punjab, and do the Baluchis and Sindhis, really care about an issue, which they perceive as relevant to a distant areas and culture? How strongly do the Tamilians or the Andhras or the Mizos feel about Kashmir?

CIVIL SOCIETY

What do we mean by civil society? It is not by chance that after decades of discussions centring on nation—and state-building the discourse has now turned to civil society. Civil society as a category of universal human society[1] means the development of intermediary forms of association, even institutions, between the

---

[1] For an overview of the debate within the context of South Asia see J.P.S. Uberoi, 'On Civil Society', *Sociological Bulletin*, vols. 48, nos. 1-2, 1999, pp. 19-39; Susanne Hoeber Rudolph, 'Civil Society and the Realm of Freedom', *Economic and Political Weekly*, 13 May 2000, pp. 1762-9; Neera Chandhoke, *State and Civil Society, Explorations in Political theory*, New Delhi/London, 1995.

family and the state. As G.W.F. Hegel saw it, civil society is an achievement of the modern world. Civil society manifests itself in voluntary societies, professional associations, networks, craft guilds, trade-unions, independent research institutions, the press and what is today called Non-Governmental Organizations (NGOs). It is a category of the secular society, not to be confounded with religious associations or political parties. In fact, where political parties fail to transmit the concerns of the citizens, civil society steps in. We are talking about the realm of citizens actively concerned with and conscious about the life of the secular community, about equality, human rights, freedom of expression, empowerment and development. Protection of the environment and consumers' rights are issues of recent origin. Civil society means interaction with rather than subordination to the state.[2] It is debatable, whether trade and business must be included.

CIVIL SOCIETY IN INDIA AND PAKISTAN

We shall look first at the state of civil society in India and Pakistan and then examine a new phenomenon: transactional civil society bridging the gulf between the two.

In both countries the history of modern civil society goes back to colonial rule, when new professions emerged, the press developed, associations were formed and laws governing both the press and associations were made. Some of these are still in force, like the Societies Registration Act of 1860,[3] and several voluntary associations founded before Independence continue to exist. Their concerns are education, social reform, art, music, literature and charity. In the 1980s a worldwide phenomenon occurred in both countries, that is, the birth of numerous new voluntary associations, now termed non-governmental

[2] S. Hoeber Rudolph, op. cit., p. 1762.
[3] I have dealt at length with NGOs in India and Pakistan in Dagmar Bernstorff. 'Why NGOs? Problems of Empowerment, Autonomy and Linkages in India and Pakistan', J. Richter and Ch. Wagner (eds.), *Regional Security, Ethnicity and Governance*, New Delhi: Manohar, 1998, pp. 164–75.

organizations. The reason for this outburst of new NGOs was frustration with the progress or better non-progress of state-centred development: 'The national governments of South Asia failed to guarantee the basic needs for the majority of their citizens, like food, housing, health services and education'.[4] During military rule in Pakistan in the 1980s many NGOs served as an alternative to political activities and some helped to bring about a return to democratic rule, only to be soon disillusioned with the government by political parties.[5] Human rights issues are foremost on the agenda of NGOs in Pakistan.

Similarly there was disillusionment in India with the government of the Janata Party in 1977–9 and NGOs opened a space for young committed activists. Indeed much work has been done by NGOs particularly in the fields of medical care, non-formal education, empowerment of women and political conscientization at the grassroots. This is not the place to discuss the conceptual and managerial problems of NGOs or the question, whether NGOs absolve governments of their duty to guarantee decent living conditions to their citizens. We are discussing their relationship with the state.

In both countries, India and Pakistan, the relationships between NGOs and other associations of civil society and the state administration are at best ambivalent, at worst strained. In Pakistan more so than in India.

In India NGOs were met at first with suspicion, but, depending on the policies of the federal states, some of them were, so to speak, adopted by the administration and their skill in carrying out developmental work was recognized. In fact, some states and the central government have budgets for NGOs and some NGOs were even founded at the instance of state governments. Such NGOs are nicknamed GONGOs. State funding though involves the danger of NGOs being influenced in their decision-making by the availability of financial resources, thanks to state programmes. NGOs have to be registered as a society

---

[4] Ibid., p. 164.
[5] See Omar Asghar Khan, 'NGOs at Crossroads in Pakistan', *Liberal Times*, vol. II, no. 3, 1994.

and their accounts must be transparent. Many NGOs succeed in obtaining foreign funds.

In the 1980s donor institutions and international NGOs became disillusioned with the erratic process of development and the sluggish functioning of state administrations; this prompted several European governments to channel part of their development cooperation funds through NGOs. Here a rigid control of such foreign-funded NGOs sets in and the foreign donor is being screened indirectly.[6]

In Pakistan the control over NGOs—foreign funded or not—is much stricter, at least on paper. They have to register under one of five acts, some dating back to colonial rule, others based on ordinances issued in different periods of military rule. NGOs are being monitored by the federal and provincial Social Welfare Boards. However, an observer thought that the state administration was just not efficient enough to implement these controls. In 1994 the government of the day tried to introduce a new bill, which was to institutionalize very strict controls over NGOs, particularly those with foreign linkages. This bill met with vehement opposition from the NGOs and could not be passed for five years. The recent military coup and the suspension of Parliament has made the bill obsolete and that is one reason why Pakistani NGOs are not altogether unhappy with the military intervention of 12 October 1999. Nevertheless, the space for NGOs is narrower in Pakistan than in India, in spite of increasing urbanization and the growth of a new middle-class.

Apart from strained relations with the state, the civil societies of both countries have enemies within society itself. Religious fundamentalisms, both of the Hindu and the Muslim variety, are on the increase. Islamic fundamentalism in Pakistan is neither in favour of human rights nor the empowerment of

---

[6] The Indian NGO has to obtain an FCRA number, that is the permission to obtain foreign funds under the Foreign Contribution Regulation Act. It is a very lengthy procedure, certainly for those without the relevant connections in New Delhi. These permissions are issued by the Ministry of Home Affairs and annual reports about the utilization of such funds have to be produced.

women, to name only a few issues. Hindu fundamentalism as propagated by the RSS, the Vishwa Hindu Parishad and other organizations of the so-called 'Sangh Parivar' denies tolerance and is outright xenophobic, certainly not pro-reconciliation with Pakistan. And what is a civil society without civic sense?

A SOUTH ASIAN CIVIL SOCIETY FOR PEACE

The positions of the governments of India and Pakistan on bilateral relations and the problem of Kashmir in particular are well known. Briefly, *Pakistan* insists on the inclusion of the Kashmir problem in bilateral talks, demands a referendum in Kashmir according to the UN Resolution of 1948 and tries to internationalize the conflict.

India maintains that Kashmir is an integral part of India as the Legislative Assembly of Jammu and Kashmir accepted the Indian Constitution in 1952 and the Kashmiris have taken part in general elections ever since. It rejects the internationalization of the conflict and holds that it is an internal issue. All governments in both countries, irrespective of which party is in power, reiterate these positions. There has been one exception, the short-lived United Front Government led by I.K. Gujral, which tried to open up a dialogue. Diplomatic relations between the two countries are cool, bilateral trade is minimal (at least the official trade), mail is slow and travel across borders difficult, the new bus between Delhi and Lahore notwithstanding.

Yet in spite of the official restrictions there are links between the two societies.

1. *Media*: The correspondent in India of the leading Pakistani newspaper *Dawn* is an Indian journalist. Similarly the reports on Pakistan in the *Times of India* were for years dispatched by a Pakistani writer. Satellite television casts Indian programmes to Pakistan and vice versa, Pakistani plays are very much appreciated by intellectuals in Delhi and Indian serials find a large audience across the border. However the Sanskritised Hindi on Doordarshan and the Arabised Urdu on Pakistan TV limit understanding. Indian films

are popular in Pakistan, but circulate illegally as videos. Pakistani films are shown in India only in film-clubs or at film-festivals with restricted audiences. At a personal level this group does network with their counterparts across the border.
2. *Music*: As mentioned earlier Pakistan Tends to identify with West Asian culture and negate the composite South Asian heritage. In the field of music this is particularly odd as Muslim musicians have contributed substantially to Indian music since the fourteenth century and still do in contemporary India. By and large there is less of an institutional infrastructure for the arts in Pakistan than in India and exchange of artists seems to be rare. When the internationally popular Qawwali singer Nusrat Fateh Ali Khan was invited for recordings in Bombay, xenophobic forces of the Shiv Sena tried to prevent this and the recording had to be done clandestinely in a hotel-room!
3. *Fashion*: There are lines of communication in the world of fashion—if the *kameez* are worn long in India, the same style prevails in Pakistan, the fashion colours of the season are alike.
4. *Literature*: Few and far between are meetings of Urdu poets from both countries, but they do happen and a dialogue takes place. However, to give an example: Urdu medium schools in India are starved for textbooks, but it would be unthinkable to use reprints of Pakistani textbooks on neutral subjects like mathematics in Indian schools.
5. *Sports*: Obviously sports, particularly cricket, provides a vast field of mutual contacts with a broad based popular echo in both countries.
6. Last not least there are still family links, but given the restrictive visa policies in both countries and the inadequate postal and telephone links, poor people particularly find it difficult to maintain their contacts. And there are illegal links in smuggling across borders in the deserts of Rajasthan and Gujarat, activities where communication does not seem to be a problem.

A SOUTH ASIAN CIVIL SOCIETY FOR PEACE

In spite of the stalemate in intergovernmental relations or perhaps because of it, citizens of India and Pakistan have started a dialogue, even many dialogues.

The publication *Beyond Boundaries. A Report on the State of Non-Official Dialogues on Peace, Security and Cooperation in South Asia*[7] lists twelve initiatives at the bilateral India-Pakistan level and twenty-eight multilateral organizations or informal channels of communication between civil societies in South Asia. These dialogues sprang from a wide range of concerns, like peace, human rights, gender issues, cultural exchanges, and bilateral trade. At the outset the authors of the study, which has been sponsored by the universities of Toronto and York in Canada, ask *why* these initiatives emerged in large numbers in the 1990s. They could identify reasons:

1. The ongoing tensions between South Asian countries,
2. The rising significance of transnational security issues, like environmental degradation, water resource management and irregular movements of people across state boundaries.
3. The growth of 'robust non-governmental organizations'.

Nowadays one distinguishes between 'track 2' and 'track 3', or 'people to people' initiatives. 'Track 2' dialogues provide a second line of communication between states at an unofficial level, which are acknowledged and sometimes even supported by governments, and they serve as testing ground for new policy concepts. Such a forum is the *India-Pakistan Neemrana Initiative* (after the Fort-Hotel in Rajasthan, where the first meeting was held), formed in 1991 with the encouragement of USIS. Former diplomats, military leaders and academics meet at regular intervals alternatively in India and Pakistan.

'Track 2' and 'Track 3' contacts, of course, often overlap. We are here primarily concerned with 'Track 3' initiatives, which try

---

[7] Navnita Chadha Behera, Paul M. Evans, Gowher Rizvi, *Beyond Boundaries. A Report on the State of Non-official Dialogues on Peace, Security and Cooperation in South Asia*, University of Toronto-York University Joint Centre for Asia-Pacific Studies, 1997.

to build bridges between citizens. These dialogues can be viewed from two positions. One, they provide an exchange of views among elites, where governments cannot participate directly, and possibly prepare the ground for policy changes. The second view holds that on the contrary 'the real dynamism of dialogues comes from the involvement of groups independent of the state, capable of creating new constituencies to reorder national security priorities and to outline alternative policy options'.[8]

The *Beyond Boundaries* . . . report analyses the constraints and obstacles as well as the achievements of these meetings. The obstacles originate in the geopolitical asymmetry of the subcontinent, the deep-seated suspicion and hostility between two countries—India and Pakistan—and the uncooperative attitude of the administration. Partly this is due to the fact, that foreign policy decision-making has always been outside the domain of public debate. Even the inputs by research institutes and think-tanks (including those founded by the governments) seem to be minimal. Officials do not welcome these alternative thought processes: 'The barriers between officials and the public are thick and often impermeable'.[9] The disinterest of some policy makers borders on contempt; they talk of 'naïve meddlers and amateurs'. Furthermore the fragility of regimes often does not allow any policy changes and there are even constituencies in the administration, particularly in the Armed Forces of both countries, which have a vested interest in maintaining a high level of tension. The roles of bureaucrats, the Armed Forces and politicians differ. In Pakistan politicians are almost subordinate to the Armed Forces and the bureaucrats. In India politicians clearly have the upper hand.

At the practical and logistical level there are problems of communication with poor telephone lines and insufficient air and train links. There have been massive complaints about the difficulties in obtaining visas, which are often granted—or refused—at the last moment.

But these dialogues are not without achievements. They do explore alternatives for conflict resolution and have even

[8] Ibid., p. 5.
[9] Ibid., p. 32.

prepared studies in support of different policy options. Public discussion of regional concerns has been influenced and in some cases public attention was awakened to escalating problems. New networks of research institutes and scholars have emerged and potential leaders have interacted with each other. Last but not least, a large number of people in India and in Pakistan have met, experienced each other's hospitality and had an opportunity to get firsthand information about the other country.

It is worth taking a closer look at three select forums of non-official dialogue among a large number of initiatives.

1. *Pakistan India Peoples' Forum for Peace and Democracy* (PIPFPD). The organization started with a preparatory meeting of concerned citizens from both countries in Delhi in 1995, followed by conventions in Lahore (1995), Calcutta (1996), Peshawar (1998) and most recently in Bangalore in April 2000. The Forum's two co-chairmen are I.A.Rahman, director of the Pakistan Human Rights Commission and Admiral L. Ramdas, who succeeded the former governor Nirmal Mukherjee in 2000. The meetings[10] follow a pattern set at the Lahore Convention. Four subjects have been selected and discussed by working groups at all conferences: 1. Demilitarization, Denuclearization and Peace Promotion, 2. Governance and Economic Cooperation, 3. Religious Intolerance, and 4. Kashmir. In addition, special groups have met, e.g. women's rights activists, trade-unionists, journalists representatives of the arts, culture, and education.

The Lahore Convention (1995) was attended by 153 delegates from Pakistan and 83 from India, the Calcutta Convention by 166 participants from Pakistan and 160 from India. In between these two conventions the PIPFPD spread from the capitals to

[10] 'Pakistan-India Peoples' Convention on Peace and Democracy, Proceedings and Recommendations', Lahore, 10–11 November 1995; Pakistan-India Peoples' Forum for Peace and Democracy, Proceedings, Recommendations and Declaration of the Third Joint Convention, Calcutta, 28–31 December 1996; Pakistan India Peoples' Forum for Peace and Democracy (PIPFPD), Fourth Joint Convention, Peshawar, 21–2 November 1998; 5th Joint Convention of Pakistan India Peoples' Forum for Peace and Democracy (PIFPD), Bangalore, 6–8 April 2000, 'Bangalore Declaration', see *Liberal Times*, vol. VIII, no. 1, 2000, pp. 57–8.

other centres. Regional chapters were formed in eight Indian cities, among them Jaipur, Varanasi, Patna and six in Pakistan, in Karachi, Lahore, Quetta, Peshawar, Islamabad and Hyderabad (Sind). A glance at the list of participants at the Calcutta Convention reveals that a large number of delegates did not come from the metropolitan cities, but from little known provincial towns. Large contingents of women from both count-ries attended the meetings.

It is not surprising that the resolutions call for a 25 per cent reduction in defence expenditure, condemn the nuclear tests by both countries and call for a nuclear weapons free world including South Asia. As the Peshawar Resolution says: 'We believe that nuclear weapons enhance neither the security nor the power or the prestige of countries in a globalising world'.[11] The forum calls on the governments to sign the CTBT, to desist from deploying the weapons already in the arsenals, and to divert their scarce resources from nuclearization to '... improving the lot of their own people, who are victims of grinding poverty, ill health and illiteracy'. Furthermore: '... The Forum expresses its deep concern over the possibilities of an outbreak of a nuclear war between the two countries as a result of accident, miscalculation or misperception'.[12]

It is fitting that the conventions devote considerable space to *religious intolerance*. The Working Group at the Lahore Convention was very ambitious and produced a long list of topics to be handled by a joint Indo-Pakistan Committee, like the promotion of street theatre, exchange of artists, syndicated articles by journalists, the preparation of a compendium on the teaching of tolerance in different religions, the exchange of students and the setting up of a watchdog group to monitor communal violence. At the Calcutta meeting a warning was heard not to attempt too much simultaneously, but to concentrate on a few topics, among them the examination of history books for prejudices and stereotypes. A committee was formed to create new stories for children, highlighting the syncretic culture of the subcontinent, and the resource materials to be sent to

[11] Peshawar Declaration, p. 5.
[12] Ibid., p. 3.

NGOs.[13] And as the Peshawar Declaration says: 'We believe that there is need for space outside the religious discourse, where individual, rational, objective, scientific thought and the spirit of inquiry can flourish'.[14]

What emerged at the Conventions regarding Kashmir? Discussions at the Lahore meeting must have been very lively with opinions clashing on the future course of action. A radical approach, like simultaneous peace marches to the border and signature campaigns in both countries was suggested, but did not find acceptance. Some wanted an opinion poll to be conducted by the PIPFPD, probably an unrealistic proposition. At the Calcutta convention it was decided to hold regular meetings between a joint committee of the PIPFPD with representatives from both sides of the LOC. To facilitate discussion at the Bangalore meeting an extensive article by Tapan K. Bose was circulated at the conference.[15] The Bangalore Declaration called 'upon the Governments of India and Pakistan to order cessation of all hostilities along the Line of Control by all forces directly and *indirectly* (italics mine) under their control' as well as on the militant organizations of Jammu and Kashmir to eschew violence and on the governments of both states and the peoples of Jammu and Kashmir *together* to find an acceptable solution in the larger interest of peace and democracy.[16]

The Calcutta Convention in 1996 was a turning point, as it was decided 'to go to the people' and 'to break into the decision-making fortresses on both sides'. A march was organized which culminated in a 'jalsa' with music and poetry readings. The breaking into the decision-making fortress in the West Bengal state succeeded in a way as the Speaker of the West Bengal Legislative Assembly was the chief guest at the inaugural meeting and hosted a dinner, at which Chief Minister Jyoti Basu mingled with the delegates.

[13] Calcutta Declaration, pp. 37–8.
[14] Peshawar Declaration, p. 5.
[15] Tapan K. Bose, 'Building Peace in Kashmir', Bangalore Convention, pp. 4–11.
[16] Bangalore Declaration, para 12.

2. The *Association of Peoples of Asia*[17] is a meeting-ground for academics and social activists. It is chaired by the Gandhian leader Nirmala Deshpande. They first met in 1996 in Delhi and evolved three principles. 1. India and Pakistan's territorial integrity needs to be respected; 2. Hindu-Muslim and India-Pakistan relations are two different issues; and 3. problems in bilateral relations need to be discussed at sub-national as well as at the international level. The Association of Peoples of Asia organized the Pakistan Peace Conference at Karachi in February 1999, where 400 participants met (about 350 from Pakistan and fifty from India and some other countries). The conference discussed problems like minorities, gender, media, but first of all peace, particularly in view of the nuclear tests India and Pakistan had carried out in 1998. A common peace march united Indians and Pakistanis in their protest.

The Association of Peoples of Asia met again in January 2000 in Calcutta[18] with participants from more countries of the region, namely, Bangladesh, Sri Lanka, Nepal, Bhutan and Turkmenistan. The meeting followed the annual conference of the Akhil Bharat Rachnatmak Samaj, a Gandhian organization, chaired by Nirmala Deshpande and thus facilitated the participation of a large number of delegates. Four retired military officers from Pakistan also attended, and seemed to have been some kind of watchdogs. The conference called for 'cessation of all forms of violent action in Kashmir, including militant activities' and the 'resumption of dialogue with active involvement of all shades of opinion of the people of Jammu and Kashmir'. The statement concludes: 'This conference reiterates that a solution to the Kashmir issue requires strict adherence to democratic precepts and practices. It will also need extending and deepening of democracy in both countries with a view to empowering the common man'.[19]

[17] 'Peace for all!' Report, Pakistan Peace Conference, Karachi, 27–8 February 1999.
[18] South Asia Peace Conference, 18–19 January 2000, Calcutta, organized by Akhil Bharat Rachnatmak Samaj and Association of Peoples of Asia.
[19] Ibid., p. 82.

3. *Women's Bus for Peace*: A novel route was taken by a group of 40 Indian women in April 2000 when they boarded the bus from Delhi to Lahore to meet with Pakistani women. The visit was reciprocated by a delegation of 60 Pakistani women at the beginning of May 2000. The underlying idea was that women are more receptive to the need for peace; they live by relationships and networking, while men live by concepts. The Indian and the Pakistani groups were warmly received in the host countries. Pakistani women greeted the Indian delegation with candles in their hands. In both countries the delegates interacted with women's organizations, with the press and with activists in the peace and human rights movements. Both foreign ministers gave them receptions. The respective high commissioners invited them. In Pakistan even the 'CEO' General P. Musharraf, saw the leaders of the Indian group. In India the Members of Parliament for Jaipur and Agra hosted the Pakistani group in their constituencies.

Seminars were held at the highest levels.[20] Amidst all the enthusiasm one also heard voices of caution, and opinions sometimes clashed. Asma Jehangir, the well-known lawyer and human rights activist, pointed out that India and Pakistan were two separate countries with their own cultures, but heterogeneity should be turned into an asset: 'If we cannot be friends, let us live as adversaries in grace and dignity', she said. By and large the Pakistani women, who live in a more difficult social and political environment, were more vocal and assertive than their Indian counterparts: 'Don't underestimate the difficulties of the peace process', warned Hina Gilani, 'but strength comes from knowing, we have the capacity to fight. We have to increase our outrage!' When Indians condemn Pakistan as a terrorist state, a delegate pointed out, they forget that democrats and liberals in Pakistan also have to live with terrorist threats and hate mail. Opinions differed whether the younger generation in Pakistan is more or less hostile towards India.

---

[20] This author attended a meeting with writers and the press on 3 May 2000. See also the *Hindu*, 6 June 2000, *Times of India*, 6 and 7 May 2000, and 20 May 2000.

On the one hand, young Pakistanis are exposed to intensive anti-India rhetoric, both in the press and in school books, and certainly in the *madrassahs*, and they usually have no direct personal experience of meeting Indians. On the other hand globalization, TV and the internet started a trend towards the levelling of differences.

The strong minded women resolved that emotional bonding is the answer to estrangement and hostility and as a symbol they exchanged bangles as symbols of peace: 'The tingling of the bangles will stop the fighting!'

THE ROAD TO PEACE

Of course the question that arises is; how effective are these 'track 3' contacts. One criticism is: these meetings are very elitist. But, with the formation of committees of professional groups, like lawyers or journalists a step towards a broadening of the bases has been made. There is also a conscious effort to involve young people, who are the potential future leaders. Second, one is tempted to ask what influence do theses interviews with political leaders really have? At least it should contribute to expanding their world outside their limited circles. Third, one may wonder what happens in the period between these meetings? As mentioned above, the PIPFPD does have branches in several cities of India and Pakistan and one can only hope that they engage in some activities. The activists think a critical mass of public opinion has to be created to be able to influence the political process.

Obviously some creative thinking has to emerge as, a departure from the petrified positions and worn out concepts. New Ideas must be born. As developments in Europe, in South Africa or in the peace process between Israel and the Palestinians have shown, this is not impossible. Innovation *does* happen in international politics. There are large numbers of scholars, writers, social activists in South Asia as well as in other parts of the world, who have in-depth knowledge of the subcontinent. In fact, South Asian Studies at American, Canadian, British, Scandinavian or German universities are frequently taught by

South Asians along with other nationals. An *international think-tank* needs to be formed, where numerous alternative solutions to strife, misery and danger of a nuclear war will be developed. It may take time, the solution to the dispute between India and Pakistan constitutes an idea, whose time has come. For the sake of its citizens South Asia must become a more peaceful place.[21]

[21] Modified versions of this paper have been read at the Department of Political Science, South Asia Institute, Heidelberg University on 5 June 2000 and at the conference on Pakistan organized by the seminar für Geschichte Südasiens, Humboldt University, Berlin on 24 June 2000. I am grateful to colleagues and participants for their comments.

Possibility of Ethnic Compromise in Sri Lanka

Partha S. Ghosh

BOWSPRIT

The war between the Sri Lankan armed forces and the Liberation Tigers of Tamil Eeelam (LTTE) has once again intensified. Ever since the restoration of state authority in November 1995, over Jaffna, the stronghold of the LTTE in the Northern Province, the military confrontation is back to square one with the LTTE regaining its hold over some important strategic areas. In the Presidential elections held on 21 December 1999 the political fallout of these developments was clearly noticeable. The impact was particularly dramatic because just three days before the elections there was an assassination attempt on President Chandrika Kumaratunga who was seeking re-election. Although the attempt failed (one of the rare failures for an LTTE suicide bomber), its impact was visible on the electoral verdict. All predictions had indicated a probable victory for the United National Party (UNP) challenger, Ranil Wickremasinghe. But some amount of sympathy wave tilted the balance decisively in favour of Chandrika; indeed the margin of victory was much less compared to the elections of 1994. In 1994 she had polled 62 per cent of the votes polled, but in 1999 the percentage fell to 51.12. What was even more important was that Sri Lanka Tamils in general seemed to desert her and unlike the 1994 elections they voted for the UNP. In the parliamentary elections that are to be held before long this trend may continue. In the given situation the pattern of relationship between the Sri Lankan state and the LTTE is going to be more or less the same.

There are, however, two important positive possibilities. One, the UNP might be more cooperative this time with the government in working out a constitutional compromise provided Chandrika reduces her tirade against that party. Throughout the campaign she abused the UNP for its alleged secret deal with the LTTE and following the abortive assassination bid on her life she used it to her advantage by indirectly attributing the incident to this conspiracy. Still, her reduced popularity may force her to be more accommodative of the UNP. The spectre of the revival of the Janatha Vimukti Peramuna (JVP) may as well contribute to this change of attitude. The JVP presidential candidate M.D. Nandana Gunathilaka did unexpectedly well at the polls in the southern Sinhala-majority provinces and garnered 4.08 per cent votes in a national count.

The other positive indication is a renewed effort on the part of some international actors to help the contending parties, the government and the LTTE to sit across the table and negotiate. Although Chandrika insists that it should be in the frame of facilitation and not mediation but that is a matter of semantics. What is important is that the efficacy of an international mediation is once again being talked about seriously. The country that is figuring most prominently in this regard is Norway.

Against this background, which throws up all kinds of possibilities and given the intractability of the problem, does peace as a value have any chance of success? Can the LTTE be persuaded, on whatever terms, to compromise on its avowed position of fulfilling its dream of an independent *eelam*? In short, can peace return to this hapless island?

Is Peace a Value?

In the parlance of statecraft peace has relevance only in an international context. Generally, an end of war or an absence of war has the connotation of peace. But now that many states are at war with their own sub-national groups it has assumed a wider national connotation as well. But whatever be the case, peace must not be confused with negation of violence. On the contrary, it may be argued that it is convoluted violence. Since peace is relevant only where there is conflict, its connotation is diametrically opposite between two conflicting parties. In the *Mahabharat* both the Kauravas and the Pandavas justified their war in the name of peace. One may recall the classic sermon of Lord Krishna to a pacifist Arjun to take up arms in defence of *dharma*, which in applied terms meant defeating the Kauravas. But who defines what is right and what is wrong? A professionally trained lawyer would find both the Kauravas and Pandavas guilty of abuse of the royal code of conduct and gender justice. In the Vietnam war America justified its unlawful involvement in it in the name of peace. Had the Americans won the war the world would have believed them, for nothing succeeds like success in politics, national or international.

Sri Lankan Context

The above formulation finds its graphic expression in President Chandrika Kumaratunga's characterization of her government's war with the LTTE as a 'war for peace'. The inherent logic is that peace is the other name of order, which can be ensured only by defeating the LTTE. Though not uttered in the same language, the LTTE's logic is the same. For them also, there can be no peace without an independent *eelam*, which is possible only through a decisive victory over the Sri Lankan army, for otherwise the dream of an *eelam* cannot materialise and the security and well-being of the Tamils cannot be guaranteed. Both arguments are logically valid. Which one is more valid depends upon one's conceptual predisposition, for peace as a concept is never value free. This author's own predisposition is for societal order in which the territorial integrity of a state is a matter of paramount importance and is just not negotiable.

Peace as a Normative Value

Drawing from the human experience of political evolution, peace has been projected as that magic wand which is expected to contribute to the dictum 'maximum good of the maximum number' without of course jeopardizing the interests of the minorities. In other words, it stands for coexistence of individuals and groups within a defined territory called state. Or, to put it differently, it connotes compromises and adjustments of individual and group interests for the larger interest of the composite community. In short, it means order and the resolution of group conflicts within the framework of a constitutional order. In simple terms, it means democratic bargaining. If so, what have been the respective contributions of the Sri Lankan state and the Tamils towards peace? The basic assumption is that Sri Lanka is a unified territory and all ethnic groups on its soil, most prominently the Sinhalese and the Tamils, for historical reasons, have equal claim on it. Any misgiving about that claim would spell disaster and eventual dismemberment of Sri Lanka. And once it is dismembered there is bound to be a massacre of both Tamils and Sinhalese as both are minorities in certain areas. The Indian experience should serve as a lesson to all those who plead for partition of plural societies on ethnic grounds.

EQUALITY OF CLAIM

Historically, both the Sinhalese and the Tamils have more or less equal claim over the island as its original inhabitants. Although the former, particularly the chauvinist variety amongst them, argue that they were the original settlers on the island, having arrived from northern India, after the establishment of Buddhism in India in the sixth century BC,[1] modern research tends to prove that even prior to that, from 900 BC onwards, there were interactions between central Sri Lanka and peninsular India. The techno-cultural remains at the Anuradhapura Citadel provide some critical evidence. Archaeological investigations into the habitations and burial sites of the age suggest that the island formed the southernmost sector of the broader Early Iron Age (900 BC to first century AD) peninsular Indian techno-cultural complex. These evidences also suggest that these habitations were not only linked with Peninsular India but through the

---

[1] According to Mahavamsa, the Sinhalese race originated in the island with the arrival of Vijaya with his 700 companions some time in the fifth century BC. K.M. de Silva, *A History of Sri Lanka*, New Delhi: Oxford University Press, 1981, pp. 3–11.

latter to the Deccan.[2] From very ancient times, therefore, Sri Lanka was a multi-ethnic society, although the south Indian component was not powerful enough to alter the essentially north Indian character of the population. In any case, as de Silva writes: 'Ethnicity was not an important point of division in society ... and it would seem that neither the Sinhalese nor the Tamils remained racially pure'.[3]

POLITICS OF TERRITORY

Did the existence of the Sinhalese and the Tamils on the island mean that particular portions of the territory exclusively belonged to the two respective communities? The answer is both yes and no. While specific areas of the present northern province were exclusively inhabited by the Tamils, insofar as the present Eastern Province is concerned, contrary to the claims put forward by the LTTE and some other Tamil groups, the evidence does not suggest so.

There is no doubt that the Tamils had contact with the island from time immemorial and as such some of them must have settled in the island long time ago; the question is how widespread were their settlements. As per available evidence, large-scale Tamil settlements took place much later. There were two stages of settlement. In the first stage, covering the eleventh and twelfth centuries, these settlements were confined to the upper half of the eastern province and parts of the western coast. These settlements did not include the Jaffna peninsula. During the second stage, primarily during the thirteenth century, following

[2] Sudharshan Seneviratne, ' "Peripheral Regions" and "Marginal Communities": Towards an Alternative Explanation of Early Iron Age Material and Social Formations in Sri Lanka', in R. Champakalakshmi and S. Gopal, (eds.), *Tradition, Dissent and Ideology: Essays in Honour of Romila Thapar* New Delhi: Oxford University Press, 1996, pp. 279, 291.

[3] De Silva, *A History of Sri Lanka*, p. 13. Interestingly, de Silva draws a distinction between 'multi-ethnic' and 'plural' societies in this context. He writes: 'Sri Lanka in the first few centuries after the Aryan settlement was a multi-ethnic society (a conception which emphasizes harmony and a spirit of live and let live) rather than a plural society (in which tension between either or other distinctive groups is a main feature)'.

the establishment of the Jaffna kingdom, there was systematic settlement of Tamils in Jaffna and Vanni regions and the northern parts of the eastern province.[4]

For decades Tamil political activists have argued that the island's north and east, corresponding to the present northern and eastern provinces, were Tamil areas and, therefore, should be designated as the 'Tamil homeland' and given full autonomy.[5] This has been challenged by historian K.M. de Silva and human geographer G.H. Peiris. De Silva argues that there was no 'Tamil homeland' as such and there were homelands in different parts of the identified area and that too not for very long periods. In any case, 'most of what is today the eastern province lay beyond the effective control of the Jaffna Kingdom and was not part of it'. De Silva finds no historical evidence to sustain the claim about the existence of 'either a Tamil state comprising the present northern and eastern provinces as the legitimate successor to a short-lived Jaffna kingdom of the past, or even for a regional unit, incorporating these two provinces as integral parts of what were once the 'traditional homelands' of the Tamils, as a large autonomous unit of a restructured Sri Lanka polity, and as a substitute for a separate state reflecting a restitution of a lost political heritage'.[6]

Peiris challenges the 'homeland' thesis from a politico-demographic perspective. He agrees that after the thirteenth century, in the northern and eastern parts of Sri Lanka, there was growth in the Tamil population, spread of Tamil language, and expansion of Tamil cultural patterns, but since north and east were

[4] K. Indrapala, 'Early Tamil Settlements in Ceylon', *Journal of the Royal Asiatic Society (Ceylon)* (Colombo), New Series, 13, 1969, pp. 60–3. See also, R.A.L.H. Gunawardana, 'The Kinsmen of the Buddha: Myth as Political Charter in the Ancient and Early Medieval Kingdoms of Sri Lanka', *Sri Lanka Journal of Humanities* (Peradeniya), 2(1), June 1976, pp. 53–62.

[5] Chelvadurai Monogaran, 'Sinhala-Tamil Relations and the Politics of Space', in *Symposium on the Plight of the Tamil Nation*, International Tamil Foundation, London, 29 June 1997, pp. 20–8.

[6] K.M. de Silva, 'The "Traditional Homelands" of the Tamils: Separatist Ideology in Sri Lanka: A Historical Appraisal', Occasional Paper 4, International Centre for Ethnic Studies, Kandy, 1995, p. 28. I have reviewed the monograph in *Pacific Affairs* (Vancouver), 69(2), Summer 1996.

not clearly defined territorial entities one cannot ascertain the claim over a territory without seeking a precise understanding of population patterns, frontiers of settlements and the geographical limits of cultural transformations.[7]

TERRITORIAL INTEGRITY

Our first and foremost assumption, therefore, is that the present territoriality of Sri Lanka should not to be questioned and all ethnic groups living within its confines should have equal rights over any portion of it, though it is possible that respective groups may have their concentrations in certain areas. What follows from this is that anybody, irrespective of his ethnic origin, can settle anywhere in the island and earn his living through legitimate competitiveness with others. This is an ideal situation and should be above controversy. But group behaviour has its own rationale and correspondingly democratic politics has its own dynamics that throw these assumptions haywire. The history of Sri Lanka during the last one-and-a-half centuries underscores this sad reality.

EVOLUTION OF THE CONFLICT

The evolution of the Sinhala-Tamil ethnic cleavage can be traced to the nineteenth century. Probably it is inherent in the process of political evolution that while democracy tends to unite peoples through mutual compromises it also sows the seeds of discord. During the colonial period the mutual suspicion between the Sinhalese and the Tamils followed the textbook pattern. As it generally happens, certain aspects of colonial policy tend to affect the majority interests more than the minority interests for the simple reason that the minorities, being already conscious of their numerically inferior status, do not react so sharply to those aspects of the policy as does the majority. But as soon as the majority reacts to those policies it indirectly harms the interests of the minority, or at least it is perceived as such,

[7] G.H. Peiris, 'An Appraisal of the Concept of a Traditional Homeland in Sri Lanka', *Ethnic Studies Report* (Kandy), 9(1), January 1991, p. 19.

and in the process a cleavage is created. The same happened in Sri Lanka also when, for example, the Morgan Commission Report of 1867 was introduced.

The Sinhalese feared that the idea was to promote Christian missionary schools and hence English education at the cost of the indigenous system of instruction. Known as the Denominational System, it gave freedom to all religious denominations to establish schools for their own children without any restrictions on religious teachings. On the face of it, it was a democratic policy but its impact was differentiated. On account of paucity of funds and lack of political support, the Buddhist or Hindu organizations were not in a position, like their Christian counterparts, to take much advantage of the situation. The actual beneficiaries were, therefore, the Christian missionaries.[8] In 1868, 65 per cent of the Sri Lankan children attending schools were Christians and only 27 per cent Buddhists. The British policy that left the development of secondary education largely to private schools after 1884 enabled the Christians to maintain this lead.[9]

The British educational policy not only disadvantaged the Sinhalese Buddhists vis-à-vis the Christians but some of its aspects also affected them vis-à-vis the Tamils. For example, in 1869, the Department of Public Instruction was opened to financially assist schools through various schemes of grant-in-aid. Following this, several Sinhalese Buddhist schools were established. This system, however, had a different kind of impact in Jaffna where it was left entirely to the Christian missionaries to promote education. As a result, the people of Jaffna benefited from the education their children received at modest cost. In due course they were so proficient in English and

---

[8] For an analysis of the growth of education in Sri Lanka, see J.C.A. Corea, 'One Hundred Years of Eduction in Ceylon', *Modern Asian Studies* (Cambridge), vol. 3, no. 2, 1969, pp. 151-65; K.H.M. Sumathipala, *History of Education in Ceylon, 1796-1965: With Special Reference to the Contribution made by C.W.W. Kannangara to the Educational Development of Ceylon*, Dehiwala, Sri Lanka: Tisara Prakasakayo, 1968.

[9] C.R. de Silva, 'Weightage in University Admissions: Standardization and district Quotas in Sri Lanka, 1970–75', *Modern Ceylon Studies* (Peradeniya), vol. 5, no. 2, July 1974, p. 151.

mathematics that they filled most of the vacancies in the public and mercantile sectors and held important professional position.[10] Under the circumstances it was no wonder that the Sinhalese enthusiasts would ask for the abolition of the denominational system. They saw in the system the root cause of their backwardness in spite of their being the majority.

LINGUISTIC CHAUVINISM

The Sinhalese resurgence also found its expression in the demand for the restoration of the their language to its pristine glory. Munidasa Cumaratunga (1887–1944), an outstanding figure on the Sinhalese literary scene between the 1920s and the 1940s, started a movement for the 'purification' of Sinhalese language by purging all borrowed European and Indian words of Pali, Sanskrit, or any other origin, and by introducing newly coined words modelled after the classical Elu idiom. He brought changes in its grammatical form reminiscent of the twelfth-century Sinhalese. His idea was to raise the Sinhalese language to the status of a cause and a mission. He called this revival Helese. The slogan 'Language, Nation and Country' actually meant 'Helese language, the Helese nation and the Helese country'.[11]

POLITICAL BUDDHISM

Like education and language, the Sinhalese resurgence found its expression in religion. Many Sinhalese Buddhist organizations, such as, the Maha Bodhi Society, the Young Men's Buddhist Association (YMBA), the All Ceylon Buddhist Congress, the Bauddha Jathika Balavegaya (Buddhist National Force), etc., emerged. They did that job which was once done by the *Sangha* but which the latter subsequently was not in a position to do effectively on account of restrictions imposed upon them by the British Government. It, however, should be noted that as the

[10] Corea, 'One Hundred Years', p. 154. See also Sumathipala, *History of Education in Ceylon*, op. cit., p. 25.
[11] K.N.O. Dharmadasa, 'Language and Sinhalese Nationalism: The Career of Munidasa Cumaratunga', *Modern Ceylon Studies*, vol. 3, no. 2, July 1972, p. 133.

mouthpiece of Sinhalese Buddhist interests the *Sangha* remained the final authority and was never actually replaced by these organizations many of which were rather short-lived.[12]

The revival of political Buddhism contributed to the crystallization of several Sinhalese myths. The Sinhalese people came to be viewed as the defenders of the faith against 'heathen' encroachments which connoted both the Europeans and the Tamils, more so the latter. The ancient Sinhalese King Dutthugamini was projected as a Sinhalese national hero who had repulsed the Tamil invaders and defended the Buddhist.

The Tamil Scene

Sinhalese resurgence was matched by Tamil resurgence. It must not be confused with Hindu resurgence for the circumstances of Sri Lanka were different. Here Buddhism did not pose any threat to Hinduism. If at all the latter faced any threat it was from the Christian missionaries. As a Hindu community the challenge that the Tamils faced from the Sinhalese Buddhists was only in the realm of social institutions. Arumuga Navalar (1833–70), who was the pioneer of Tamil resurgence, emphasized on the return to orthodoxy which included the institution of untouchability.[13] The pre-eminence of the Vellalas of Jaffna, who had for centuries dominated the political and economic affairs of the Tamils, was highlighted. This Vellala consciousness conceived the Sinhalese numerical dominance as a threat to its basic values because it tended to intervene into the Tamil social system on the pretext of weeding out its undesirable features.[14]

[12] Bruce Mathews, 'The Sinhalese Buddhist Attitude towards Parliamentary Democracy', *Ceylon Journal of Historical and Social Studies* (Peradeniya), vol. 6 (New Series), no. 2, July-December 1976, pp. 40–1.

[13] Navalar's contribution to Tamil renaissance has been seriously challenged on the ground that he stood primarily for the cause of Vellala pre-eminence. Navalar's Hindu College, for example, did not admit a non-Vellala until the 1960s. See S. Ratnajeevan H. Hoole, 'C.W. Thamotharanpillai, Tamil Revivalist: The Man behind the Legend of Tamil Nationalism', *Nethra* (Colombo), 2(1), October-December 1997, pp. 1–45.

[14] Bryan Pfaffenberger, 'The Cultural Dimension of Tamil Separatism in Sri Lanka', *Asian Survey* (Berkeley), vol. 21, no. 11, November 1981, pp. 1150–3.

Tamil Nationalism

While Hinduism did not play a significant role in building the Tamil consciousness, the community's historical image contributed considerably to its shaping. It drew its inspiration from concepts pertaining to territory, dynasty (the Nallur Kingdom) and language. Over the years these concepts got rigidified by the mythology of 'the other'—'Sinhalese bucolic hordes, bent on brutal oppression'.[15] Radhika Coomaraswamy captures this deep-seated hatred in these words:

> At this point of history, the Tamils do not have a State and cannot perpetuate this myth through official school texts. However, if indeed a separate state is established, I have no doubt that the 'Sinhalese bucolic hordes' will make an early appearance in the pages of school texts.[16]

Ethnicity and The Nationalist Movement

Unlike the Indian nationalist movement under Gandhi's leadership, the Sri Lankan movement was essentially elitist which included both the Sinhalese and Tamil elite. But this elitism was also marked by a strong presence of ethnicity in which one community considered its gain as the other's loss and vice versa. This distrust was noticeable during the formation of the Ceylon National Congress in 1919. With the introduction of universal adult suffrage in 1931 this suspicion grew and the Tamils started demanding 'balanced representation' in the legislature, which meant 50 per cent reservation for the minorities that largely consisted of the Tamils. Against this background, any talk about Sri Lanka being multiracial or multiethnic appealed to them. A 1937 memorandum of the All-Ceylon Tamil Conference sent to the Secretary of State for the Colonies stated, *inter alia*:

> The conception of corporate unity . . . in the minds of the Sinhalese is in the nature of a merger, an absorption, of the minorities in the major community. A just and more correct idea of a united Ceylon is that of a rich and gorgeous many-coloured mosaic, set and studded

---
[15] Radhika Coomaraswamy, 'Power Nationalism and Ideology', *Lanka Guardian* (Colombo), vol. 7, no. 19, 1 February 1985, p. 19.
[16] Ibid.

with the diversities of communal consciousness within a glorious one-minded solidarity....[17]

INDEPENDENCE AND AFTER

After independence the Sinhala-Buddhist majoritarian politics had a field day. The two main pressure groups in the forefront of this movement were the Buddhist Committee of Enquiry, an unofficial body of prominent Buddhist monks and laymen appointed by the All Ceylon Buddhist Congress in 1954 to enquire into the state of Buddhism in Sri Lanka, and the Eksath Buddhist Peramuna (EBP), the United Front of the Buddhist monks.[18] In 1956, the Buddhist Committee of Enquiry published its report under the title *Betrayal of Buddhism*. It was a severe indictment of the ruling United National Party for its neglect of Buddhist interests and for its pro-Christian bias. Its major demands were: the creation of a Buddha Sasana Council; the repeal of the section in the constitution dealing with protective clauses pertaining to the minorities; the take over of all government-aided schools and training colleges by the state; and the termination of the services of Christain nuns working in government hospitals.[19] In the same year, another major event took place that was also in the same direction. It was the celebration of the 2500th anniversary of the passing away of the Buddha and that of the arrival of the Sinhalese race in the Island. The celebrations highlighted the legitimacy of the Sinhalese Buddhists to rule the country as the original race on the island.[20]

---

[17] Michael Roberts, 'Ethnic Conflict in Sri Lanka and Sinhalese Perspectives: Barrier to Accommodation', *Modern Asian Studies*, vol. 12, no. 3, 1978, p. 359.

[18] For a detailed account of these developments, see W. Howard Wriggins, *Ceylon: Dilemmas of a New Nation*, Princeton: Princeton University Press, 1960, Chaps. 7 and 9; Donald E. Smith, 'The Sinhalese Buddhist Revolution', and A.J. Wilson, 'Buddhism and Politics, 1960–5', both in Donald E. Smith, ed., *South Asian Politics and Religion*, Princeton: Princeton University Press, 1966.

[19] S.V. Kodikara, 'Communalism and Political Modernisation in Ceylon', *Modern Ceylon Studies*, vol. 1, no. 1, 1970, p. 102.

[20] One is convinced of such thrusts if one reads documents such as, the Lanka Bauddha Mandalaya (The Buddhist Council of Ceylon) and the

1956: THE WATERSHED

When S.W.R.D. Bandaranaike came to power in 1956 the Buddhist chauvinists found in him a leader who was willing to identify with their sentiments and one who was seen in the light of the 'charismatic rulers of the past glorified in the chronicles'.[21] Bandaranaike committed himself to abide by the Ten Commandments drawn up by the Buddhist clergy. The most important component of these commandments was to make Sinhalese the official language. The establishment of the Ministry of Cultural Affairs in 1956, for the first time in Sri Lanka's history, clearly indicated the government's pro-Buddhist commitment.[22]

During Bandaranaike's time the Tamil fear of suppression of their interests intensified. The decisions that affected the community both politically and economically were those pertaining to language, education and settlement schemes. By making Sinhalese the sole official language in 1956, by abolishing the denominational system in 1960, and by introducing the weightage system for technical and higher education the interests of the Tamils were affected materially. The centrally-sponsored settlement schemes hurt their interests politically.[23]

Government of Ceylon: The Ministry of Home Affairs, *An Event of Dual Significance* (Colombo, n.d.).

[21] H.L. Seneviratna, 'Affairs of a New Nation', *Ceylon Journal of Historical and Social Studies*, vol. 8, nos. 1 and 2, January-December 1965, p. 94. See also, Heinz Bechert, 'S.W.R.D Bandaranaike and the Legitimisation of Power through Buddhist Ideals', in Bardwell L. Smith, ed., *Religion and Legitimisation of Power in Sri Lanka*, Chambersburg, Pa: Anima Books, 1978, pp. 199–211.

[22] Ibid., pp. 95, 102.

[23] Since there issues have received considerable academic attention, no effort has been made here to recapitulate them. See, for example, Robert N. Kearney, *The Politics of Ceylon (Sri Lanka)*, Ithaca: Cornell University Press, 1973; A. Jeyaratnam Wilson, *Electoral Politics in an Emergent State: The Ceylon General Election of May 1970*, London: Cambridge University Prerss, 1975; Robert N. Kearney, 'Language and the Rise of Tamil Separatism in Sri Lanka', *Asian Survey*, vol. 18, no. 5, May 1978; S.J. Tambiah, 'The Politics of Language in India and Ceylon', *Modern Asian Studies*, vol. 1, no. 3, 1967; Urmila Phadnis, 'Ethnicity and nation-Building in South Asia: A Case Study of Sri Lanka', *India Quarterly*, vol. 35, no. 2, April-June

Tamil Response

On 19 August 1956, the Federal Party, the principal Tamil party, at its Annual Convention held at Trincomalee, made the following four demands:

1. The replacement of the present pernicious constitution by a rational and democratic constitution based on the federal principle and the establishment of one or more Tamil linguistic state or states incorporating all geographically contiguous areas in which the Tamil-speaking people are numerically in a majority as federating unit or units enjoying the widest autonomous and residuary powers consistent with the unity and external security of Ceylon.
2. The restoration of the Tamil language to its rightful place enjoying absolute parity of status with Sinhalese as an official language of the country.
3. The repeal of the present citizenship laws and the enactment in their place of laws recognizing the right to full citizenship on the basis of a simple residential test of all persons who have made this country their home.
4. The immediate cessation of colonizing the traditionally Tamil-speaking areas with Sinhalese people.

The Convention declared:

Unless the Prime Minister and the Parliament of Ceylon take the necessary steps to constitute a Federal Union of Ceylon by the Twentieth Day of August One Thousand Nine Hundred and Fifty Seven, the Kadchi will launch Direct Action by non-violent means for the achievement of this objective.[24]

1979; Vijay Samaraweera, 'Land, Labour, Capital and Sectional Interests in the National Politics of Sri Lanka', *Modern Asian Studies*, vol. 15, no. 1, 1981, p. 150. For a study of the settlement schemes and internal migration in Sri Lanka, see Nihal Amerasinghe, 'An Overview of Settlement Schemes in Sri Lanka', *Asian Survey*, vol. 16, no. 7, July 1976, pp. 620–36 and O.E.R. Abhayaratne and C.H.S. Jayewardene, 'Internal Migration in Ceylon', *Ceylon Journal of Historical and Social Studies*, vol. 8, nos. 1 and 2, January-December 1965, pp. 68–90. These papers, however, deal only with the structures and not their implications for ethnic relations.

[24] Quoted in Ketheshwaran Loganathan, *Sri Lanka: Lost Opportunities:*

Bandaranaike responded to this by a dual strategy. On one hand he showed his keenness to go by the Sinhalese popular sentiments while on the other he demonstrated his willingness to accommodate the Tamil grievances. The first tendency was visible when he refused to provide police security to the Tamil leaders who had gone on fast in Colombo's Galle Face esplanade. As a result, these leaders were subjected to mob heckling including violence. As part of his second strategy, Bandaranaike tried to introduce the Regional Council Bill and make amends in the language policy through the Bandaranaike-Chelvanayagam (B-C) Pact of 1957.

Neither the B-C Pact nor the subsequent Dudley Senanayake-Chelvanayagam (D-C) Pact of 1965, though well intentioned, could do much to contribute to harmonize the relations between the two communities. As a result, Tamil disaffection grew steadily finding its clear manifestation in the election of 1977. The results showed that the Tamil United Liberation Front (TULF) had a massive popular support in the north and somewhat less emphatic support in the east. The net result was that in the Northern Province the TULF bagged all the 14 seats with 68.5 per cent votes while in the eastern province it won 3 seats out of 4. The only constituency it lost was a Muslim majority constituency.

The election was followed by the outbreak of communal riots in many parts of the island leaving an estimated 300 Tamils killed and thousands rendered homeless. The UNP government took effective steps to suppress the riots and when the first session of the new parliament opened in August 1977 a statement of Government Policy declared that 'there are numerous problems confronting the Tamil-speaking people. The lack of a solution to their problems has made the Tamil-speaking people support even a movement for the creation of a separate state'.[25]

Past Attempts at Resolving Ethnic Conflict, Colombo: Centre for Policy Research and Analysis, 1996, pp. 17–18.

[25] Robert N. Kearney, 'Ethnic Conflict and the Tamil Separatist Movement in Sri Lanka', p. 907; Robert N. Kearney, *The Politics of Ceylon*, pp. 533–4.

Rise of Tamil Extremism

In the evolution of the Tiger movement the years 1977-8 were of crucial importance. Shortly before the 1977 elections two important elder politicians of Jaffna, namely S.J.V. Chelvanayagam, the founder leader of the Federal Party, and G.G. Ponnambalam, founder of the Tamil Congress, had passed away. They had been a great integrative and moderating force among the Tamils. In their absence the militant groups which were already in the field, and which had made their presence felt in the killing of SLFP mayor of Jaffna, Alfred Duraiyappah, in 1974, were unleashed. Their arrival on the centre-stage of Tamil politics was signalled by the murder of four policemen in Velvettithurai in April 1978. The incident triggered off a confrontation with the government that injected a new and most complex dimension to Sri Lanka's ethnic problem and eventually plunged the country into a virtual civil war.

The Jayewardene government, confusing the effect with the cause, resorted to military suppression of the guerrillas without undertaking corresponding measures to meet the challenge politically. As a response to the Velvettithurai incident the government first proscribed the LTTE and similar other groups in May 1978 and then declared emergency in Jaffna in January 1979 which continued, except for June-July, till January 1980. Even as the government dealt with the terrorist problem militarily the National Assembly adopted the Anti-Terrorism Bill on 19 July 1979. There was no opposition to the bill since the TULF members were on a boycott of the House at that time in protest against the administrative adjustment of the Vavuniya district and although the SLFP attacked the bill on the floor none of its members actually voted against it. The reason for the SLFP acquiescence may have been the call issued by the Minister of State for Information, Ananda Tissa de Alwis, to the SLFP to sink party differences when the entire Sinhalese majority was being attacked by the minority.[26]

The bill did not curb terrorism. On the contrary, it radicalized

---

[26] Asian Recorder, 27 August-2 September 1979, p. 15058. For a critical analysis of the act, see Nihal Jayawickrama, 'Eruption of Ethnic Violence', Lanka Guardian, vol. 7, nos. 23-4, 1 April 1985, p. 20.

the extremists and boosted their popularity among the Tamils. Besides the LTTE, there were five active Tamil guerrilla groups, namely, the People's Liberation Organisation of Tamil Eelam (PLOTE), the Tamil Eelam Liberation Organisation (TELO), the Tamil Eelam Liberation Army (TELA), the Eelam People's Revolutionary Liberation Front (EPRLF), and the Eelam Revolutionary Organisation of Students (EROS). Their ideological differences and internal factionalism notwithstanding, these groups were averse to political bargaining and sought an armed solution to the Tamil problem. Their relative success *vis-à-vis* the TULF to draw the government's wrath raised their popularity among the Tamils. The LTTE ridiculed the TULF as 'Tamil United Lawyers' Front'.[27]

1983 Riots

All efforts to resolve the ethnic conflict through constitutional and political means came to a grinding halt when the country was rocked by anti-Tamil riots in July 1983. Riots had taken place earlier also but the 1983 riots were unprecedented in the sense that in this case even the elite members of the Tamil community were targeted. Following the riots the Jayewardene government was under tremendous pressure from the Tamils of Sri Lanka behind whom were the government of India and the fifty-five million Tamils of Tamil Nadu. Jayewardene realized that time was running out and something must be done. Hereafter India became an important variable in Sri Lanka's ethnic politics.

It is not necessary to go into the details of all that happened after 1983. To put the subject of this paper in perspective it would suffice here to highlight some of the important landmarks in the evolution of the inter-ethnic dialogue. These landmarks are: the Thimpu Talks (1985), the Indo-Lanka Accord (1987), the Mangala Moonesinghe Select Committee (1991), and lastly, the devolution proposal announced by President Chandrika

[27] For an analysis of the Tamil guerrilla activities, see Dagmar Hellman-Rajanayagam, 'The Tamil "Tigers" in Northern Sri Lanka: Origins, Factions, Programmes', *Internationales Asien Forum* (Munich), vol. 17, nos. 1–2, 1986, pp. 63–85.

Kumaratunga (1995–7). It may be noted that when all this was happening the Tigers were intensifying their militancy.

The Thimpu Talks

In late 1983 there were a series of talks between the Indian and the Sri Lankan governments, the result of which was the so-called Parthasarathi Plan contained in the Annexure C proposal. Following Rajiv Gandhi's assuming power as the prime minister, Parthasarathi's role was assumed by Foreign Secretary Romesh Bhandari. He held several parleys with the Sri Lankan authorities which resulted in a summit conference in New Delhi in June 1985. The upshot of the summit was not clear, but at least it paved the way for the Thimpu talks of July 1985 between the representatives of the Sri Lankan government and those of the six Tamil groups which included the moderate TULF and five extremist groups, namely, LTTE, TELO, EPRLF, EROS and PLOTE.

At the talks the proposals put forward by the Sri Lankan government were the old ones dealing with devolution through district councils which the Tamil delegation rejected. It announced four cardinal principles as the basic minimum to solve the problem, which again were the reiteration of old Tamil demands, namely,

1. Recognition of the Tamils of Sri Lanka as a distinct nationality.
2. Recognition of an identified Tamil homeland and the guarantee of its territorial integrity.
3. Based on the above, recognition of the inalienable right of self-determination of the Tamil nation.
4. Recognition of the right to full citizenship and other fundamental democratic rights of all Tamils, who look upon the Island as their country.

Indo-Lanka Accord

By the end of May 1987, a rumour spread in Jaffna that the Sri Lankan authorities were preparing to launch an 'invasion' of Jaffna. The Tamil areas were already subjected to bombings and military operations and the supply of essential commodities to Jaffna had been stopped. There was strong pressure from the Tamil Nadu government for an Indian military intervention. Faced with diplomatic as well as internal pressure India decided to send relief supplies to Jaffna by boat. When the Sri Lankan navy prevented the boats from reaching Jaffna India decided to airlift the cargo. On 4 June, the cargo plane took off escorted by Mirage 2000 fighters. An Indian foreign office statement declared that 'any resistance would be met by force'. No resistance was offered and the transport plane air dropped its cargo, dry rations and vegetables, near Jaffna and safely returned to India.

The mission drew sharp reactions from Colombo. Prime Minister R. Premadasa contemptuously said that 'the dogs had shat on the Jaffna peninsula'. Calling the Indian action an act of 'cowardice' he said: 'The Sri Lankan people unitedly condemn the act of India and express their opposition and hatred'.[28] On 5 June, Sri Lanka lodged a protest with the United Nations Secretary-General against the entry of the Indian Air Force 'in violation of the country's sovereignty, independence and territorial integrity'.[29]

India's message, however, was clear to Colombo. The day the airlift took place, the Sri Lankan government lifted the six-month old fuel embargo on Jaffna peninsula. The National Security Minister, Lalith Athulathmudali, announced 'operation goodwill' which provided for the distribution of 900 tons of food to the Tamils in the Vadamarachi region over which the Sri Lankan army had gained control.

Following the relief mission, attention again shifted to the possibility of finding a political solution to the strife. On 19 July 1987, President Jayewardene proposed the creation of an autonomous state comprising the northern and eastern provinces. The proposal envisaged the creation of a single province consisting of the northern and eastern provinces which would have one Governor and one Chief Minister. The two provinces, however, would remain distinct for administrative purposes. There would

[28] *Hindu*, 5 June 1987.
[29] Ibid., 6 June 1987.

be 36 seats in the northern provincial council and 35 in the eastern. If the scheme was accepted there would be a special referendum in the Eastern Province to decide whether or not it wanted to merge with the Northern Province. It was further proposed that the militants should surrender their weapons before the provincial council elections and the army should return to their barracks. An independent committee headed by the Chief Justice should monitor the elections. India agreed to underwrite the scheme and promised assistance in eliminating residual violence from any parties against the settlement.

Jayewardene's proposal galvanized the peace process that soon culminated in the signing of an accord between India and Sri Lanka on 29 July 1987. The importance of the accord lay not only in its provisions but also in the exchange of letters between the two governments that was almost simultaneously undertaken. The accord had essentially two aspects. The first dealt with India's commitment to uphold Sri Lanka's sovereignty and territorial integrity on the condition that the latter agreed to grant a reasonable amount of autonomy to the Tamils to their satisfaction. The second dealt with Sri Lanka's commitment to disallow any extra-regional power to dabble in its affairs which had either a known or a potential intention to harm India's security interests in the region.

Following the signing of the Indo-Sri Lankan accord, India sent a peace keeping force to ensure that peace returned to the strife-torn Tamil areas. In operational terms this meant the disarming of the LTTE cadres. Politically, the Sri Lankan government commenced preparations for working out a model through which power could devolve on the reorganized provincial councils. The model envisaged the eventual amalgamation of the northern and eastern provinces, the area that was claimed by the Tamils as their 'traditional homeland'.

There was an inherent flaw in the accord because the LTTE had not approved it. Vellupillai Prabhakaran, the LTTE supremo, explained that the accord did not address any of the Tamil demands, namely, an end of the illegal Sinhala colonization, recognition of the Tamils as a nation, the permanent merger of the northern and eastern provinces, and the withdrawal of Sri

Lankan troops from the province.[30] There was strong opposition to the accord even amongst certain sections of the Sinhalese. Prime Minister Premadasa was himself opposed to it. Many Sri Lankans viewed the IPKF as an 'occupation army'. So strong was the sentiment that the JVP, which was generally feared and looked down upon by the elite circles because of its ultra extremist Trotskyite line, came to be regarded with greater equanimity because of its stand against the accord. The President's popularity plummeted and there was an attempt on his life.

The relations between the Indian government and the LTTE touched an all time low. The political power of the LTTE emanated from its guns and, understandably, it refused to surrender them without any credible guarantee that political power would be handed over to it. 'It took us 12 years to build this organisation', Prabhakaran said, 'and it just can't be dismantled in 72 hours'.[31] As events proved Prabhakaran was being modest.

Mangala Moonesinghe Select Committee

On 9 August 1991 the Sri Lnkan Parliament passed a unanimous resolution to set up a Parliamentary Select Committee (PSC) to 'recommend ways and means of achieving peace and political stability in the country' under the chairmanship of senior SLFP MP Mangala Moonesinghe. The PSC commenced its function on 20 August 1991 and called for written representations, 253 of which were received. Curiously, neither the UNP nor the SLFP submitted any.[32]

From the beginning the PSC got bogged down with one single issue: whether or not to agree with one merged north-eastern

[30] *India Today*, 15 August 1987, pp. 78–9. Subsequent reports, however, suggested that the LTTE was consulted prior to the accord. For details, see Editorial, *Hindu*, 26 April 1988. It may also be noted that support for the accord came from other Tamil leftist groups such as EPRLF, PLOTE, TELO and ENDF. For details, see L. Ketheswaran (official spokesman of EPRLF), 'The Peace Accord—A view from Tamil Left', *Lanka Guardian*, vol. 11, no. 1, 1 May 1988, pp. 23–5, 50.

[31] *India Today*, 15 August 1987, pp. 78–9.

[32] For details of the PSC experience, see Loganathan, *Lost Opportunities*, pp. 167–83.

province. While the Tamil parties including the Ceylon Workers Congress (CWC) went on repeating their demand for the merger the Sinhala parties including the SLFP and UNP members within the PSC kept opposing it. During the course of the deliberations it became obvious that the Sri Lanka Muslim Congress (SLMC) had emerged as an interested party and it wanted to have its share of the cake too, which meant that it was not in favour of north-eastern merger without sufficient safeguards for the interests of Muslims in the provinces.

On 17 June 1992, the PSC circulated a 'Concept Paper' which contained the following points:

1. Two separate Councils, one for the northern province and another for the eastern province.
2. An 'Apex Assembly', to be elected by members of the respective Councils 'to plan common policies for both Councils, and coordinate programmes relevant to the two Councils, etc.'
3. A 'National Chamber', comprising of the respective Chief Ministers. The main function would be to 'establish harmony and coordination between the Centre and the Peripheral Units with a view to integrating the National firmly'.
4. As an interim measure, a 'separate institution should be established to supervise the immediate implementation, smooth functioning and monitoring of all devolved powers'. In this context, the 'Concept Paper' suggested the appointment of an Interim Administration for the northern and eastern provinces, comprising representatives of political parts within and outside parliament.[33]

On the same day, the Tamil parties (EPRLF, TULF, ENDLF, TELO, EROS, all represented in parliament, as well as PLOTE and ACTC, not represented in parliament, presented to the PSC their four-point Formula:

1. A Unified Politico-Administrative Entity for the permanently merged north-eastern province.
2. Substantial devolution of power ensuring meaningful autonomy to that unified unit.

[33] Ibid., p. 174.

3. Institutional arrangement within the larger framework of the unbifurcated north-eastern province for the Muslim people ensuring their cultural identity and security.
4. The Sinhalese people (in the north-eastern province) to enjoy all the rights that other minorities have in the rest of the country.[34]

The hiatus between the two sides was quite manifest. But the 'Option Paper' that the PSC circulated on 14 October 1992 indicated some compromise. It recommended:

1. A Regional Council for the entire north-east region constituted by the two elected Provincial Councils.
2. The Regional Council to be headed by a Chief Minister for the entire north-east region. The two Executive Ministers for the two provinces shall each year alternatively function as the Chief Minister of the entire Region.
3. There shall be one Governor for the Region.
4. In each province, the rights of ethnic and religious minorities shall be guaranteed by Constitutional arrangements.[35]

There was one point made in the 'Option Paper' which was rather ambiguous. Almost in passing it mentioned that the Regional Council would be constituted only 'when the two Provincial Councils meet together on matters pertaining to the entire region'. There was no certainty whether the two Provincial Councils should function as a single Regional Council on specified subjects.[36]

During the entire period of the PSC there was only once that some dent was noticeable on the solid Tamil plank of north-east merger. On 11 November 1992, K. Srinivasan, an MP from Jaffna, who contested on an ENDLF ticket in alliance with TULF (later expelled from the ENDLF), submitted a proposal to the PSC under the title 'A Realistic Solution to the National Crisis'. Its main elements were:

1. The unitary nature of the Sri Lankan Constitution be converted into a federal one, subject to a national referendum.

[34] Ibid., pp. 172–3.
[35] Ibid., pp. 175–6.
[36] Ibid., p. 176.

2. The de-merger of the northern and eastern provinces into distinct units of devolution and substantial devolution.
3. Special institutional arrangements be made for the security of the Muslims of each unit.
4. State land to be alienated, in keeping with the demographic composition in each district, and to maintain the ethnic balance of each unit as at the year 1971, without displacing Sinhalese settlements that had already taken place.[37]

The proposal received support from the UNP, SLFP, LSSP, SLMC and CP so far as the de-merger of north-eastern province was concerned but not on making Sri Lanka a federal state as was evident in the PSC meeting held on 11 December 1992. The Tamil parties any way had viewed the Srinivasan proposal as a 'horse deal' engineered by UNP's Muslim leader A.C.S. Hameed to sabotage the on-going talks between the TULF and the SLMC. Soon afterwards, on 14 December 1992, the Tamil parties in a Joint Statement declared:

It is now abundantly clear that the entire process of the PSC had been designed to give effect to the promise, contained in the UNP Manifesto for the Presidential Elections of 1988, to de-merge the presently merged North-East Province. This design suited the SLFP as well.[38]

The PSC, however, did not take notice of the Tamil parties' view and two days later, on 16 December 1992, issued its Interim report entitled 'Matters Agreed Upon By A Majority of the Members'. The agreement were (a) on the establishment of two separate units of administration for the northern and eastern provinces, (b) to adopt a scheme of devolution on lines similar to those obtaining in the Indian Constitution, and (c) to devolve more subjects that are in List III (Concurrent List) or to dispense with the list. On the same day the Tamil parties rejected these 'agreements' and declared that they confirmed the 'lack of will of the Sinhala polity represented in Parliament, regardless of whether it is the ruling UNP or the major opposition, the SLFP, to come to grips with the legitimate grievances and aspirations of the Tamil People'.[39]

[37] Ibid., p. 177.
[38] Ibid., p. 179.
[39] Ibid., p. 180.

The failure of the PSC was fore-ordained because neither the Sinhalese nor the Tamils were willing to budge from their uncompromising positions about the north-east merger. But there were other organizational problems also. The size of the committee, consisting of forty members, was too large to do any meaningful business. The political parties did not prepare working papers nor were there technical experts to guide the committee on specific issues. Radhika Coomaraswamy was right when she said that 'the failure of the Parliamentary Select Committee on the ethnic question is the failure of politics and the style of politics that does not allow for the resolution of conflict'.[40]

The Chandrika Plan

As promised during the parliamentary and presidential campaigns of 1994, President Chandrika Kumaratunga came out with a detailed devolution package within the framework of a proposed new federal constitution. It proposed to give the federating units much more power than any time in the past. It also talked about the permanent merger of the northern and eastern provinces in which the Tamils would have their say. But since the People's Alliance (PA) government was under pressure from the UNP in particular and the Sinhala-Buddhist forces in general it retracted from the original textbook type federalism and went in favour of more safeguards for the central authority. It was seen that the power of the centre was not diminished and the integrity and security of the nation was not compromised. Any disintegrative tendency was to be nipped in the bud by interfering in regional affairs if the situation so demanded. The idea of the so-called Tamil homeland was also diluted beyond recognition through providing various possibilities in respect of the territorial reorganization of the eastern province. Since the Muslims were an important political force this engineering was easily possible.

The biggest mistake that the PA did while proposing the devolution plan was that it did not consider the fact as to how the

---

[40] Radhika Coomaraswamy, 'Select Committee: The Failure of Politics', *Pravada* (Colombo), 2 (10), November-December 1993, p. 20.

plan could be passed when it had only a thin majority in the parliament. A minimum of two-thirds majority was required to pass it for it amounted to an amendment to the Constitution. Without UNP's support, therefore, it was not possible and no political effort was made to enlist it.[41] The other problem was that Chandrika became overconfident after the initial military reverses of the LTTE in 1995 which included the restoration of state power in Jaffna to totally ignore them and trying to find a solution by talking to other groups only. It was of course a difficult choice and it is to always easy for anybody to criticize events from the advantage of hindsight.

Does Peace Have A Chance?

More than five years have passed since the 1994 presidential election and yet another has been held in December 1999. But the conflict between the government and the LTTE remains where it was. Is peace going to be restored to this hapless land? Since the LTTE calls the shots it would primarily depend on its future role and capacity. Moderate Tamils have lost their clout because ultimately it is the LTTE that has to be given a share in governance. But would they be satisfied with that small role. Their dream of *eelam* is as fresh in their mind as it was three decades ago. Merely governing a province of Sri Lanka is no compensation for that dream.[42] In this situation peace as a value has little meaning for it would ultimately be the respective fire power of the Sri Lankan army and the LTTE which would determine the future of Sri Lanka. It is a sad situation but that is the hard reality.

---

[41] This author had predicted the political difficulty facing the proposal almost immediately after it was announced. See Partha S. Ghosh, 'Chandrika's Federal Package: A Political Analysis', *Mainstream* (New Delhi), 16 September 1995, pp. 9–12. Reproduced in *Lanka Guardian* (Colombo), 1 October 1995, pp. 9–11.

[42] On this point, see Partha S. Ghosh, 'The Two Scenarios for Sri Lanka', *Times of India* (New Delhi), 16 May 1995.

Nobody's Communiqué: Ethnic Accords in North-eastern India

Samir Kumar Das

As the failures of ethnic accords whether in India or in other parts of South Asia become increasingly apparent, peace audit exercises are gaining a certain currency amongst the socially-minded scholars as well as serious social activists. Such exercises seem to oscillate between the politics of accusations and what may for want of a better term be described as 'non-politics' of committing mistakes. While state counsellors and its protagonists have otherwise been highly self-critical, they often attribute the failures to a section of ethnic leaders whose wooden-headed intransigence is believed to have torpedoed the accords, one after another. Thus, while referring to the Shillong Accord of 1975, Subodh Chandra Dev—widely recognized as one of its principal architects, expresses his anxieties in these terms: 'The biggest problem in the implementation of the accord is to make a section of (the China-returned) insurgents accept the Shillong Accord and to make them lay down their arms on the border itself'.[1] Nari Rustomji and Ved Marwah—both with a vast experience of having served in different parts of the region at different points of time—also find fault with all those whose apathy and lack of imagination have driven some ethnic communities to 'extremes of paranoia',[2] But Rustomji in particular,

---

[1] S.C. Dev, *Nagaland: The Untold Story*, Calcutta: Gauri Dev, 1988, p. 124.
[2] See, Nari Rustomji, *Imperilled Frontiers: India's North-Eastern Borderlands*, New Delhi: Oxford University Press, 1983, p. 71. Also, Ved Marwah, *Uncivil Wars: Pathology of Terrorism in India*, New Delhi: Harper-Collins, 1995, pp. 303–5, *passim*.

urges the tribal members to forgive and forget the past as a tribute to the value systems that they have evolved for themselves throughout the centuries. Writing in 1983, his observation on the Shillong Accord still betrays an optimism that is uncharacteristic of most of the run-of-the-mill social scientists: '... if they will cherish in their hearts with sincerity the Christian doctrine of forgiveness and atonement, the working out of the drama to its conclusion, but a happy and not a tragic conclusion, may yet prove a reality despite the bruises they have suffered'.[3]

Others however accuse the state of having turned accords into mere scraps of paper or 'those accords' as Samaddar puts it. Kumar Rupesinghe for instance, argues that accords may simply be regarded as instruments through which a state 'imposes its will' on the body positie.[4] Kumar Sanjay Singh draws our attention to the eternal paradox that the states *per se* face all over the world: while status quo necessarily works against the disadvantaged, any state assigns to itself the task of upholding and maintaining it. Accords as Singh argues, may be likened to 'a strategy' that the state deploys in order to 'replicate the status quo and retain its legitimacy' in the eyes of the disadvantaged.[5] Although Samaddar invokes time and again Foucauldian concept of 'governmentality', his comment that accords are 'a technique of governance' smacks of the traces of an otherwise instrumentalist view of power that Foucault has by his own admission taken the pains of distancing himself from. By saying that accords are a means of 'managing a set of norms' and their management is what enables 'the rulers to rule' Samaddar brings in a logic that equates governmentality with 'a techniqaue of governance'.[6] Governmentality for Foucault, is more a commitment on the state's part, to the modernist framework of rationality than

[3] Rustomji, ibid., p. 71.

[4] Kumar Rupesinghe, 'Strategies of Conflict Resolution: The Case of South Asia', in Kumar Rupesinghe and David Kumar (eds.), *Internal Conflicts in South Asia*, London: Sage, 1996, p. 180.

[5] Kumar Sanjay Singh, '*Naga Accords: An Instance of Domination through Negotiation*' (1999), mimeo.

[6] Ranabir Samaddar, ' "Those Accords": A Bunch of documents', SAFHR Paper Series 4, Kathmandu: South Asia Forum for Human Rights, 1999, p. 7.

simply a tool or 'technique of governance'. Such a commitment is 'peculiar' to the West for which it is more of a 'passion' than anything else. As Barry Allen puts it: 'There is something peculiar about the Western passion for government. It arises from or at least is constantly reinforcing and reinforced by the idea we have cultivated as to what it means to be "rational" in matters of political government'.[7] Commitment to rationality for him, is an end-in-itself rather than a means-to-an-end.

If one of the parties could secure its interests by making the accords that it had itself entered into, fail, their success could have served their mutual interests better. Failure according to this argument, is imputed to the mistakes that both parties commit much to the detriment of their intercloking interests. Horam for instance, makes this comment on the Shillong Accord: 'There have been mistakes and blunders on both sides and the results of which were far from happy for either parties'.[8] If politics is regarded as a rational pursuit of interests, then cumulative mistakes and blunders create, albeit unintendedly, a non-political domain in which the parties involved are destined to lose because of the simple fact that they are not capable of pursuing their interests rationally. Both the politics of accusations as well as the non-politics of committing mistakes revolve around the question of whether the failure of ethnic accords serve the interests of the rivalling parties better or their success. Coupled with these, there is also the somewhat tricky question of whether their interests are of common and interlocking nature to the extent that each has a vested interest in making it successful or are sufficiently isolated, so much so that each can attain its interests only to the exclusion of the other, thereby making the accord fail. It is essentially the definition of their interests that sets these two positions apart.

In spite of all these differences, they both take what I have called an instrumentalist view of accords. Accords are seen primarily as instruments that the contending parties seek to make

[7] Barry Allen, 'Foucault and Modern Political Philosophy', in Jeremy Moss (ed.), *The Later Foucault*, London: Sage, 1998, p. 188.

[8] M. Horam, *Naga Insurgency: The Last Thirty Years*, New Delhi: Cosmo, 1980, p. 205.

use of, whether in isolation or in their combination, in a bid to serve their respective interests. I propose to look upon accords more as constructs that the rivalling parties have made for themselves, which, once they are entered into, seem not only to exist relatively independently of whatever the signatories think about them but shape and mould their thoughts and practices, 'subjectifying' themselves as it were, by laying down the modalities on the basis of which their affairs are supposed to be conducted in future.

Such an understanding of accords is predicated on two very closely inter-related assumptions: first, the Indian state has by and large been incapable of imposing its will on the larger body politic as much as none of the ethnic communities, howsoever sizeable it is, has been in a position to unilaterally and decisively influence it. The thesis of a highly 'communalized' state spreading its tentacles throughout the length and breadth of India's body politic appears to have been blown out of proportion. The state at present is far too weak to undergo such transformations. The assumption is grounded in one of Stanley Tambiah's arguments that the countries of South Asia have not yet been permeated by the moral economy of a coherent nation-state-ideology:

> Modern South Asian ethnic conflicts take place in an environment that lacks a crystallized and coherent nation state ideology and a body of political norms and practices deriving from it that is acceptable to and shared by all (the majority of) the components and members of body politic. That there is crisis of the nation state in South Asia today is patently clear.[9]

In the absence of a crystallized and coherent moral economy, the actors seem to be engaged in what looks like an inordinately protracted and indecisive battle in which none is strong enough to assert its interests and wipe others out. Accords, instead of putting an end to the battle that we are referring to, reflect its continuing nature. The battle, in other words, is embedded in the accords: on the one hand, they help in setting forth the rules

---

[9] Stanley Tambiah, *Levelling Crowds: Ethnonationalist Conflicts and Collective Violence in South Asia*, (New Delhi: Vistaar, 1996, p. 322.

within which the battle is sought to be carried out and conducted and bringing about the semblance of an order in what otherwise could have degenerated into 'a war of all against all'. In simple terms, the signature of accords also results in certain transformations in the nature of subjects who made them. On the other hand, all accords, being texts agreed upon by the contending parties, are bound to be open-ended and to use a term which is currently fashionable in linguistic circles, polysemic and hence, leave ample scope for reading rather unforeseen and, may we say, even unforeseeable, political practices into them. A good deal of these apparently enigmatic political practices turn the rules by their head and produce new and hitherto unknown subjects working on the accords. Since the accords embody the battle that itself is protracted and indecisive, they pertain to nobody. Again, all accords are necessarily preceded by ethnic discords while all discords do not necessarily culminate in accords. Within the scope of this brief paper, we propose to confine ourselves to an analysis of those ethnic discords in northeastern India which have led to the signature of accords.[10] The distinction between discords that produce or are likely to produce accords and those that do not or are unlikely to do so, however should not be exaggerated. There are indeed many conjunctural factors which contribute among other things, to the conversion of the latter into the former and they need to be analysed on a case by case basis. Of course, that is much beside our scope here.

The present paper is organized into three very closely interconnected sections: The first focuses on the parties—more particularly, their nature—that are involved in the process of accord making. What is the nature of the ethnic communities or more accurately, the organizations claiming to act on their behalf that the Indian state is interested in making peace with? Or similarly, what is the nature of the state itself that shows an eagerness in making peace with the other? Both these questions are complementary and are discussed in the first section. The second section seeks to point out how the process of accord

[10] For the texts of these accords, I have depended on P.S. Datta, *Ethnic Peace Accords in India*, New Delhi: Vikas, 1995.

making—otherwise very long and tortuous—contributes to the reconstruction of subjects, and a re-negotiation of their relationships. Subjects do not create accords, accords create subjects. Accords also offer to the subjects the opportunity of reading their changing subjectivities into them and work out a variety of subject positions within them. The third section proposes to concentrate on the open and polysemic character of the texts of accords in north-eastern India.

The Threshold Within the Nation

The argument that the nation during the early years of independence did not acquire a determinate form and that the Indian state was by and large groping in the dark for it did not know for certain what the constituent elements of the nation would be, has to be taken with utmost caution. According to this argument, the state struck deals and signed accords, albeit implicitly, with whatever elements it had to encounter in the immediate aftermath of India's independence. Such an openness made the Constitution an ensemble of accords.[11] While the argument draws our attention to the distinction between the nation and its other, it hardly sensitizes us to an unacknowledged, albeit very formidable threshold that divided the nation internally. Even if there were millions of unsigned accords encoded in the law of the land, the state knew how to make a distinction between those who were capable of making accords—the potential accord makers—and those who were not. Indeed their capability was so taken for granted that they did not have actually to sign off an accord to prove it. The nation was—to borrow a term coined by Mahmood Mamdani for describing the colonial world of African societies—'bi-furcated': 'Citizenship would be a priviledge of the civilized; the uncivilized would

---

[11] Such an argument has been advanced by many, of whom Rajni Kothari seems to be the pioneering spokesman. See, Rajni Kothari, 'Integration and Performance: Two Pivots of India's Model of Nationbuilding', in Rajni Kothari (ed.), *State and Nationbuilding: A Third World Perspective*, Bombay: Allied, 1976.

be subject of an all-round tutelage.'[12] The threshold, in other words, split the nation into two asymmetrical spheres—those of the civilized and the uncivilized, of the citizens and the subjects one on top of the other. The spheres are also of uneven size.

The 'civilized' sphere of the citizens is precisely the society of potential accord-makers. For it consists of people who are both willing and able to enter into accords and contracts. In fact, the concept of citizenship is founded on the theory of contractualism: the citizens are entitled to the security of their 'life, liberty and pursuit of happiness' only in exchange of their acquiescence to the state. On the other hand, there is the 'uncivilized' sphere of the subjects. By virtue of being so, they are permanently kept outside the scope of contract. Since subjects do not deserve to enjoy the right to security of their life, liberty and property, their acquiescence to the state is bound to precede their entitlement. There cannot be any equivalence between acquiescence and entitlement in their case. The notion of equivalence is otherwise considered to be central to contractualism. Trust is what determines their relationship with the state and the state is supposed to act as their trustee. For them it is more a 'moral duty' than a 'rational practice'.[13]

Accordingly, the state does not seem to have any doubt about what the possible constituent elements of the nation would be and has embraced and encapsulated them as 'natural' elements. The notion of the 'natural' underlies the processes of integration of the Princely States as well as of the reorganization of states on a linguistic basis since the early 1950s. It is interesting to note that the term 'natural' figures over and over again in Sardar Patel's speeches on the integration of Princely States. The Princely States which have subsequently integrated themselves into India are called 'natural' because their integration not only facilitates the

---

[12] Mahmood Mamdani, *Citizen and Subject: Decentralized Despotism and the Legacy of Late Colonialism*, New Delhi: Oxford University Press, 1997, p. 17.

[13] For a Theoretical exploration of this point, see, John Dunn, *The History of Political Theory and Other Essays*, Cambridge: Cambridge University Press, 1996, Chap. 5.

'secular' and 'democratic' process that has already been set off within them but is also compatible with the self-definition of the newly born Indian state. Patel did not find any difficulty in identifying either the states that can be regarded as the 'natural' elements of the Indian nation or such states that are likely to accede to Pakistan.[14] Similarly, we all know that the States' Reorganization Commission never recognized language as a rule-of-thumb principle of reorganization of states in India. While conceding to the demands of language-based communities for reorganizing the states on a linguistic basis, the commission realized the importance of a threshold: 'The problem is essentially one of determining how far the free play of provincial sentiment deriving from a consciousness of cultural and linguistic distinctiveness is a factor making for unity or diversity.'[15] Thus, Assam, for reasons spelt out in the report, was never recommended for any further reorganization. That the state was subjected to frequent surgical operations is however a different story.

The state's policy towards the so-called uncivilized sphere of the subject was basically three-fold: first, it did not hesitate to declare that they were not the 'natural' parts of the Indian nationhood. In fact, a certain celebration of their difference was considered to be strategic to their incorporation into the framework of the Indian nation.[16] Second, the state's policy was not only to establish the difference but to hierarchize it and to locate it within what in Classical Development Theory is called, 'an evolutionary schemata'. The state was imbued as it were with a modernist zeal and the subjects were required to gradually follow without raising any question the rules that govern the civilized sphere and be 'benefited' by it. V.P. Menon, associated for long with the process of integration in India, for instance, does not feel the necessity of granting to the subjects the right of signing accords: 'With regard to the tribes located on the

[14] See, *For a United India: Speeches of Sardar Patel 1947–50*, New Delhi: Publications India, 1949, *passim*.

[15] *Report of the States Reorganization Commission*, New Delhi: Publications Division, 1955, p. 30.

[16] See, Samir Kumar Das, 'Tribes as the Other: A Critique of Political Anthropology of Northeastern India', *Journal of Politics*, vol. III, December 1996.

north-east frontier, there were no formal treaties and engagements; the Government of India's policy had been merely to extend gradually to those areas the benefits of settled administration.'[17] Subjects only understand the language of 'benefits' and not of rights. Third, since the process of extension of settled administration is only too gradual, so much so that it does not adversely affect the already fragile balance of these societies, their acquiescence to the state and integration into the nation are bound to predate the accrual of actual benefits to them. The implication is that they do not enjoy any right to be consulted or taken into confidence. The Naga leaders initially were not averse to the idea of trusteeship. In a memorandum submitted to the British authorities on 20 February 1947, the Naga National Council, for instance, made a stong plea for establishing an 'interim government' for a period of ten years at the end of which the Naga people should be left to choose any form of government they would think appropriate for them. The council in the memorandum openly stated that a constitution drawn up by people having no knowledge of the Naga Hills and its people would be quite 'unsuitable and unacceptable' to the Nagas. The fear of being boxed within the territorial confines of either of the two newly born states in South Asia without correspondingly enjoying any contractual right of voicing opinions and of being consulted haunted the minds of not only the Nagas but also many other ethnic communities including the plains tribals of then undivided Assam.[18]

The so-called civilized sphere of the citizens is governed by what Mark Kingwell might call, 'socio-linguistics of politeness'.[19] The uncivilized sphere comprising the subjects remains outside

[17] V.P. Menon, *The Transfer of Power in India*, New Delhi: Orient Longman, 1957, p. 407.

[18] For an understanding of the problem of the plains tribals, see, Girin Phukon, *Assam: Attitude to Federalism*, Delhi: Sterling, 1984. Also, Girin Phukon, *Politics of Regionalism in Northeastern India*, Guwahati: Spectrum, 1996, pp. 9–10. Also, Girin Phukon, 'Politics of Ahom Identity', *The Calcutta Journal of Political Studies*, Special Number, 1999, pp. 52–61.

[19] Mark Kingwell, *A Civil Tongue: Justice, Dialogue, and the Politics of Pluralism*, Pennsylvania: Penn. State University Press, 1995, p. 198. His analysis, though commendable in many respects, is seemingly oblivious to the relations of power.

its scope. Let us see how. In order to illustrate the point, we may refer to the 'talk' that took place on 14 June 1977, two years after the Shillong Accord was signed, between Morarji Desai, the then Prime Minister of India and A.Z. Phizo, the father of Naga insurgency in London. A detailed transcript of their talks is now available in M. Horam's book on Naga insurgency, though of course there is a difference of opinion about the ontological status of these talks. As Horam writes: 'Phizo claimed that he had tape-recorded the "talk" at this meeting and the text of the Phizo-Desai talks was soon circulating in Nagaland. Mr. Desai called it a "garbled" version of his conversation with the Naga leaders.'[20] Both of them, however, agreed that it was a non-official conversation. The reference to the Naga question and the state of the Naga people as well as Phizo's claim of representing them were two very crucial issues that virtually prevented the 'talks' from taking off.

Phizo's first substantive remark that 'I have come to meet the Prime Minister of India because my people have been suffering for a long time' invited strong rebuttal from Desai on two major counts: First, Phizo's tacit claim of pushing the point as an uncontested representative of the Naga people was questioned by Desai primarily because he was a 'foreigner' and 'was staying in a foreign country'. No modern state can acknowledge the right of the subjects to be represented by a foreigner, let alone, a foreign country. Hence, their dilemma is: while they have to remain as subjects, they cannot identify themselves as foreigners. They are an integral part of the nation, but very much outside its civilized sphere. Besides, there is also a difference between the two representations of the Naga people offered by both Phizo and Desai respectively. While making the claim of representing them, the Indian state actually keeps in mind only a section of the Nagas that has been invested with citizenship and contractual rights—thanks to the creation of the state of Nagaland within the Indian Union back in 1963.

The creation of the state of Nagaland may be regarded as the first great step towards 'the extension of settled administration'. As Desai puts it: 'It was the Nagas who came and asked for a

[20] Horam, op. cit., p. 188.

state and it was given to them'. In other words, the state felt obliged to respond to the demands of those who reportedly made it a point to raise the demand within the framework of the Indian state. Since acquiescence here is rewarded with rights, we may say that a section of the Nagas has nevertheless been inducted into the civilized sphere. Desai reiterates the state's commitment to the 'protection of citizens': 'By way of promising to exterminate the Naga rebels, we are protecting our citizens'. His distinction between (Naga) citizens and '(a few) Nagas persisting on independence', in fact, sets forth the parameters of talks: '. . . if you want to talk only about Naga Independence, I won't talk to you'. Phizo, on the other hand, refers to the Nagas as a homogeneous collectivity. As he says: 'The Government of India may claim something on their part and the Nagas uphold something on their part and there may be a wide gap between us'. In other words, it is only that the Indian state inflicts this so-called division on what Phizo holds to be a homogeneous community of Nagas. It simply means that unless the sociolinguistic rules of civilization, citizenship and politeness are complied with, Phizo is unlikely to be heard. The only way to communicate the grievances is to observe these rules and it is ironic that the observance of these rules at the same time makes the grievances incommunicable. For they are grievances which cannot be communicated without breaking the rules.

Desai's second objection to Phizo's first substantive remark centres on the issue of the suffering of the Naga people. The issue is not so much whether the Nagas are suffering or not. It is on the contrary, hinged on the authority over the information of suffering. Desai claims that by virtue of his being the prime minister of India, he has a privileged access to this information and this is what authorizes him to say the last word: 'You are a foreigner. You are staying in a foreign country. You receive reports and talk about it. I have all the reports and there is no problem. I know everything. I am the Prime Minister of India. Nobody needs to tell me that there is a problem'. The state in simple terms, arrogates to itself the invincible capacity of 'knowing everything'. Hence, the Nagas have 'no problem' because the prime minister of India says so and he and only he is authorized to make a statement on this. It is power that invests knowledge with its 'truthfulness'. Thus, it is no wonder that even within the brief span of a three-and-half page talk, Phizo had tried to raise the question of suffering not less than five times and at each time Desai had threatened to break off the talks. It points to a strange dilemma: you want to talk because there is a problem; but you are not allowed to talk if you bring in the problem. The rules of socio-linguistics lead to a metamorphosis of their agenda.

THE PROCESS OF SUBJECTIFICATION

To say that accords and discords are the poles of the same continuum and that the former reflects the perpetuation of the latter is however not the same as saying that the same discords are reproduced through accords. An understanding of the distinction between pre- and post-accord discords will enable us to appreciate how the process of peace-making through such means as talks, dialogues and confidence-building, etc., entails a change not only in the agenda of ethnic communities or organizations staking the claim of representing them but also in the mutually contending subjects involved in the process. It may be suggested that the discords that are likely to produce accords involve a certain assertion of some degree of independence. The term 'independence' might at first sight appear to be a misnomer; but for purposes of convenience we may use it in two rather distinct senses: first, we may come across communities that assert their identity as separate 'nations' and by virtue of their being so, they consider themselves to be entitled to complete self-determination and fully sovereign statehood. The United Liberation Front of Assam (ULFA) has challenged the Indian state not because it has subjected Assam to the 'colonialism of New Delhi', though of course this question is secondary to its central critique, but because it is the Indian state and hence, kept Assam constantly out of the civilized sphere. ULFA's anti-statism springs from the 'truth' that the state is an 'external agency' and hence, has no authority to rule over Assam.[21] Assam to ULFA has never been a part of India before the British annexation. The same view has

[21] For an elaboration of this argument, see, Samir Kumar Das, *ULFA: A Political Analysis*, New Delhi: Ajanta, 1994, p. 97.

been reiterated by the National Socialist Council of Nagaland (I-M): 'Nothing is more inalienable for a nation, big or small, than her sovereignty. . . . The sovereign existence of Nagaland is more at peril than ever before'.[22] Independence defined in this sense hinges on a counter-factual argument that, had the Indian state performed well and not turned the fringe regions into its colonial hinterlands, the fight for independence would have remained the same in essence. Besides, communities engaged in discords may assert a very different kind of independence. Here, independence is understood to mean a certain re-negotiation and re-adjustment of their relationships within the Indian Union. What the communities do in this case is either to demand a share in the country's power structure or to make the state honour its commitment to a free and thriving society or even both. Almost all the accords of north-eastern India focus on these two issues. They have led to the formation of either new states, as in the cases of the 16-point Agreement of 1960, or the Mizo Accord of 1987, both resulting in the birth of the state of Nagaland and Mizoram respectively, or new district councils as in the cases of Bodo Accord (1993), Agartala Agreement (1993) signed with the All-Tripura Tigers' Force, Rabha Hajong Accord (1995), Mishing (Tiwa) Accord (1995), Karbi Tripartite Agreement (1995) etc. Some of the accords have also made categorical provisions for the protection of the language and nature of certain ethnic communities or the peoples living within the jurisdiction of states and councils who feel threatened by the alarming influx from outside. Article 6 of the Assam Accord for instance, declares: 'Constitutional, legislative and administrative safeguards, as may be appropriate, shall be provided to protect, preserve and promote the cultural, social, linguistic identity and heritage of the Assamese people'. On the other hand, the Accord (1994) signed with the Hmar People's Convention leading to the formation of Sinlun Development Council, proposes to give adequate autonomy to the Council for social, economic, cultural and educational advancement of the people under its

[22] Manifesto of the National Socialist Council of Nagaland (I-M) dated 31 January 1980. Quoted in Luingam Luithui and Nandita Haksar (eds.), *Nagaland File: Violation of Human Rights*, New Delhi: Lancer, 1984, p. 112.

jurisdiction and not only of the Hmars (Article 3). Not all accords are equally exclusionary. Mizo insurgency, viewed in this light, may be regarded as a case *sui generis*. The Memorandum submitted by Mizo National Front to the prime minister of India on 30 October 1965 exudes a strain of independence in the first sense: 'Nationalism and patriotism inspired by the political consciousness has now reached its maturity and the cry for political self-determination is the only will and the aspiration of the people, *neplus ultra*, the only final and perfect embodiment of social being for them'.[23] The Mizo Declaration of Independence signed on 1 March 1966 is framed in a manner that conveys the second sense. It is the state's inability to respond to the popular demands of the Mizos that is believed to have pushed them to the extreme course of independence. The text identifies as many as 12 areas including the protection of human rights in which the state has failed miserably. Does it mean that a better performance by the Indian state could have saved Mizoram from the imbroglio?

It is the assertion of independence on the subjects' part that makes them eligible for making explicit and categorical accords and contracts with the state. For unless their demands are couched in ethnic-territorial terms, the state does not find any reason to respond to them. Being persistently denied of any access to the so-called civilized sphere governed by the socio-linguistics of politeness, they are left with no other alternative but to make ethnic-territorial demands to attract the state's attention. Even the installation of an oil refinery requires two highly popular social movements in Assam. Although the movement demanding the recognition of Manipuri (Meitheilon) as one of the scheduled languages of India is very old, unless it comes to a head, the state does not feel the necessity of responding to it. While the state refuses to apply rules of the civilized sphere to them, it has to evolve special rules or at least to make normal rules appear special or both by way of entering into accords with the subject ethnic communities. Almost every accord by rule includes what may be called a cultural protection clause. The whole idea behind it is that the state or any of its authorized bodies promises

[23] Quoted in S.N. Singh, *Mizoram*, New Delhi: Mittal, 1994, p. 258.

to take 'special care' or make 'special attempts' for protecting the language and culture of some ethnic communities or peoples living under the jurisdiction of a state or a district council. The Hydari Agreement of 1947 sets forth the trend in this respect. The agreement among other things, made two very special provisions concerning adjudication of disputes and protection of tribal lands. Article 1 for instance announces:

All cases whether civil or criminal, arising among the Nagas in the Naga Hills will be disposed of by duly constituted Naga court according to Naga customary law, or by such law as may be introduced with the consent of duly recognised Naga representative organizations, and where a sentence of death or transportation has been passed there by right of appeal to the Governor.

Article 4 on the other hand seeks to protect the tribal land: 'The land with all its resources in the Naga Hills should not be alienated to a non-Naga without the consent of the Naga Council'. The provisions are special because the normal rules of the civilized sphere cannot be or better say, allowed to be extended to them. Conversely, sometimes accords also include provisions which are otherwise governable by normal laws of the land so much so that they do not deserve attention in these documents. The accord signed with the Tribal National Volunteers in 1988 may serve as a case in point. It makes provisions for 'skill formation of tribal youths of Tripura', 'increasing the duration and content of the All-India Radio programmes in tribal languages or dialects of Tripura', 'self-employment of tribal youths' and 'subsidised distribution of rice, salt and kerosene'. Interestingly, three odd articles have been added to the Assam Accord below the signatures as an appendix. These articles pledge for establishment of an oil refinery and an I.I.T. in Assam and urges on the concerned governments to reopen Ashok Paper Mill and the Jute Mills. By way of incorporating them into accords, they are to look highly special.

Pre-accord discords are characterized by a craving on the part of subject communities for recognition of this independence and speciality. Their status as independent and special subjects is a prerequisite for their role as accord-makers. This is not exactly the same kind of freedom and independence that Classical

Liberal Theory à la John Locke, talks about: For one thing, while Lockean contractualism draws our attention to the irreducibility of the individual as the accord-maker, the claim of the ethnic organizations to act on behalf of certain ethnic communities is too serious to be brushed aside. For another, the craving for independence and speciality according to Locke, is governed by certain obligations enshrined in the contract. It is true that he grants to the individuals what he calls, 'a right to rebellion'. But, even if it is a rebellion, it aims at making the state honour the obligations that it has committed itself to while making the contract.[24] On the other hand, we have already pointed out that the state's claim to obedience from the subject communities is made free from any contractual obligations. We must keep in mind the crucial distinction between independence of the citizen and that of the subject. While the former is considered to be rational, the latter is not. That one is independent does not necessarily mean that one is rational too.[25]

What are the transformations that accords bring about in the nature of independent and special subjecthood of the concerned ethnic communities? First of all, the accords seek to disarm them, sever their connections with other armed organizations and propose to restore the status quo ante of the supposedly pre-insurgent era. Usually, accords announce wholesome packages for the rehabilitation of the insurgents. All the four clauses of Article 4 of the Hmar Accord deal with the provisions for restoration of the order. While the first clause intends to disarm the armed cadres of Hmar People's Convention, the second one assigns to it the responsibility of taking immediate steps 'to amend as may be necessary, its articles of Association Constitution so as to conform them to the provisions of law'. Clause 3 vests the Government of Mizoram with the responsibility of rehabilitating the rebels who have come overground before 18 December 1992. Clause 4 obtains the promise from HPC that it will not

[24] See, John Locke, 'An Essay Concerning the True Original, Extent and End of Civil Government', in Sir Ernest Barker (ed.), *Social Contract: Essays by Locke, Hume, Rousseau*, London: Oxford University Press, 1958.
[25] See, Jon Elster, 'Rational Choice Theory', in *The Polity Reader in Social Theory*, Cambridge: 1994, pp. 121–5.

extend any support to such organizations as ULFA and NSCN (I-M). Articles 2 and 3 of the TNV Accord mentioned earlier have announced the same provisions. The accords of the northeast seem to be scripted on the same proforma.

Second, while the state helps a lot in organizing the subjects into closely knit communities by keeping them outside the civilized sphere, the process of peace-making in general and accords in particular seem to disarticulate and disintegrate them. We have already seen that Desai's insistence on treating the Nagas as Indian citizens in fact strips them of their identity as Nagas. The division between the pacifists and the hostiles virtually cuts every community into at least two pieces. The formation of Nagaland as a separate state as per the Agreement of 1960 has been interpreted by a commentator as a ploy to divide the Nagas and thereby decimate them as a community:

> The creation of Nagaland as a separate state has intended to take the sting out of the rebellion—it was to put in place a new moderate leadership which would accept the Indian Constitution and its control over Nagaland for substantial concessions in terms of autonomy.[26]

Considering that the Naga society is not a monolith, their prospects of being organized into a community are critically contingent on free exchange and circulation of opinions, on dialogues as means of resolving their disagreements and differences, on what Craig Calhoun calls, 'discourse about social arrangements: The members of a community need to engage themselves not only with others but also amongst themselves in discourse about social arrangements.'[27] Luingam Luithui and Meredith Preston in a recently written paper have critically reviewed the post-Shillong Accord scenario and shown how free circulation and exchange of opinions and views on it were censored and crippled.[28]

---

[26] Subir Bhaumik, 'The Accord that Never Was: A Critique of the 1975 Shillong Accord', 1999, mimeo.

[27] Craig Calhoun, 'Nationalism and Civil Society', in Craig Calhoun (ed.), *Social Theory and the Politics of Identity*, Cambridge: Blackwell, 1994, p. 327.

[28] Luingam Luithui and Meredith Preston,'The Politics of Peace in Nagaland Today', 1999, mimeo.

Third, accords also led to a certain fragmentation of the preaccord agenda of ethnic communities. The packages offered through the accords under all normal circumstances, do not pertain to the communities *per se* but to Indian citizens who may just happen to be the members of certain communities. Thus, the agenda of the community for its collective well-being always remains unaddressed. I have shown elsewhere, how the signature of the Assam Accord amounted to a certain de-ethnicization of the demands underlying the movement (1979–85).[29] While accords are made only when the demands are made in ethnic-territorial terms, accords do not take care of the ethnic communities as subjects. An understanding of the pre-Shillong Accord scenario may be instructive in this connection. President's Rule was clamped on 25 March 1975. This, according to S.C. Dev, then a Deputy Commissioner of Nagaland, 'created for the bureaucrats opportunities to show their determination and commitment to principles, ideals and values'.[30] They adopted what Subir Bhaumik calls, 'a tribe-by-tribe approach' to what the Naga National Council construed as a pan-Naga problem. The whole idea was to depend on the intermediaries, like the *gaonburas*, the village elders, the *dobhashis*, the leaders of the public and most importantly, family members of the hostiles and to ask them to get in touch with the underground, failing which unlimited state repression would be unleashed against them—sometimes, entire villages and finally, to get them to surrender by way of accepting demands which are essentially of local nature, like construction of metalled roads, bridges, rural employment, etc.[31] The whole exercise was intended to fragment and thereby decimate what was a comprehensive agenda of self-determination.

Accords certainly do not leave the state unaffected either. They lead to a transformation in its nature, in itself as a signatory to them. The state that puts its signature on the document and the one that is supposed to implement its provisions are not exactly

---

[29] Samir Kumar Das, 'On Institutionalizatioin: A Reconsideration of the Assam Movement (1983–1995)', *Journal of Politics*, vol. 4, 1998, pp. 68–72.
[30] S.C. Dev, op. cit., p. 137.
[31] Ibid, pp. 98–114.

the same. The conclusion of both the Assam Accord and the Mizo Accord was complemented by a change of regimes. The implication was that in both cases, those who had hitherto been on the wrong side of the fence were called upon to share the responsibility of implementing the accords. The Assam Accord in particular set forth the parameters within which the Asom Gana Parishad-led government, especially during 1985-90, was supposed to operate. We all know how the accord proved to be a stumbling bloc to its functioning and how the party took pains to distance itself from it.[32] We also know that the accord was supposed to address itself to the foreigners' issue and the crisis that the government faced and of course continues to face, is: to the extent it pushes the issue, to that extent it alienates the ethnic minorities especially Bengali Muslims—already a sizeable vote bank—who are afraid of being called foreigners and facing all the consequences that will follow upon it. But to the extent it distances itself from the issue, it alienates the Assamese-speaking Varna Hindus who actually harbour the fear of being swamped by them.

Accords in short, are sites where the parties meet together as friends and 'take up' their roles as friends.[33] Accords in other words, subjectify them as friends and hence, subject them to the tangled web of friendship.

THE CONTESTATION

It is sometimes argued that since accords have a character of their own—existing independently of what the actors otherwise would have thought and practised, serving in the process nobody's (pre-accord) interests—the only way to get out of this tangled web is to do away with them. Hostility to accords is as much rampant today as the euphoria with them. Collective emancipation in other words is defined as an assertion of the

[32] For a detailed analysis, see, Samir Kumar Das, *Regionalism in Power: The Case of Asom Gana Parishad (1985–1990)*, New Delhi: Omsons, 1998, Chap. 6.
[33] The words 'take up' are borrowed from Derrida and are used in the same Derridean sense. See, Jacques Derrida, *Politics of Friendship*, tr. George Collins, London: Verso, 1997.

peoples' right to transgress and break accords. This argument views emancipation and accords as not only different but opposed to each other. By siting resistance and emancipation beyond the purview of accords, this argument denies the latter of what may be called, their textuality. That the accords being over and above texts, account for a variety of subject positions including the more radical and subversive ones and allow them to be worked out and played around with within their corpus, is a point hardly understood by this argument. On the one hand, subjectification by its very nature generates resistance. Indeed, Foucault's notion of social dialogue is sensitive to this duality:

> Foucault's human beings are active bodies that exist in the midst of the world, and to be in the world in this way is to be wholly and inescapably open to influence and transformation by other forces, to be 'totally imprinted by history,' as Foucault puts it. At the same time, because forces are always imposed on other forces, this imposition requires the overcoming of those other forces, a subduing or taming of them; and there is also resistance, struggle against the limits such overcoming imposes, and the everpresent possibility of reversal.[34]

It is the notion of textuality that on the other hand, shows how 'such struggle against the limits' may be conducted within the 'limits' and how it can be read into the texts of accords. Accords in other words, embody what Roland Barthes might call, 'stereographic plurality':

> The text is plural. This does not mean just that it has several meanings, but rather it achieves plurality of meanings, an irreducible plurality. The text is not coexistence of meanings but passage, traversal, thus it answers not to an interpretation, liberal though it may be, but to an explosion, a dissemination. The text's plurality does not depend on the ambiguity of its contents, but rather on what could be called the stereographic plurality of the signifiers that weave it.[35]

---

[34] Christopher Falzon, *Foucault and the Social Dialogue: Beyond Fragmentation*, (London: Routledge, 1998, p. 45.

[35] Roland Barthes, 'From Work to Text', in Josue V. Harari (ed.), *Textual Strategies: Perspectives in Post-Structuralist Criticism*, London: Methuen, 1980, p. 76.

By way of concluding this paper, we may just refer to two kinds of examples showing how the 'limits' set forth by the accords are sought to be transcended without necessarily doing away with them: first, once an accord is signed, representatives of the ethnic communities have invariably expressed their resentments against its non-implementation or maybe, its half-hearted or inadequate implementation. First, the struggle for implementation or in some cases adequate and proper implementation has been as strong as that characterizing the pre-accord era. While doing all this, they may tend to retain the prerogative of defining what implementation involves or the propriety and adequacy of it. The leaders of the Assam movement could not realize that the Illegal Migrants (Detection by Tribunals) Act of 1983 would prove to be an insurmountable obstacle to the process of detection, disenfranchisement and deportation of foreigners promised by the Assam accord. Their experience in government led them to realize the gravity of the situation and suggest some amendments to it. The AGP-government finally called for repealing the act altogether for a proper implementation of the accord.[36] The present AGP-government has conveniently forgotten its early stand on the act and simply stopped referring to it any longer. Sometimes, leaders press for completing the obligations left incomplete by the accords. The excruciating brevity of the Shillong Accord became an object of fierce resentment. It comprises only three articles of which the first two spell out the obligations to be fulfilled by the underground organizations, i.e. 'acceptance of the Constitution of India by their own volition' and their disarmament. The concluding article keeps the other issues for 'discussion for final settlement' under suspended animation without fixing a deadline. The issue was revived by a number of Naga leaders who wanted 'the other issues' to be thrashed out, discussed and settled. However, the level of disillusionment was so high that the struggle did not cut much ice among the Nagas.

Second, the accords may sometimes be observed in a way that turns them on their head. Ironically, the very observance of

[36] Das, *Regionalism*, pp. 124–6.

their provisions amounts to their subversion. The Bodo Accord provides a classic illustration of this point. When the Assam government refused to entrust the Bodo Autonomous Council with a jurisdiction over a little more than 1,000 villages that the Bodos claimed for themselves back in 1993 on the ground that the Bodos do not constitute a numerical majority in those areas (nor are these areas contiguous with the proposed Bodoland), the leaders got the message, went deep inside the disputed villages and cleansed them of the non-Bodos—particularly, the Muslims and the Santhals—in a bid to tilt the demographic balance in their favour. Observance of this so-called democratic-majoritarian principle in fact made a mockery of the principle itself and deprived it of what was hitherto construed to be its essence. Liberal democracy's insensitivity to the cultural rights of the ethnic communities or what Carl Schmitt calls, their 'way of life' turned out to be only too expensive in this case.[37]

All these subversive political practices can however be referred back to the accords. The accords give credence to all such political practices. The foes within the friends are never allowed to come into the open and indulge in a free for all.

---

[37] Andrew Norris, Carl Schmitt on Friends, Enemies and the Political', *Telos*, 112, Summer 1998. For an excellent analysis of Liberal Democracy's incompatibility with cultural particularities, see, Bhikhu Parekh,'The Cultural Particularities of Liberal Democracy' in David Held (ed.), *Prospects of Democracy: North, South, East and West*, Stanford, Calif.: Stanford University Press, 1993, pp. 165–75.

Identity, Movements and Peace: The Unquiet Hills in Darjeeling

Subhas Ranjan Chakraborty

The politics of Darjeeling, even when it touched the sensitive issues of ethno-linguistic identity, was generally not violent. The quiet, but occasionally volatile, political ambience was disturbed in the mid-1980s when the movement launched by the Gorkha National Liberation Front (GNLF) turned violent. The repression unleashed by the state compounded the situation, leading to more violence and the hills were literally aflame for a few years. Continuous efforts to defuse the situation and to find a solution through negotiations among the GNLF and the state and central governments bore fruit when the Darjeeling Gorkha Hill Council (DGHC) accord was signed. This agreement, it was hoped, would not only bring peace to Darjeeling but would serve as a model to resolve conflicts of a similar nature in other parts of the country. This essay seeks to explore the development of the identity crisis and the ways in which the problem was sought to be solved by the people of Darjeeling. It also examines the attitudes of the central and state governments and the final resolution, at least for the time being, of the conflict through the accord.

I

The district of Darjeeling as it stands today was acquired by the British in stages. Parts of the district were the territory of the Raja of Sikkim, who was engaged in a struggle with the new kingdom of Nepal, which was unified after 1767. Between 1780 and 1810 the Nepalese made successful inroads into the Sikkimese territory and advanced eastward as far as the Teesta. Nepal also managed to annex the Terai, i.e. the territory between the Mechi and the Teesta rivers. A conflict between an expanding kingdom of Nepal and the British was on the cards; it eventually led to a war in 1814. At the end of the war, the tract between the Mechi and the Teesta was ceded to the British by Nepal by the treaty of Sagauli to be eventually handed over to the Raja of Sikkim, who was also reinstated. This arrangement was confirmed by the treaty of Titaliya. Thus it was British intervention which prevented an absorption of Sikkim and its territories in Darjeeling by Nepal. Sikkim was now to be retained as a buffer between Nepal and Bhutan. While the Company now guaranteed the sovereignty of the Raja of Sikkim, the Raja, on his part, was obliged to submit for arbitration by the Company any dispute between him or his subjects with Nepal ten years later, a dispute arose and this was duly referred to the Company. The Company deputed Captain Lloyd to effect a settlement. Lloyd visited what he described as 'the old Gorkha station called Darjeeling' for six days in February 1829 and was immediately 'struck with its being well adapted for the purpose of a sanitarium'. The advantage that Darjeeling offered as a strategic acquisition and as a centre of trade was realized by Lloyd and he impressed upon the Governor-General Lord Bentinck the wisdom of acquiring this land for the Company from Sikkim. After some negotiations, the Raja of Sikkim 'out of friendship for the Governor-General' presented Darjeeling to the East India Company on 1 February 1835. Darjeeling meant all land 'south of the Great Rungeet river, east of the Balasun, Kahail and Little Rungeet rivers, and the west of the Rungnoo and Mahanadi rivers'.[1]

The relations between the government of Sikkim and the Company, however, were not always smooth. In 1850, after some trouble, the Company annexed the Sikkim Terai. At the same

[1] This brief survey is based on L.S.S. Omalley, *Bengal District Gazetteers*, Darjeeling (1907, repr. 1987), pp. 19–34. Also see Dr. K. Pradhan: *The Gorkha Conquest* (Calcutta, 1991), Part 3; Dr. K. Pradhan: *Pahila Pahar* (in Nepali), Darjeeling, 1982, pp. 1–50.

time, a tract in the hills bound by the Rammam on the north, the Great Rangit and the Teesta on the east and by the Nepal frontier on the west was also acquired. The territory now under the British precluded any access for Sikkim to the plains except through territories under the British. The British territory now had a frontier with Nepal on the west and Bhutan on the east; it was also connected with the districts of Purneah and Jalpaiguri.

A fresh treaty was signed with Sikkim in March, 1861 and this put an end to the troubles that had continued to plague relations between Sikkim and the British and it also put Sikkim more firmly under the British.

The British were next involved in a war with Bhutan. At the end of the war, the British succeeded in obtaining the Bhutan Dooars along with the passes leading to the hills. They also acquired territories in the hills on the eastern banks of the Teesta. Thus Kalimpong was acquired and added to the district of Darjeeling.

II

After the cession of Darjeeling in 1835, General Lloyd and Dr. Chapman were sent to explore the country and after receiving their report it was decided to adopt Darjeeling as a sanitarium. In 1839 Dr. Campbell, the British resident in Nepal, was appointed the Superintendent of Darjeeling. In this capacity he was incharge of political relations with Nepal and Sikkim besides being incharge of the civil, criminal and fiscal administration of the district. Under his able guidance Darjeeling attracted an increasing number of settlers from the neighbouring states of Nepal, Sikkim and Bhutan as also from the plains and the population grew to about 10,000 by 1849.[2]

Darjeeling remained under the non-regulation scheme of administration before the passing of the Indian Council's Act of 1861. The Act abolished the distinction between the regulation and non-regulation provinces and districts. An Act of 1870 restored the pre-1861 position and the Governor-General and the Lt. Governor were now empowered to legislate by means of

[2] Omalley, op. cit., p. 22.

executive order for the less advanced districts. Darjeeling, under the Act of 1870, was to be under the non-regulated scheme for the preservation of the indigenous system of the native population. The Act XV of 1874 converted Darjeeling into a scheduled district. Such districts were kept outside the purview of general laws prevalent in the rest of the country.[3] A large number of acts relating to land-tenure, inheritance, transfer and sale of land, etc., were kept out of operation in the scheduled districts. Darjeeling now shared this special status with four other districts of Bengal. This position continued till 1919, when the Act of 1919 changed the nomenclature of 'scheduled district' to 'backward tract'. Art. 52A(2) of the Act stipulated that the governor of the province under the direction of the Governor-General would have the sole responsibility of administering such 'backward tracts'. The governor was also to decide if any law passed by the provincial legislature was to have effect in such areas.

The Government of India Act, 1935, changed the term 'backward tracts' to 'excluded' and 'partially excluded' areas. Here again it was stipulated that:

no act of Federal legislature or of the provincial legislature shall apply to an excluded area or a partially excluded area, unless the governor by public notification so directs, and the governor in giving such a direction with respect to any act may direct that the act shall in its application to that area . . . have effect subject to such exceptions and modifications as he thinks fit.

In the case of a partially excluded area the governor had to consult the council of ministers but in the case of an excluded area his discretion was final. Darjeeling now became a 'partially excluded area' within the province of Bengal.[4] After independence, Darjeeling continued to be a district of West Bengal, though there was a demand for inclusion in Assam.

Darjeeling provides enough evidence of the anxiety of the colonial administration to preserve the separateness of Darjeeling

[3]D. Chakraborty, *Gorkhaland: Evolution of Politics of Segregation*, University of North Bengal, mimeographed, 1988, pp. 6–20.
[4]Ibid., p. 14.

and to emphasize its distinction from the people of the plains. The ostensible reason was the unique ethnic and linguistic character of the majority of settlers in Darjeeling, though in fact British policy was inspired by strategic considerations relating to a frontier district. This unique and isolationist character was also a ploy to keep the people of Darjeeling away from the mainstream nationalist movement. Indeed, the emerging elite in Darjeeling were always encouraged to preserve their isolationism and to demand a separate status. However, their aspirations for self-determination or at least self-government in the hills remained frustrated as Darjeeling, by and large, remained outside the reforms introduced elsewhere.[5]

III

The social history of Darjeeling in the nineteenth and twentieth centuries was shaped by several factors. Campbell noted that there were about 100 people around 1835.[6] Fairly rapid demographic growth has generally been attributed by scholars to immigration from Nepal, Sikkim, Bhutan and the plains. The growth of population was as follows:

1891	2,29,914
1901	2,49,117
1931	3,19,635
1951	4,45,260
1971	7,81,777

In attracting such immigration the growth of Darjeeling as a hill station was a substantial contributory factor. Among the pull factors were the beginning and growth of tea cultivation in the Darjeeling hills, the recruitment of the Gorkhas into the

[5] D.K. Sarkar and D. Bhaumik, *The Darjeeling Gorkha Hill Council: An Alternative Politico-administrative Arrangement at a Sub-State Level* (ICSSR project). I am indebted to Dr. Sarkar for kindly permitting me to use the typescript of the final report.
[6] It has been suggested by some scholars that this estimate refers only to the Observatory Hill and the surrounding area. The population of Darjeeling was larger. See K. Pradhan, *Pahila Pahar*; and *Study on Gorkhaland*, Review no. 2, Study Forum, Darjeeling, 1987.

British army and general opportunities for trade and commerce and sundry employment. The possibility of clearing forests and acquiring cultivable land was also an important factor. What, in this regard, has often escaped notice is the effect of the political and social evolution in Nepal. The political and social consequences of the unification of the kingdom of Nepal may be seen as the push factor. Among these may be mentioned the emergence of a new political elite in Nepal, evolution of new land-tenurial systems in supersession of the old communal land tenures and the plight of the tribal groups, particularly in eastern Nepal. There was a fairly large-scale immigration from eastern Nepal and, as a result, these groups were soon to outnumber the autochthonous Lepchas and the Sikkimese Bhutias (in the present Darjeeling and Kurseong sub-divisions) and the Bhutanese (in the present Kalimpong subdivision).[7]

The British authorities gave a preferential treatment to the migrants from Nepal. One reason was that the Nepalis, compared especially to the Lepchas, were more hardworking and adopted social and technological innovations more quickly. Coming from Nepal they were likely to be loyal subjects as the British and Nepal were on good terms. The British also needed the Gorkha soldiers for their army.[8] The early Nepali settlers through enterprise and hard labour evolved a community of their own, and developed characteristics which were peculiar to Darjeeling. It did not remain an undifferentiated society and an elite, comprising both the Nepalis and the Bhutias, emerged. It must be remembered that the evolution of the Nepali society in Darjeeling was quite different from that of Nepal. For one thing, the Bahun-Chhettri domination was not all that apparent in Darjeeling. And indeed tribal exclusiveness was shed in favour of an inclusive Nepali identity. The cementing factor was the use of the Nepali language or the *khas-kura* which was used increas-

---

[7] K. Pradhan, *The Gorkha Conquest*, and *Pahila Pahar*: L. Caplan, *Land Tenure and Social Change in East Nepal*, London, 1970; M.C. Regmi, *Land Tenure and Taxation in Nepal*, vol. I, Berkeley, 1968.

[8] K. Pradhan, *The Gorkha Conquest*, p. 190; B. De and P. R. Ray, *Notes on the History of Darjeeling District*, Indian History Congress, Waltair Session, 1979.

ingly as the common language in preference to the tribal dialects or languages. Religious differences were preserved with Hinduism and Buddhism remaining the dominant religions; animism was not practised in a large way. In Darjeeling, missionary educational institutions were opened, but the common Nepali did not have easy access to them. Those who did still manage to receive such education, in Darjeeling or in Calcutta, gradually constituted the new indigenous elite in Darjeeling.

The demand for white-collar jobs in the circumstances was met largely by the Bengali *bhadralok* from the plains. They filled the positions in the lower and middle echelons of the administration, became clerks in the tea-gardens and were also to provide professionals like teachers, lawyers, doctors and engineers. The wholesale and retail trade were taken over by the Marwaris and the Biharis. It is important to note that the immigration from Nepal was supplemented by the migrants from the plains of India as well. Thus a potential source of social conflict was created as both the economic and professional domains were dominated by the non-Nepalis. Demand for education and for prestigious white-collar jobs was on the rise. In the meanwhile, the hill people resented the domination of the plainsmen in the decision-making process. This can be seen as a negative factor that helped identity-formation.

This was one aspect of the evolution of a separate identity among the people in the hills. The plains people could easily be constructed as the other to emphasize the identity of the hill people. The distinct ethos that grew had other dimensions as well. People of various linguistic and ethnic groups, who had originally come as immigrants, settled in various *bastis* and *kamans* and adjusted to a new life. Nepali was accepted the common language and, as we have mentioned earlier, tribal exclusiveness was shed in search of a new overarching identity as Nepalis.[9] Other linguistic groups, however, were not totally obliterated. Indeed, census figures are interesting. In 1901 there were only about 45,000 *khas-kura* or Nepali speaking people. But if one included other dialects like Gurung, Murmi, Magar,

[9] K. Pradhan, *Pahila Pahar*, pp. 1–50.

etc., then the total number was one and a half lakh.[10] All these groups, however, gradually accepted Nepali as their language. Thus, according to the census figures of 1961, the number of Nepali-speaking people were 3.52 lakh out of a total population of 4.04 lakh in the hill areas of the Darjeeling district. Indeed, Nepali has become the *lingua franca* of the entire eastern Himalayan region. Thus we see that a strong linguistic foundation for a separate identity was laid down over the decades and this may be seen as the product of the historical evolution of Darjeeling.

It was only a minority among the hill people who were able to appreciate and articulate such perceptions of a separate identity. This new elite now clearly felt the need to have an institutional framework to assert and preserve such identity. They did find an appreciative response among the Europeans in the colonial administration. We find the terms 'hill people' or 'hillmen' in the memoranda that these people started submitting to the British since the beginning of this century.

The years after 1905 witnessed an emotional turmoil in the plains of Bengal following the partition of Bengal by Lord Curzon. It may be purely coincidental, but it was only after this upsurge of the Bengali identity which protested so strongly against fragmentation that, in 1907, on behalf of the hill people of the district of Darjeeling a memorandum was presented to the British Government demanding a separate administrative unit for the district.[11] It was a rather inchoate demand without the meaning and the content of the 'separate administrative unit' clearly delineated. It is, however, significant that the separate identity of the 'hill people' was sought to be asserted through a form of self-governance. The fact that the district, as a non-regulation district, did enjoy a separate status was quite forgotten. It is possible to see the memorandum as an expression of some unformatted aspirations of the 'hill people', but that such a separate identity was constructed and asserted is significant for this study.

[10] *District Census Handbook*, Darjeeling, 1951, pp. xxxix-xliii.

[11] A Memorandum of the Demand of Autonomy to the Government of India and Parliament, 24 December 1957.

A more formulated demand came in 1917 when a deputation of the representatives of the hill people led by S.W. Laden La and Kharga Bahadur Chhettri waited on Mr. Montagu, the Secretary of State and Lord Chelmsford, the Viceroy. Lord Chelmsford, in a private letter to Lord Ronaldshay, the Governor of Bengal, told him that the nationalists should not be allowed to monopolize the attention of Montagu.[12] Lord Ronaldshay's initiative may have worked in arranging the meeting. In the meeting they demanded a separate and independent administrative unit comprising Darjeeling and the Dooars portion of the Jalpaiguri district. It is interesting to note that the Bengali nationalists plainly misunderstood the import of the demand. Surendranath Banerjea wrote in 'Bengalee', 'So the trumpet-call of self-government has awakened even the Gorkhas . . . the fact that even the Gorkhas are for Home Rule proves how fallacious is the argument put forward by the Anglo-Indian press about the military races in India not being in favour of Home Rule'.[13] Banerjea did not quite understand the aspirations of the 'hillmen' in making the demand they did. There was even a suggestion for creating a North-Eastern Frontier Province (NEFP) including Assam Dooars and hill territories to the east of Bhutan.[14] It is important to note that the Darjeeling elite looked towards the British for a favour and not to the nationalists to wage a fight for securing their demand. This non-communication between the two sets is crucial to understanding the failure of more effective integration of the periphery.

The move for the presentation of the memorandum was made by the Hillmen's Association (founded in 1917). The first President was Laden La, who rose in the police service to became an additional superintendent of police of Darjeeling. After his retirement he was honoured with the title of Sardar Bahadur and was for some time the chairman of the Darjeeling Municipality. Other prominent members included Rupnarain Sinha, Rai Saheb M.K. Pradhan. These leaders were all educated, anglicized urban gentlemen who enjoyed the confidence of the

[12] J. Broomfield, *Elite Conflict in a Plural Society*, Bombay, 1968 p. 101.
[13] *Bengalee*, 20 December 1917.
[14] D. Chakraborty, op. cit., p. 10.

colonial administrators. This is seen clearly when in March 1920 the Darjeeling Planters' Association, European Association and Hillmen's Association in a joint meeting demanded that Darjeeling, including the portion of Jalpaiguri 'annexed from Bhutan in 1865' should be excluded from Bengal. It is interesting to note that the Kalimpong Samiti, the Gorkhas under Bhimlal Dewan and the People's Association, Darjeeling, opposed the exclusion of Darjeeling from Bengal. They also expressed the view that the continuation of the scheduled district status would result in perpetual backwardness of the district. Among the supporters of this view were Dr. Parasmani Pradhan and Dal Bahadur Giri.[15]

In 1929 the Hillmen's Association submitted a memorandum to the Simon Commission demanding: (a) Darjeeling be taken out of the list of 'backward districts', and (b) at least three seats in the provincial and central legislatures be reserved for the hillmen of Darjeeling. The Hillmen's Association seemed to have been swaying between two ideas: to remain in Bengal with special safeguards or to leave Bengal. In 1934 the Hillmen's Association again submitted a memorandum to Sir Samuel Hoare, the Secretary of State and Sir John Anderson, the Governor of Bengal demanding both reforms and special safeguards. In fact, they would have preferred to combine a measure of local self-government with preferential treatment.[16] Later in 1935 the Hillmen's Association, under the signature of its president Laden La, submitted another memorandum to the Secretary of State demanding the total exclusion of the district from Bengal and its conversion into a separate administrative unit.[17] These demands were not conceded and Darjeeling continued to enjoy a special status within the province of Bengal. Under the Act of 1935, elections to the provincial legislature were held and Dambar Singh Gurung was elected as the representative of the hill people.

[15] Ibid., pp. 10–12; De and Ray, op. cit.
[16] C.K. Kar, *Sub-Regional Movement in India, A Case Study: Political History of the Gorkhas of Darjeeling District*, Calcutta, n.d. Appendix A and B.
[17] Memorandum of 1917.

The Hillmen's Association did not prove to be a successful negotiator for the hill people for they secured nothing by way of concession for the district, though they personally enjoyed the patronage of the British. They raised the demand of a NEFP again in 1938, but no longer held the allegiance even of the elite in Darjeeling. Some middle class leaders now began to pay greater attention to social service and literary organizations like the Gorkha Dukha Nivarak Sabha or the Nepali Sahitya Sammelan. Through these organizations they tried to expand their constituency to include the common people. The influence of the Hillmen's Association was clearly on the wane. Yet, they continued with their representations and in 1942, in a memorandum to Lord Pethick-Lawrence, the Secretary of State, demanded Darjeeling's separation from Bengal and its constitution as a separate administrative unit under the governor-general with a Chief Commissioner at its head. It is interesting that the local Planters' Association and the Europeans' Association consistently supported the demands of the Hillmen's Association. Osborne Smith, a local planter who played a role in the drafting of the 1934 memorandum, was active in 1942 as well. The European civil service community also generally backed the Hillmen's Association.[18]

D.S.Gurung, though associated with the Hillmen's Association, soon distanced himself from the organization. He was a traditionalist, with a deep love for the Nepali language and heritage. He opposed the idea of separation from Bengal and instead put forward the demand for autonomy of the district. He also wanted to mobilize the people for political action. Gurung took the initiative of forming an alternate political organization and convened a meeting of the representatives of various social service and literary organizations and prominent individuals as the President of the Gurkha Association. Gorkhas from other places in the country also joined the convention. The convention took the decision to form a political party—the All India Gorkha League (AIGL)—with Gurung as its president and Randhir Subba as its secretary. The original constitution of the party referred to Nepal as the motherland of the Gorkhas, but in

[18] De and Ray, op. cit.

1948 the clause was deleted.[19] The AIGL sought the protection of the culture and political rights of the Indian Gorkhas and of the Nepali language and demanded recognition as citizens of India. It demanded regional autonomy for Darjeeling within the framework of an Indian province rather than separation.

The accent on Nepali in the political agenda of the AIGL could have alarmed the non-Nepali sections of the hill people, but the AIGL leaders were aware of this and sought to allay their apprehensions by saying that they were mindful of the demands and the linguistic and cultural interests of such groups. The Hillmen's Association repeated, in a representation to Lord Casey, the governor of Bengal, the demand for a Chief Commissioner's province, while the AIGL demanded autonomy but favoured inclusion within Assam. It could be seen as part of a grand strategy, as Assam with a number of minority groups was likely to grant self-government to such groups in a not too distant future.

D.S.Gurung was elected to the Constituent Assembly, but after his death in 1948 his brother filled up the resultant vacancy. Thus on the eve of Indian Independence the AIGL became the focal point of Darjeeling politics so far as the demand for autonomy was concerned. The Hillmen's Association did not prove to be more than a collaborative organization of the colonial administration, devoid of a mass base as it was. Their demands found concordance in the demands of the European pressure groups, particularly the planters. But the new professional and educated middle classes were also looking at other variables in this identity such as language and culture. They also felt the need, not necessarily shared by the Hillmen's Association, to mobilize the people for more effective political and social action. Since there were deep socio-economic differences in the Nepali society and since the majority of the leadership was not prepared to address the issue of class, language was an important factor in mobilization.

The issue of language became important around 1926–7 when the question of the medium of instruction in schools was taken up. Nepali, it was demanded by some social and literary organizations, should be the medium of instruction in the schools. While

---

[19] D. Chakraborty, op. cit. p. 15.

the Bhutias and Lepchas did not oppose this demand they asserted the right to be educated through the medium of their own language. At the same time Nepali litterateurs like Parasmani Pradhan took care to develop the language and literature. To coordinate such efforts he along with Dharanidhar Sharma and Surya Bijram Gewali founded the Nepali Sahitya Sammelan . In a speech Pradhan noted: 'We are Nepalese made up of many denominations: Chhetri, Bahun, Newar,Gurung, Rai, Limbu, Tamang, Bhutia, Lepcha, Tharu, Sunwar and so on. We all have our own languages, but since Nepali is the only common language we must develop Nepali first'.[20] In 1930 the Nepali textbook committee, appointed by the Director of Public Instructions (DPI) Bengal recommended the adoption of the Nepali language as the medium of instruction up to the middle school or the junior high school level. These efforts revealed a mentality that was quite different from that of the leading members of the Hillmen's Association. These leaders were seeking a more comprehensive socio-cultural identity, not merely a separate administrative set-up.

What is generally missing in the narratives of Darjeeling that I have had a chance to look at is the relationship between the nationalist movement that was gathering momentum elsewhere in India and the new elite or the people of Darjeeling. One reason why the colonial administration was keen to support the quest for a distinct identity was to keep them away from the nationalist movement. But the question that would bother me is this: did the elite or the people construct such identity against the Indians in general or Bengalis in particular or perceived such identity as distinct from yet complementary to the larger Indian identity? We have evidence to suggest that the mainstream nationalist movement did find significant echoes in Darjeeling and that there was a distinct strand that accepted the overarching Indian identity and adopted an anti-imperialist stand as well.

The non-cooperation movement of Gandhi did attract some support in Darjeeling. Dal Bahadur Giri became a member of the Congress and led the non-cooperation movement in the hills. He did share the belief that true emancipation would not come

[20] I. Pradhan, *Parasmani Pradhan*, Sahitya Akademi, 1970, pp. 29–31.

so long as Indians were under foreign rule. This was a new awareness to which some in the hills at least subscribed and it was not obsessed with a separate status for Darjeeling. Printed donation receipts in the form of 'currency notes' with Gandhi's portrait on it were sold for 1, 2 and 4 annas to raise funds for the non-cooperation movement. Giri brought out processions in Darjeeling and Kalimpong. He was arrested though his effort at mobilization was not a great success. He died some time after his release, but K.B. Bista tried to rejuvenate the Congress in Darjeeling after him. This was also a failure on the part of the mainstream nationalist movement to enlist the support of the minorities by persuading them to accept the nationalist ideology. This is, at least negatively, significant for we shall see that after independence the people of Darjeeling provided significant electoral support to the national parties for a long time.

Local aspirations and the national ideology remained things apart. In spite of the failure to mobilize a large number of people during the non-cooperation movement it was not without significant effect. The Presidential address at the annual general meeting of the Hillmen's Association in May 1923 clearly condemned the non-cooperation movement. The address noted,

the unfortunate incidents at some of the gardens in which some amount of violence and threat were used by the coolies. The first such incident occurred at the Kalej Valley Tea Estate when the coolies fell out with the assistant manager resulting in riot. . . . This trouble at Kalej Valley seemed to be the outcome of the wage question. . . . This was followed by riot at the Nagri Farm Tea Estate. This seemed to be purely mischievous for which the non-cooperation . . . propaganda was to a great extent responsible.[21]

This address would prove that the non-cooperation movement did send some signals of alarm to the elite.

Another important leader was Helen Ahmed, a Christian Lepcha lady from Kurseong, who joined the Congress and participated in the Champaran *satyagraha*. Maya Devi Chhettri, who later became a Member of Parliament, joined the civil disobedience movement in the 1930s.[22] They, however, succeeded

---

[21] Quoted in De and Ray, op. cit.
[22] De and Ray, op. cit.

neither in creating a stable organization nor in attracting a large number of supporters. The point is that the Congress, as the representative of the mainstream nationalist movement, at least had a significant presence in Darjeeling, but it failed to enlist the people of Darjeeling as a whole for the national movement.

The revolutionary movement also spread to Darjeeling. In 1934 there was an attempt on the life of Sir John Anderson, the governor of Bengal at the Lebong race course. It is difficult to gauge the reaction of the local people in the absence of any evidence, but the Hillmen's Association presented an address to the governor assuring him 'of our readiness to respect any call on our people at all times and in any emergency'.

The communist movement also found some support in the hills, particularly in some tea garden areas. Sushil Chatterjee was a pioneer in organizing working class movements in the area, ably supported by Satyendra Narayan Majumdar. He also recruited men like Ratanlal Brahman, Bhadra Bahadur Hamal, G.L. Subba from the hills.[23] The communists supported the claim of the 'national minorities' for self-determination and this could find a sympathetic chord among the people in the hills. They had even suggested the creation of a greater Gorkhastan covering a large tract of the Himalayas and the sub-Himalayan zone. The memorial submitted by the district committee of the Communist Party of India (CPI) to the Constituent Assembly stated, '... the CPI, therefore, demands that after making necessary revisions of the existing boundaries, the three contiguous areas of Darjeeling district, Sikkim and Nepal be formed into a single zone to be called Gorkhastan'.[24] The CPI later shifted its stance to a demand for regional autonomy for the national minorities in 1951.

IV

After Independence, Darjeeling continued to be a province of West Bengal. The question of a separate identity for Darjeeling had not been resolved. Indeed, Indian Independence in a way

[23] S.N. Majumdar, *Patabhumi Kanchanjangha* (in Bengali), Calcutta, 1983.
[24] 'Why Gorkhastan' *Pranta Parishad*, Darjeeling, 1986, pp. 31–2.

marked a new phase in the struggle for autonomy for Darjeeling. The question of reorganization of states assumed new urgency after Independence and the minorities for some time hoped for a fulfilment of their aspirations.

The All-India Gorkha League submitted a memorandum to Jawaharlal Nehru, the prime minister, in Kalimpong on 29 April 1952, in which it suggested three alternatives: (a) a centrally administered unit; (b) a separate province comprising Darjeeling and the neighbouring areas, and (c) the district of Darjeeling and the Dooars areas of Jalpaiguri to be merged with Assam. The league also demanded the constitutional recognition of Nepali. Thus the old issue of autonomy remained; to it was added the issue of language in a new way. It is significant that the question of citizenship, raised later by the GNLF as a central issue, was not mentioned.

The issue of language had two aspects: recognition of Nepali as the official language for the hills and the inclusion of Nepali in the Eighth Schedule of the Constitution. In the late 1950s the issue of language was raised in the West Bengal Assembly, but the West Bengal government did not immediately concede the demand. It is interesting that the 1951 census indicated that the Nepali-speaking people constituted a mere 19.98 per cent of the people of Darjeeling. What happened was that the census enumerated the different linguistic affinities of the ethnic groups. For example, the Magars, Gurungs, Rais, Tamangs, etc., were not recorded as Nepali-speaking people, but as speaking a separate language. This was clearly not a reflection of reality. But the Chief Minister Dr. B.C. Roy used the census figure to suggest that one should wait till the 1961 census before a decision could be taken.[25] The 1961 census recorded an absurd growth: the Nepali-speaking people now constituted 59.9 per cent of the people. The anomaly is explained by the fact that the old tribal groups were no longer enumerated as speaking a distinct language. The demand for the recognition of Nepali as the official language grew as a result. In 1961 the West Bengal Assembly, by the West Bengal Official Languages Act, adopted Nepali as the official language for the hill subdivisions of

[25] D. Chakraborty, op. cit., p. 28.

Darjeeling. This was at least a minor triumph for the people of Darjeeling.

The demand for the inclusion of Nepali in the Eighth Schedule of the Constitution grew stronger over the next two decades. Suniti Kumar Chatterjee, a member of the Official Languages Committee and an eminent scholar, submitted a minority report in which he suggested the expansion of the Eighth Schedule to include languages like Nepali and Sindhi. The demand was veritably transformed into a movement when the All-India Nepali Bhasa Samiti assumed the leadership of the language movement. They coopted members from other areas of the country where sizeable Nepali-speaking people lived. They succeeded in mobilizing public opinion through agitation and propaganda and enlisted the support of many non-Nepali intellectuals as well. The Samiti tried to set up organizations even in the remote village areas and I would argue that they succeeded in mobilizing the people at the grassroots level. The awareness they created was to be exploited later by the Gorkha National Liberation Front (GNLF) movement. The Government of India was not very responsive to this sensitive demand and indeed Morarji Desai, as Prime Minister, alienated many by referring to Nepali as a foreign language during a visit to Darjeeling in 1979.

The success of the mobilization by the Bhasa Samiti could be seen in the spontaneous outburst of public anger in Darjeeling. A mammoth meeting was held at the GDNS grounds where I.B. Rai put a simple postulate to the government: 'You will take our land, but not us'. The language movement now acquired a militancy that was new in the hills. The Left Front government which came to power in West Bengal in 1977 supported this demand and the Assemblies of West Bengal, Sikkim and Tripura adopted resolutions supporting the demand in 1977 and 1978. The demand was conceded only after the GNLF movement had totally transformed the politics of Darjeeling.

Meanwhile the question of autonomy was raised by all the political parties, but the contours of the autonomy were not clear. The institution of the States Reorganisation Committee raised hope. The AIGL repeated the demands made in the memorandum of 1952, but the CPI now favoured regional autonomy. The government of West Bengal strongly opposed any suggestion to separate Darjeeling from West Bengal. It stressed that such a separation would be fraught with dangerous consequences, because 'it is all too likely that this is only the thin end of a much bigger wedge intended to foster future claims for merger with Nepal'.[26]

By 1955 even the Congress had come round to the opinion that a district council with statutory powers might be the answer to the demand for autonomy. The three main parties submitted a memorandum to Nehru again in 1957 demanding autonomy. In 1967 the Gorkha League joined the United Front ministry in West Bengal.

D.P. Rai was a minister in three successive governments between 1967 and 1971, but did not succeed in securing Darjeeling's administrative autonomy. In fact, the nature and the details of such autonomy had really not been properly addressed. There were several and rather vague ideas about autonomy. The Congress favoured the concept of an autonomous district council and hill council suggested by the Patashkar Committee (1965) for Assam. In 1972 the Congress government in West Bengal set up a nominated Hill Council and established a branch secretariat in Darjeeling for Hill Affairs. This non-statutory body satisfied very few in Darjeeling.

The Left Front government came to power in 1977 and the CPI(M) was now obliged to address the issue of autonomy they had supported for a very long time. In 1981 the Assembly passed a resolution requesting the Centre to suitably amend the Constitution to grant autonomy to Darjeeling. A CPI(M) Member of Parliament brought unofficial bills in Parliament seeking to amend the Constitution, but the bills were rejected. The bill, brought by Ananda Pathak, proposed:

Notwithstanding any-thing in the Constitution, Parliament may by law, form within the state of West Bengal, an autonomous region comprising such areas, as may be specified, of the district of Darjeeling and neighbouring district where the Nepali-speaking people are in a majority and create for the administration of such region a district council.

[26] Government of West Bengal Memorandum to the States Reorganisation Committee.

The central government did not appear to be sensitive to the demand and thus the Left Front government failed to introduce any change on its own. By now there was a consensus among the national and the regional parties that the people's quest for an identity is best served by the creation of statutory autonomy for Darjeeling. It was also the bitter experience of the people that constitutional agitation and even a sympathetic government in the state had not secured their demands. This was the situation in the hills when the militant GNLF movement took virtually everyone by surprise.

Before concluding this section, I would like to look briefly at the electoral politics in Darjeeling between 1952 and 1987.

Constituency	Darjeeling	Jorebungalow/Kurseong	Kalimpong
1952	GL	GL	CPI
1957	GL	CPI	IND.
1962	GL	CPI	GL
1967	GL	GL	CONG.
1969	GL	GL	GL
1971	GL	CPM	GL
1972	GL	GL	CONG.
1977	GL	CONG.	GL
1982	CPM	CPI(M)	GL
1987	CPI(M)	CPI(M)	CPM[27]

Electoral Politics in Darjeeling 1952-87.

The performance of the AIGL had been consistent till 1977. But the national parties like the Congress and the CPI/CPM also had substantial share of electoral support during these decades and even managed to win seats. Subash Ghising managed to poll a mere 269 votes when he contested in 1977. The picture changes violently after the beginning of the GNLF movement. The boycott call given by Ghising had overwhelming response in 1987. Total polling was: Darjeeling-15,843; Kalimpong-1,100 and Kurseong-7,802. This abnormally poor voter turnout

[27] D. Bannerjee, *Election Recorder*, Calcutta, 1990.

explains CPI(M) winning all the seats for the first time. The communist parties had their bases in the tea garden areas in Darjeeling and Kurseong, but even the Congress had a good share of the popular votes. The AIGL did not have more than 50 per cent of popular votes in all the constituencies except in 1969. In other years its support varied between 64.4 per cent (Jorebungalow, 1952) to 26.5 per cent (Jorebungalow, 1957).[28]

This electoral support for the national parties may be seen as the reflection of the desire to remain in the mainstream of national politics. The support extended by these parties to the demands for autonomy and linguistic recognition sustained such a desire. But essentially the failure to secure the demands exposed the limitations of moderation. The GNLF movement, no doubt, took lessons from this experience.

V

The early 1980s witnessed, for the first time, a persistent demand for a separate state.[29] The organization that gave this call for the first time was the Pranta Parishad, more a platform than a political party, set up by people belonging to the AIGL, the Congress and some other small parties. It was established in the same year as the GNLF but enjoyed the advantage of being led by known political leaders like Madan Tamang. The Parishad submitted a memorandum to the prime minister on 13 April 1980 demanding the separate state of Gorkhaland. They even gave a call for boycotting the elections in 1981 and 1982, but the call evoked a lukewarm response. They, however, succeeded in creating an impression, for the first time, that a separate state was the only solution to the demands of the hill people for their identity, material development and cultural distinctiveness. Their documents clearly stated that 'they attach no value to the so-called regional autonomy preferred by the Left Front govern-

[28] C.K. Kar, op. cit., p. 60.
[29] For this section various documents and reports in newspapers and periodicals have been used. See Gorkhaland Agitation, An Information Document (Government of West Bengal, 1986); Nagendra Gorkha: Gorkhaland Andolan (in Nepali), Darjeeling, 1993–4.

ment of West Bengal and the Union Territory status as demanded by the Darjeeling District Congress(I) leaders'.

But the thunder they expected to produce was stolen by the GNLF, led by Subash Ghising. The rise of the GNLF and of Subash Ghising is a phenomenon that can hardly be fully explained. How did a man who could muster no more than 269 votes in the 1977 elections, suddenly emerge as the undisputed leader of Darjeeling in 1986? There were quite a number of factors that favoured the emergence of militancy and violence in Darjeeling. The failure of long constitutional agitation comprising submission of memoranda, resolutions by the state assemblies and propaganda to achieve the demands is to be counted among them. There were some extraneous factors as well. The creation of Sikkim as a state of India after the merger obviously emboldened some people in Darjeeling also to ask for a separate state. The state of Assam was broken up and new states created. This served as an example of what militancy could achieve. The Mizo accord also reinforced such sentiments. Finally, the anti-foreigner agitation in Assam and Meghalaya in which a large number of Nepalis were forced to leave those states raised the question of basic insecurity of the Indian Gorkhas.

This is where the Ghising-led GNLF made an entirely new point by raising the issue of citizenship along with the status of the Indo-Nepal treaties. The whole history of Darjeeling from the formation of the district by the British was recalled to underline the anomalies of the present. Ghising effectively made the point that the Indian Gorkhas are a people without an identity, without a home as it were. He demanded the scrapping of Clause VII of the Indo-Nepal Treaty of 1950. This clause allowed 'on a reciprocal basis' the nationals of one country the right to acquire property, to participate in trade and commerce, of residence and other related privileges. The GNLF contended that this blurred the distinction between the Indian Gorkhas and the subjects of Nepal. Thus it is 'a curse and a permanent political blockade to the ill-fated Indian Gorkhas who are here in present India for centuries with their own language, culture, tradition and historical homeland'.

We the whole aboriginal and the settled Gorkhas of India have always been loyal to the country all along and continue to be so. Besides ... the communal and colonial rule of the West Bengal government, the Gorkhas have been forced to suffer innumerable humiliations and indignities in different parts of the country on account of the unfortunate ambiguities created by clause vii of the Indo-Nepal Treaty of 1950.

They also raised the issue of a separate regiment for Indian Gorkhas so that they are not confused with the recruits from Nepal and thus considered as mercenaries.

Our people are facing a crisis of identity since independence. We want clearly and unambiguously to be identified as Indian nationals.... We believe that the creation of a separate state of Gorkhaland within the Indian Union will give us a clear Indian identity and distinguish us from the people of Nepal.[30]

This is where the GNLF movement broke fresh grounds. They were looking for an Indian identity, as Indian Gorkhas as distinct from the Gorkhas of Nepal. It is this distinct identity that history had indeed forged among the people of Darjeeling, most of whom had originally come from Nepal but who had evolved an ethos in Darjeeling quite different from that of Nepal. This is where he was able to touch a responsive chord among the people. He acquired a mass base almost overnight. The CPI(M) quickly lost the ground it had gained since 1977. Mass fronts of the GNLF like the Gorkha National Women's Organisation (GNWO); Gorkha National Student's Federation (GNSF); Gorkha National Youth Organisation (GNYO) and Gorkha National Employees' Organisation (GNEO) were established. The students and employees joined the movement in large numbers and a special feature of the movement was the large-scale participation of women. The movement started with continuous strikes and protests against the government of West Bengal. Later, however, clashes with the CPI(M) and, indeed, with anyone who did not fall in line, started. The government decision to treat the movement as a law and order problem and the deployment of central forces like the CRPF, the BSF, the EFR

[30] C.K. Kar, op. cit., Appendix G; Gorkhaland Agitation, Appendix A and B.N. Gorkha, op. cit.

and the SAP made matters worse. Darjeeling, for nearly, two years witnessed violence like it had not seen before. The CPM was able to retain its hold over some tea garden areas and particularly in Bijanbari area. But the GNLF movement snowballed. Even the lone Gorkha League MLA from Kalimpong resigned. The hills were literally on fire. Normal life remained disrupted for nearly three years.

From the beginning of 1987 negotiations among the state and central governments and the GNLF started. After protracted negotiations and some hard bargaining by all the sides a consensus emerged that favoured the creation of an elected hill council. Several subjects would be transferred from the state to the council which would enjoy autonomy. Finance would come from state and central funds, routed through the state. The nomenclature of the council that was finally agreed upon by all sides was the Darjeeling Gorkha Hill Council (DGHC). Twelve *mouzas* between Sukna and Lohagarh in Siliguri sub-division would be transferred to the council. The agreement was finally signed on 22 August 1988.

Thus was fulfilled the long search for a separate identity in Darjeeling. Three years of militancy and violence achieved what constitutional agitation could not in nearly a century. Thus Ghising's phenomenal rise was crowned with success, though at the end of the day he had to be content with nothing more than the old demand of regional autonomy. It is possible to argue that Ghising displayed political wisdom in accepting what appeared to be in the realm of possibility, perhaps deferring his original agenda. He abandoned his demand for a separate state, though such a demand was periodically renewed, particularly when a conflict arose over the implementation or interpretation of the accord of 1988. The other demands about citizenship, the Indo-Nepal treaty and the Indian Gorkha regiment were also relegated to the background.

The accord of 1988 produced a shift in the politics of Darjeeling as well. The CPI(M) was split and the splinter group in the hills, the Communist Party Revolutionary Marxist (CPRM), now supports the demand for a separate state, though these were the people who fought Ghising very hard during the GNLF movement. The Congress, the AIGL and other smaller parties have been virtually marginalized. Efforts to put up a united front against the GNLF have not succeeded so far.

VI

The DGHC Act (Act XIII of 1988)[31] provided the institutional framework for regional autonomy for Darjeeling. This called for certain changes in the existing framework, like the abolition of the Zilla Parishad. A separate Mahakuma Parishad was set up for Siliguri, but the municipalities and the panchayat institutions in Darjeeling were brought under the general supervision of the DGHC. The older Hill Development Council and the District Planning and Coordination Committee were also merged with the DGHC.

The DGHC has a general council and an executive council. The general council consists of 28 elected and 14 nominated members. It is strange that a provision was made for the nomination of one-third members. The nominated councillors may include the MPs, MLAs and chairmen of the municipalities in the area. Members of the Scheduled Castes and Scheduled Tribes and women may also be represented. An amendment of the Act in 1994 provided for the nomination of three of such members by the chairman. This provision may have proved to be satisfactory for all concerned. Yet, one suspects that it is a reflection of the anxiety of the state to exercise effective control over the council through the principle of nomination. Ghising did express an apprehension that the nomination of the executive councillors showed that the 'state government is hell bent to exercise control over the council from outside'. He called the nominated members 'watchdog of the state government'.[32] The decisions were still taken on the basis of consensus as far as practicable, according to Ghising. The chairman is virtually the chief minister of the hill areas of Darjeeling.

The exercise of regional autonomy is dependent on the

---

[31] DGHC Act (Act XIII of 1988), corrected up to 1 January 1997, Hill Affairs Department, Government of West Bengal.

[32] Interview with Subash Ghising, quoted in Sarkar and Bhaumik, op. cit., pp. 40–4.

powers and functions of the council as much as on the resources available to it. The Act of 1988, as amended up to 1994, transferred twenty subjects to the jurisdiction of the council. Besides, the state government may by notification place under the control and administration of the general council any other matter. The council shall also be responsible for (*i*) formulation of integrated development plans for the district, and (*ii*) implementation of the programmes for the development of the hill areas.

Initially, the functioning of the council was not smooth as the chairman complained of 'a lack of political will and commitment on the part of the state government to implement decentralization at DGHC level'.[33] He even submitted a memorandum to the Union Home Minister asking for the formation of an Appraisal Committee consisting of the representatives of the central and state governments and of the DGHC to review the issue of transfer of power.[34]

Adequate financial resources are a *sine qua non* for effective functioning of the council. There are three principal sources of finance: assigned revenue, shared revenue and grants-in-aid. The last would mean state and central assistance. The DGHC is also charged with the formulation and implementation of the development plans for the areas under the jurisdiction of the council, often in collaboration with the agencies of the state and central governments. Since the DGHC can hardly be expected to generate a significant amount of revenue from the sources assigned to it, it has to depend largely on grants from the central and state governments.

There had not been a steady flow of fund from these sources initially. For example, central assistance for tourism was not available between 1988 and 1991, but the grant for the next three years had been 6, 10 and 5 lakh of rupees respectively. Such grants were arbitrary and not based on the needs of tourism in Darjeeling. Likewise, allocation under the state plan varied from 15 crore for 1991–2 to 32 lakh for 1992–3. On the other hand, the total grant from the state and central sources under EAS for

[33] Ibid., p. 43.
[34] Ibid.

the year 1994-5 could not be spent.[35] There is also the problem of meeting the growing non-plan expenditure. But this is a problem faced by the central and state governments in India and is not unique to DGHC. These problems were gradually sorted out and something of an equilibrium exists for the present. It is the perception of the state finance minister, Asim Dasgupta, that finance does not pose a major problem now.[36] Differences have been settled and the flow of funds has been satisfactory. As a result the DGHC has been able to pursue its development efforts.

Yet, some basic problems remain. One of them is the perennial financial constraint. This is likely to produce situations of confrontation in the future. The DGHC does resent that two of the most lucrative sources of revenue—tea and timber—remain outside its ambit.

Institutional arrangements under the Act (of 1988) embodies elements drawn from constitutional provisions of Autonomous state (Art 244A) and sixth schedule without any improvement whatsoever. There exists a number of areas which are not clearly defined.... The Autonomous district councils under the sixth schedule are vested with law making powers subject to the assent of the governor, but such power has been denied to the DGHC. In other words, DGHC remains as a contrived structure not with adequate finances and functions.[37]

There was conflict over the holding of elections to the panchayats, but this was also resolved, clearly revealing an willingness on the part of both the parties to live and let live.

After more than a decade of functioning the DGHC, it may not be unfair to suggest, has been able to overcome the hiccoughs and some sort of *modus vivendi* between the state government and the council has been achieved. It would have been natural for this experiment to take some time to acquire roots, but given the political will to achieve this it would be realistic to expect it to survive, even flourish. The unquiet hills are quiet again. After 1989 there has not been a major law and

---

[35] Ibid., p. 83.
[36] Interview with the author.
[37] Sarkar and Bhaumik, op. cit., p. 75.

Identity, Movements and Peace | 279

order problem. The long quest for autonomy has met with success. The Gorkha identity and its association with Darjeeling has been established by the name of the council. The three elections to the DGHC have returned the GNLF members with an overwhelming majority. Among the national and other regional parties, only CPI(M) has been able to retain some foothold in the council. The united front of some other parties failed to dislodge the GNLF in the latest election held in 1999.

But certain basic questions relating to identity raised by the GNLF have not been resolved. They appear to have been dropped for the moment, but Ghising has neither totally disclaimed the demand for a separate state nor has he totally given up other demands. A DGHC pamphlet in 1996 raised some of these issues again.

Until and unless the Art. VII of the Indo-Nepal treaty is erased it is impossible to incorporate the ceded land of Darjeeling in the Indian Union . . . until and unless the Indo-Bhutan treaty of 1949 is rectified the leasehold lands of Kalimpong, western Dooars and Assam Dooars cannot be incorporated in the Indian Union.[38]

This perception is not shared either by the state or the central governments, yet the issue is kept alive as a political bait. One reads in the newspapers report about an occasional claim to ultimate sovereign status and decision to issue separate currency and postage stamp. If there is more than idle wishful thinking in this, the DGHC is unlikely to provide a permanent solution to the problem of identity in Darjeeling. The entire area is strategically sensitive and the politics of Nepal and Bhutan may have the impact of internationalizing the issue. After all, Ghising did write to many heads of state and even the Secretary-General of the UNO during the GNLF movement.

I have tried, in this paper, to understand the question of identity in terms of the history of Darjeeling and the evolution of a separate Gorkha or Nepali identity in this area. The aspirations to have a separate administrative framework in Darjeeling may have been met by the DGHC. Conversely, such identity can have satisfaction only with the establishment of a new state.

[38] Quoted in ibid., pp. 104–5.

One feels the question cannot be resolved unless a more clear conceptual understanding of the role of the ethno-linguistic minorities in the making of the Indian nation emerges. It is also linked up with the nature of Indian federalism. For, demands of statehood, if conceded in one place, cannot be postponed in other places for all time to come. Thus peace may conceivably be disturbed again. For the present at least, the first decade of DGHC does give some hope. It has ended the confrontation and brought peace back to Darjeeling; it may well preserve it for a long time, given the political will on all sides. The question of identity is another matter. The responsibility for establishing such identity rests as much on the centre as on the periphery.

I am grateful to Professor Dipankar Basu for providing me with some valuable materials.

Perspectives of the Indus Waters Treaty

K. Warikoo

The Indus Waters Treaty was signed by India and Pakistan in September 1960 after more than eight years of negotiations to resolve the dispute over the usage for irrigation and hydel power of the waters of the Indus water system. It is the treaty quite some time now that has been publicly denounced by the Jammu and Kashmir government for being 'discriminatory' to the Indian state of Jammu and Kashmir.[1] The state government has been contending that in spite of having an untapped hydro-electric potential of 15,000 MWs, the state has been suffering from acute power deficiency due to restrictions put on the use of its rivers by the Indus Treaty. And when the chief minister of the state, Dr. Farooq Abdullah, or his officials point to the losses accrued to the state by virtue of this treaty, they are not indulging in any rhetoric. In fact their views that the requirements of the J & K state were not taken into account while negotiating the Treaty with Pakistan are shared largely by the intellectual, the media and public circles in Jammu and Kashmir. Not only that, some people go further in suggesting that the central government has been insensitive to the state's problems. It is against this background that the Indus Waters Treaty is being seen here. That the treaty has been in force for nearly 40 years is ample justification for making an appraisal on whether it has really

[1] Arun Joshi, 'J & K to Denounce Indus Waters Treaty', *Hindustan Times*, 19 December 1998.

served the larger purpose of bringing India-Pakistan amity and cooperation on other fronts.

The Indus Basin

The Indus system of rivers comprises the main river Indus, known as the river Sindhu in Sanskrit, and its five tributaries from the east, the Jhelum, Chenab, Ravi, Sutlej and the Beas, and three tributaries from the west, the Kabul, Swat and the Kurram rivers.[2] The great Indus river is 2880 km. long and the length of its tributaries as mentioned above is 5600 km.[3] Historically, India has been named after this great river. The main Indus river rises in Tibet and after flowing through the Indian state of Jammu and Kashmir enters Pakistan. The river Jhelum originates in Verinag in the valley of Kashmir and enters Pakistan. The Chenab river rises in Lahaul in Himachal Predesh state of India and after flowing through Jammu province enters Pakistan. The Ravi river rises near Kulu in Himachal Pradesh and flowing through Punjab enters Pakistan. The Sutlej rises in Tibet and flows through Punjab before entering Pakistan. River Beas rises in Himachal Pradesh and flows wholly within India. The Kabul and Kurram rivers rise in Afghanistan. The Kabul river is joined by the waters of the Swat in Peshawar valley.

Though the Indus basin is known to have practised irrigation since ancient times, it was the British who developed an elaborate network of canals in the Indus system of rivers. However, their emphasis was that lands belonging to the Crown should receive such irrigation so that the British Indian government would earn revenue from water cess as well as from the sale of crown wastelands.[4] In this manner, the Indus system waters were used to irrigate annually about 23.4 million acres in the Indus plains and 2.6 million acres above the rim stations before Partition.[5]

[2] Rushbrook Williams, 'The Indus Canals Water Dispute', *Leader*, Allahabad, 5 June 1955; S.K. Garg, *International and Interstate River Water Disputes*, New Delhi, 1999, p. 79; N.D. Gulhati, *Indus Waters Treaty: An Exercise in International Mediation*, Bombay: Allied, 1973, pp. 18, 24.
[3] S.K. Garg, op. cit., p. 79.
[4] Rushbrook Williams, op. cit.
[5] N.D. Gulhati, op. cit., p. 39.

PARTITION AND ITS AFTERMATH

The immediate aftermath of the partition of the Indian subcontinent and the creation of two Dominions of India and Pakistan in 1947 was that the bulk of the irrigation canals developed on the Indus system went to Pakistan. Out of 26 million acres of land irrigated annually by the Indus canals, 21 million acres lay in Pakistan and only 5 million acres in India.[6] As per the 1941 census, the population dependent on the Indus system waters was 25 million in Pakistan and 21 million in India.[7] Besides, India had 'another 35 million acres of lands crying out for irrigation from the Indus basin sources'.[8] Thus the partition gave independent India much less undeveloped area in spite of the fact that it was an upstream country with control over Ravi, Beas, Sutlej, Jhelum and Chenab. India had not only to cater to the food requirements of 21 million people but also those millions who migrated from irrigated areas in West Punjab and Bahawalpur, now in Pakistan, all of whom were dependent on the Indus waters.

The dispute over sharing of Indus waters came to the fore immediately after Partition because the existing canal headworks of Upper Bari Doab Canal (UBDC) and Sutlej Valley canals fell in India (state of East Punjab), while the lands being irrigated by their waters fell in Pakistan (West Punjab and Bahawalpur state). In order to maintain and run the existing systems as before Partition, two Standstill Agreements were signed on 20 December 1947 by the Chief Engineers of East Punjab and West Punjab. These interim arrangements were to expire on 31 March 1948, after which East Punjab started asserting its rights on its waters. It was on 1 April 1948 that the East Punjab Government, in control of the headworks at Madhopur on the Ravi and at Ferozpur on the Sutlej, cut off water supplies to the canals in Pakistan fed by these headworks, after the Standstill agreements expired on 31 March 1948. In fact, East Punjab had formally notified West Punjab on 29 March 1948 that the 'Standstill Agreements' would expire on 31 March, and had accordingly invited

[6] Ibid., p. 59.
[7] Ibid.
[8] Rushbrook Williams, op. cit.

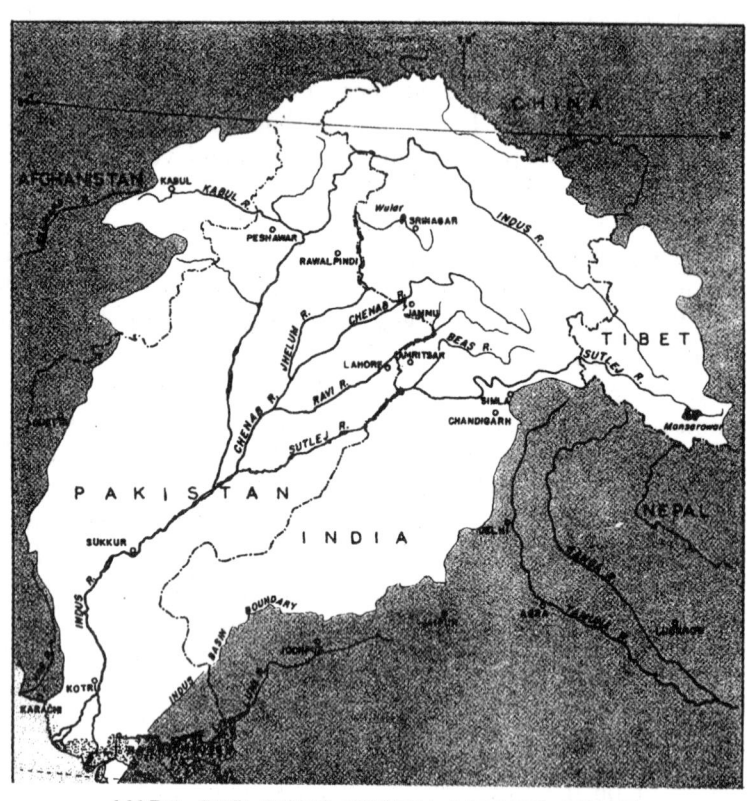

MAP 1: THE INDUS REGION (NOT TO SCALE)

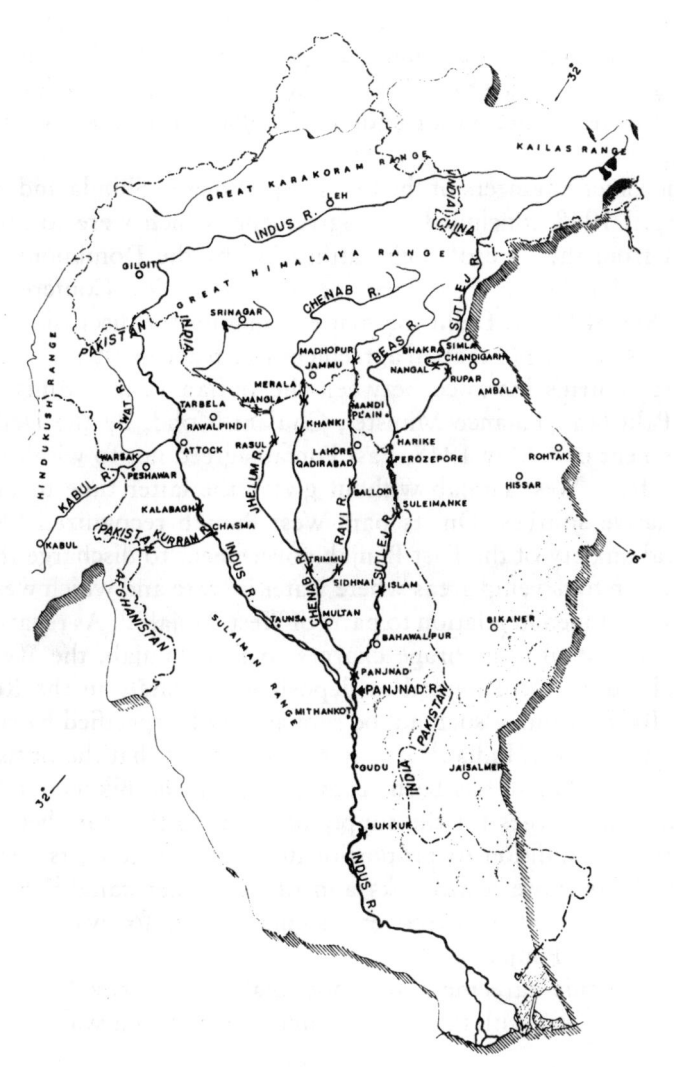

MAP 2: THE INDUS BASIN (NOT TO SCALE)

the Chief Engineers of West Punjab to Shimla for negotiating an agreement for resumption of water supplies.[9] According to Rushbrook Williams, the water supplies were cut because 'the canal colonies in Pakistan served by these headworks did not pay the standard water dues. The people incharge of the head works were applying exactly the same kind of sanction that they would have applied in an undivided India—no canal dues, no water'.[10]

The Chief Engineers of the two Punjabs met in Shimla and on 18 April 1948 concluded two agreements which were to take effect from the date of their ratification by the Dominions of India and Pakistan. Finally at the inter-Dominion Conference on 3 May 1948 at Delhi the matter came up for discussion. It was on 4 May 1948 that an agreement was reached after a meeting at Nehru's instance between the Indian Prime Minister and Pakistan's Finance Minister, Ghulam Mohd. By the Delhi Agreement of 4 May 1948, East Punjab agreed not to withhold water from West Punjab without giving the latter time to tap alternative sources. On its part West Punjab recognized 'the natural anxiety of the East Punjab government to discharge the obligation to develop areas where water is scare and which were underdeveloped in relation to parts of West Punjab'.[11] As regards the payment of seigniorage charges to East Punjab, the West Punjab government agreed to deposit immediately in the Reserve Bank of India 'such adhoc sum as may be specified by the Prime Minister of India'.[12] It may be pointed out that the British Province of Punjab has been recovering from the Bikaner state seigniorage charges for the supply of water to the state before Partition in addition to proportionate maintenance costs, etc., of the Ferozepore headworks and of the feeder canal.[13] East Punjab now wanted to recover a similar charge for water supplied to West Punjab.

Though this agreement was not final, it did provide some basis for dealing with the vexed problem. But soon it was found

[9] N.D. Gulhati, op. cit., pp. 64–5.
[10] Rushbrook Williams, op. cit.
[11] N.D. Gulhati, op. cit., p. 69.
[12] Ibid.
[13] Ibid., p. 68.

that Pakistan was unwilling to stick to the agreement, as it was seeking to use the Indus Water dispute as a political tool in the battle over Kashmir being fought at the United Nations. Pakistan also sought to create anti-India hysteria in Pakistan over this issue. As such Pakistan unilaterally abrogated the May 1948 Agreement saying that it was signed 'under duress'.[14] Besides, Pakistan refused to pay the dues to India even after a year of the agreement.[15] Pakistan now asked for a reference to the International Court of Justice for a final verdict, which was objected to by India. Pakistani media and politicians launched a campaign over the issue of canal waters dispute to create a scenario of serious crisis in Indo-Pakistani relations. All along, Pakistan's policy was to seek third party adjudication, which India was opposing.

The Lilienthal Proposal and World Bank Initiative

It was in this atmosphere of mutual distrust and contrived tensions, that David E. Lilienthal, formerly Chairman of the Tenessee Valley Authority and the U.S. Atomic Energy Commission visited India and Pakistan in February 1951 on a supposedly private visit. Before embarking upon this visit Lilienthal had met the then U.S. President Truman, the U.S. Secretary of State, Dean Acheson, Pakistan's Foreign Minister, M. Zafrulla Khan and Secretary General of Pakistan's Delegation to the U.N., Muhammad Ali.[16] While in India, Lilienthal was a guest of Prime Minister Nehru and he also held talks with Sheikh Abdullah on Kashmir. In Pakistan, Lilienthal discussed Kashmir and the 'economic warfare' between India and Pakistan with Prime Minister Liaquat Ali Khan. Liaquat Ali was reported to have told Lilienthal that 'unless the Kashmir issue is settled it is unreal to try to settle the issues about water or about evacuees'.[17] On his return to America, Lilienthal wrote an article titled 'Another

[14] Sisir Gupta, 'The Indus Waters Treaty, 1960', *Foreign Affairs Reports*, vol. 9, no. 12, December 1960.
[15] Ibid.
[16] N.D. Gulhati, op. cit., p. 92.
[17] Ibid., p. 93.

"Korea" in the Making' analysing the Indo-Pakistani relations. He prefaced his article with a loaded comment:

> India and Pakistan are on the edge of war over which shall possess Kashmir—a fight the U.S. might be forced to enter.... The direct issue is whether the historic region of Kashmir and Jammu shall be part of India or Pakistan. On one of this disputed region's frontiers lies Red China, on another Red Tibet. Along another frontier is Soviet Russia.[18]

Explaining the importance of the Indus waters for ensuring food security to millions of people in India and Pakistan, Lilienthal proposed that the canal waters dispute could be solved by India and Pakistan by working out a programme jointly to develop and operate the Indus basin river system. He wrote:

> Jointly financed (perhaps with World Bank help) an Indus Engineering Corporation, with representation by technical men of India, Pakistan and the World Bank, can readily work out an operating scheme for storing water wherever dams can best store it, and for diverting and distributing water.[19]

Lilienthal, who appeared to be concerned about the presence of Communist China and Soviet Union on the borders of Kashmir, was hoping to become the head of the proposed Indus Engineering Corporation.[20] Whereas Lilienthal sent copies of his article to the Indian Ambassador and the Pakistani Counsel on the water dispute, he also pursued the proposal with the U.S. State Department.

Interestingly, around the same time, Eugene R. Black, then President of the International Bank for Reconstruction and Development, Washington (World Bank) and a close friend of David Lilienthal[21] became interested in the Lilienthal proposal. In September 1951, the World Bank formally offered its good

---

[18] David Lilienthal, 'Another "Korea" in the Making', *Colliers Magazine*, 4 August 1951.
[19] Ibid.
[20] N.D. Gulhati, op. cit., p. 445.
[21] G.T. Keith Pitman, 'The Role of the World Bank in Enhancing Co-operation and Resolving Conflict on International Watercourses: The Case of the Indus Basin', in *International Water Courses: Enhancing*

offices to both India and Pakistan to work out a solution to the Indus waters issue on the basis of the Lilienthal proposals. The World Bank offer was conditioned by the 'essential principle' that 'the problem of development and use of Indus Basin water resources should be solved on a functional and not a political plan, without relations to past negotiations and past claims, and independently of political issues'.[22] Both countries accepted the suggestion after the World Bank President, Eugene R. Black, personally met both the Indian and Pakistani prime ministers. By May 1952 the first of a long series of conferences opened at Washington which were continued at Karachi and Delhi. But it soon became clear that Lilienthal's proposal of a joint Indus Engineering Corporation could not be realised. Instead, it was found necessary to replace the existing supplies from alternative sources. So in February 1954 the World Bank officials proposed to India and Pakistan the division of rivers.

The three eastern rivers (Ravi, Beas and Sutlej) would be available for the exclusive use and benefit of India, after a specified transitionary period. The Western rivers (Indus, Jhelum and Chenab) would be available for the exclusive use and benefit of Pakistan, except for the insignificant volume of Jhelum flow presently used in Kashmir.... Each country would construct the works located on its own territories which are planned for the development of the supplies. The costs of such works would be borne by the country to be benefitted thereby.[23]

Whereas India accepted the World Bank proposals, in spite of its sacrifices, Pakistan vacillated and accepted 'in principle' only after the Bank pressed her for a reply. In his letter of 22 March 1954 to the World Bank president, the prime minister of India while conveying his general acceptance to the principles governing the Bank proposals as the basis of agreement stressed that 'the actual agreement which would be worked out with the assistance of the Bank authorities will naturally deal with a number of details including the question of the small require-

---

Cooperation and Managing Conflict, ed. M.A. Salman and Laurence Boisson de Chazournes, Washington, World Bank Technical Paper, no. 414, p. 159.
[22] Ibid., p. 160.
[23] Gulhati, op. cit., p. 137.

ments of Jammu and Kashmir'.[24] On the other hand, Pakistan continued to ask for clarification of details and further technical studies, thereby taking several years in the negotiations.

India's acceptance of the World Bank proposals was based on the hope that in five years' time India would be able to make use of the waters of the eastern rivers. This was, however, frustrated by Pakistani procrastination. Pakistan was seeking a comprehensive replacement-cum-development programme in Pakistan involving high investment of about 1.12 billion US dollars.[25] And in 1959 the World Bank, USA and certain Western countries were ready to foot the bill for this huge construction programme in Pakistan, so that the vexed canal waters dispute between India and Pakistan could be solved. It was on 1 March 1960 that the World Bank made a public announcement of the financial plan it had evolved for the replacement and development works of the Indus system. It was estimated to cost about 1000 million dollars (partly in foreign exchange and partly in local currencies). The Bank announced that the requisite expenditure would be contributed by Australia, Canada, New Zealand, Germany, United Kingdom, United States, the World Bank besides the contributions by India and Pakistan. Ironically as it may sound, the bulk of this financial plan was meant to be spent in Pakistan (691 million dollars out of 747 million of grants and loans with India getting only 56 million dollars as loan for the Beas Dam, as against Pakistan getting all her development underwritten by the Bank's financial plan).[26] Besides, the World Bank press release did not mention the additional US grant of 235 million dollars (in local currency).[27] Yet, India stuck to its commitment to conclude the Indus Waters Treaty based on the World Bank proposals. And the treaty was duly signed on 19 September 1960 at Karachi by Jawaharlal Nehru, the prime minister of India, President Ayub Khan of Pakistan and W.A.B. Iliss of the World Bank.

[24] Cited in ibid., p. 147.
[25] A.G.T. Keith Pitman, op. cit., p. 161.
[26] Gulhati, op. cit., pp. 277–8.
[27] Ibid.

The Treaty

The main features of the Treaty are as follows:[28]

1. The waters of the three eastern rivers—the Ravi, the Beas and the Sutlej—would be available for unrestricted use by India, after a transition period.
2. The waters of the three western rivers—the Indus, the Jhelum and the Chenab—would be allowed to flow for unrestricted use by Pakistan except for some limited use such as (a) domestic use, (b) non-consumptive use, (c) agricultural use, (d) generation of hydro-electric power (run-of-river-plants) in Kashmir.
3. During the transition period of ten years, India would continue to give Pakistan some supplies from the eastern rivers, in accordance with detailed regulations set out in the Treaty. The period may be extended at Pakistan's request up to a maximum of another three years. If so extended, India would deduct from its contribution Rs. 4.16 crore for one year's extension and Rs. 8.54 crore for two years' extension and Rs. 13.13 crore if the extension is sought for three years.
4. Pakistan would build works in the transition period to replace, from the western rivers and other sources, waters she used to get in her canals from the eastern rivers.
5. Non-consumptive use, domestic use, etc., would be permitted in all the rivers by both the countries, but such use should not in any way affect the flow of rivers and channels, to be used by the other party.
6. India would contribute in ten equal annual instalments the fixed sum of Pounds Sterling 6,20,60,000 to the Indus Basin Development Fund towards the cost of replacement works in Pakistan.
7. Both countries have recognized their common interest in the optimum development of the rivers, and declared their intention to cooperate by mutual agreement to the fullest possible extent.

[28] For full text and annexures see ibid., pp. 373–410.

8. The two countries would regularly exchange data regarding the flow in and utilization of waters of the rivers.
9. A Permanent Indus Commission would be constituted with the Commissioners for Indus Waters of the two countries— a post which should be filled by a high-ranking engineer competent in the field of hydrology and water use. Each Commissioner will be the representative of his Government for consideration of all matters arising out of the Treaty. The purpose and functions of the Indus Commission would be 'to establish and maintain cooperative arrangements for the implementation of this Treaty and to promote co-operation in the matter of development of the rivers'.
10. If the Indus Commission fails to reach agreement on any matter pertaining to the Treaty it would be referred to a Neutral Expert. If the difference is in the nature of a dispute and the Neutral Expert certifies it to be so, the matter would be dealt with by the two Governments and might be referred to a Court of Arbitration.
11. Nothing contained in the Treaty, and nothing arising out of the execution thereof shall be construed as constituting a recognition or waiver (whether tacit, by implication or otherwise) of any rights or claims whatsoever of either of the parties.

CRITICAL REVIEW

The Indus Treaty was signed by Nehru in the fervent hope of ushering all round improvement in India-Pakistan relations and resolution of all outstanding problems including Kashmir. Perhaps Nehru was impressed by Ayub's offer of joint defence with India made in early 1959 in the wake of deteriorating India-China relations.[29] Ayub's offer, however, needed to be viewed in the light of Pakistan being a member of SEATO and CENTO, which made him susceptible to Western prescriptions for regional peace and cooperation. At that time the US and its friendly Western nations viewed the Communist Block—USSR and China— as a greater threat. Although India did not accept the concept of

[29] *Dawn*, 25 April 1959.

joint defence, it sought to improve relations with Pakistan by agreeing to substantially pay for the cost of irrigation programmes in Pakistan, besides surrendering the use of three western rivers. India treated the Indus waters issue as a technical and engineering problem. On the other hand, Pakistan exploited it as a political weapon in her Cold War against India. At the same time Pakistan succeeded in extracting huge financial assistance of about one billion dollars from the World Bank, USA and other Western countries, using the geopolitical environment in the region to its advantage.

Nehru went to Karachi on 19 September 1960 to sign the treaty hoping to begin a new chapter in the history of Indo-Pak relations. Though the joint communique issued at the end of Nehru-Ayub talks on 23 September 1960, revealed little progress on Kashmir, both sides agreed to work for promotion of friendly and cooperative relations and resolve the outstanding differences. However, Pakistan did not hide its disappointment that there was no progress over Kashmir. The Pakistani press continued to harp on the theme of 'free and impartial plebiscite to determine the choice of the people of Kashmir'.[30] The Indian press meted highlighted the positive aspects of the joint communique. The *Times of India* even suggested that, 'in the interests of a lasting settlement this country may be prepared eventually to accept the status quo in the State and agree to slight changes in the present cease-fire line to make it a viable international frontier'.[31] Hardly a month had lapsed after Nehru's visit to Karachi, that President Ayub of Pakistan, at a public meeting in Muzaffrabad (Pak occupied Kashmir) in early October 1960, declared that 'Pakistan could not trust India until the Kashmir question was settled and that the Pak army could never afford to leave the Kashmir issue unsolved for an indefinite period'.[32] In this way Indian hopes of building up mutual trust and confidence with Pakistan were belied. What followed is too well known to be repeated. Pakistan launched Operation Gibralter in 1965 to wrest Kashmir. There was yet another war in 1971 and ever since 1989 Pakistan

[30] Ibid., 19 September 1960.
[31] *Times of India*, 30 September 1960.
[32] *Dawn*, 6 October 1960.

has been engaged in a deadly proxy war against India in Kashmir and elsewhere. More recently India had to encounter the Pakistani armed intrusion in Kargil. As such Nehru's assertion in the Lok Sabha on 30 November 1960 that 'we purchased a settlement, if you like; we purchased peace to that extent and it is good for both countries',[33] was not borne out by the subsequent events. Members of Parliament belonging to both the Congress, PSP and Jana Sangh pointed to the glaring mistakes committed in the conclusion of this treaty. Congress MPs from Punjab and Rajasthan, Iqbal Singh and H.C. Mathur called the treaty disadvantageous to India stating that both their home states 'had been badly let down'.[34] Ashok Guha, another Congress MP, lamented that the 'interests of India had been sacrificed to placate Pakistan'. Ashok Mehta, the leader of the PSP in the Lok Sabha described it as a 'peculiar treaty under which Pakistan, already a surplus area, would be unable to make full use of her share of the Indus Water and would have to allow it to flow into the sea. On the contrary, India after the fullest development of the water resources, would still be short of supplies'.[35] But Nehru's efforts at creating goodwill and understanding with Pakistan by giving concessions through the Indus Treaty, did not bear fruit. That Nehru himself realized this soon after, is confirmed by N.D. Gulhati, who led the Indian delegation during the negotiations over Indus. Gulhati recalls: 'When I called on the Prime Minister on 28 February 1961, my last day in office, in a sad tone he said, "Gulhati, I had hoped that this agreement would open the way to settlement on other problems, but we are where we were".'[36]

In retrospect, it can be stated that India was too generous to Pakistan, both in terms of allowing use of the waters of the western rivers and by making a payment of more than 62 million pounds sterling (i.e. about Rs. 430 crore in current value) to Pakistan. It is also surprising why the World Bank advanced such disproportionate proposals to India, 'particularly when the

[33] Cited in *Indian Express*, 1 December 1960.
[34] Ibid.
[35] Ibid.
[36] Gulhati, op. cit., p. 345.

eastern rivers given to India carried 20 to 25 per cent of the total flow of the Indus Basin as against the 75 to 80 per cent in the three western rivers allocated to Pakistan'.[37] Out of the total annual flow of 168.4 million acre feet (m.a.f.) of water in the Indus system of rivers, the total requirement for irrigation water was 96.36 m.a.f. for the entire cultivable area of the Indus basin, thereby leaving a surplus of 72.02 m.a.f. of water which would be going to the sea. Since the cultivable area on the three eastern rivers was 22.856 million acres, little less than on the western rivers (25.100 million acres), the mean annual supplies made available by the eastern rivers was only 32.8 m.a.f., that is 13.57 m.a.f. less than the actual water requirement of 46.37 m.a.f. In stark contrast to this, the mean annual flow in western rivers was 135.6 m.a.f., i.e. 85.59 m.a.f. more than its requirement of only 50.01 m.a.f. of water. It is quite intriguing as to why the Indian government delegation involved in the prolonged negotiations over Indus waters, agreed to much lower share of water available in the eastern rivers, particularly when the concerned officials were in the know of the facts.[38] However, it appears that the Jammu and Kashmir government, particularly its irrigation and power development departments, had not done their homework of studying and quantifying the existing and future water requirements for irrigation, hydel power generation and other uses inside Jammu and Kashmir. As such the Indian delegation failed to secure the necessary safeguards in the treaty for future consumption of water for hydel power purposes, excepting by run-of-the-river methods. Gulhati himself admits that 'since no study had ever been made until then, of the development locally possible, above the rim stations, none of us had, at that time, any real idea of the quantum of future developments in the upper reaches of the western Rivers. Nor did we

[37] S.K. Garg, op. cit., p. 85.
[38] A.N. Khosla, former Chairman of the Central Water and Power Commission who was responsible for water resources development including the Indus dispute, published details of the Indus basin and water flow in various Indus rivers two years before the agreement was signed. See his 'Development of the Indus River System: An Engineering Approach', *India Quarterly*, vol. 14, no. 3, July-Sept. 1958, pp. 234–53.

have any idea of the irrigation from the Indus in Ladakh. As regards hydro-electric development we felt that, being a nonconsumptive use, it was not covered by the Bank proposal which dealt only with irrigation uses'.[39] Moreover, it is not the number of rivers but the quantum of water which was to be distributed. Besides, the World Bank did not include the Kabul river while dividing the six rivers among the two countries.

If we consider the internationally accepted Helsinki Rules framed by the International Law Association which postulate the equitable utilization of waters of an international drainage basin—taking into consideration various factors such as the extent of the drainage area, hydrology of the basin, economic and social needs of each basin state, population dependent on the waters of the basin, avoidance of unnecessary waste in utilization of waters of the basin—then India did not get a fair deal. According to S.K. Garg, who has computed the respective entitlement of India and Pakistan on the basis of the population, drainage areas, length of rivers and culturable area, India should have been given 42.8 per cent share in the waters of the Indus Basin, as against the actual allocation of 20 to 25 per cent, flowing in the three eastern rivers.[40]

It may be worthwhile to mention that in a somewhat similar problem of water distribution that occurred in Central Asia after the disintegration of the USSR, the Inter State Commission for Water Coordination amongst the Central Asian countries has been regulating the allocation, consumption and exchange of water for natural gas, coal, oil or their monetary equivalent. For instance, as per existing agreements, Kyrgyzstan released from Toktogul reservoir to Kazakhstan and Uzbekistan 3.25 ckm of water for each country in exchange of 1.1 billion kWh of power (either electricity or coal) valued at 22 million dollars from Kazakhstan and 400 million kWh of power (electricity) plus 500 million m^3 of natural gas valued at 48.5 million dollars per year from Uzbekistan.[41] Besides, agreements were worked out

---

[39] Gulhati, op. cit., p. 149.
[40] S.K. Garg, op. cit., p. 85.
[41] USAID, Central Asia Mission, *Energy and Water Round Table: Analysis and Preparation for September 8–12, 1997 Meeting*, 22 August 1997.

for supporting the operation of Toktogul reservoir in Kyrgyzstan in the irrigation mode out of compensation payable to Kyrgyzstan. All parties agreed to be guarantors for compensation and monetary exchanges.

It becomes clear that the Indian state of Jammu and Kashmir in spite of being the upstream area, has suffered due to restrictions placed by the treaty on the unhindered usage of its river waters (of Jhelum, Chenab and Indus). The irony of the matter is that the state, being rich in its hydel resources, has been facing a perennial problem of shortage of hydro-electric power, more particularly during the winter months and due to the dry spell in the valley. Power generation goes down drastically due to the considerably low levels of the river Jhelum. For instance, the run-of-the-river Uri Hydel Project, built at a cost of more than 800 million US dollars, is currently producing only 70 MW as against the 480 MW installed capacity.[42] Since the Indus Treaty does not allow building of storage dams which could ensure the provision of requisite water flow, these high cost hydel projects generate electricity much below their installed capacity. As such the state is unable to meet its demand of about 700 MWs, even after importing 230 MWs of power from the northern grid.[43]

Similarly, work on the construction of Tulbul Navigation Project started by the Jammu and Kashmir government in 1984 in order to raise the level of water in the Wullar lake for facilitating transport on the river Jhelum, was stopped in 1987 after objections were raised by Pakistan.[44] Whereas the Tulbul Project cannot diminish or change the flow of water to Pakistan, it can keep the Jhelum river navigable for a considerable stretch thereby bringing economic benefits to the people in the valley. It is therefore understandable that there has been growing concern and anger in Jammu and Kashmir over the negative consequences of the Indus Treaty for the state. Both the official and public circles

---

[42] Shujaat Bukhari, 'Serious Power Shortage Stalks J & K', *The Hindu* 18 January 2000.

[43] Ibid.; Rashid Ahmad, 'Incessant Power Cut takes Valley into Dark Age', *Pioneer*, 21 January 2000.

[44] Bharat Bhushan, 'India-Pakistan Talks: Tulbul Navigation Project', *Hindustan Times*, 5 November 1998.

in the state have been pleading for a review of this treaty, so that the legitimate water requirements of state for hydel power generation, deepening of rivers for navigation purposes, erecting protective bunds for floods, and building adequate water reserves for irrigation are fulfilled.

Yet another associated problem has been the revenue loss of millions of rupees to the state, as a result of the floating of timber logs from Jhelum and Chenab across the LoC into Pak-occupied Kashmir. This author learnt from some responsible officials of some insurance companies operating in the state, that the local timber merchants have been claiming million of rupees of insurance compensation in lieu of their timber losses on this account.

And in Pakistan itself, experience has shown that its portion of Indus basin has been suffering from acute problems of waterlogging and salinity due to excess availability of Indus waters and consequent canal seepage and percolation of excess amount of water. According to a study, in Punjab alone, '5 million ha have already gone out of cultivation due to salinity caused by waterlogging, 690,000 ha are in an advanced stage of deterioration and 2 million ha are affected to a lesser degree'.[45]

To conclude, Indian efforts to buy peace from Pakistan by giving concessions through the Indus Waters Treaty failed miserably. The manner in which the Treaty was negotiated and concluded gives the impression of external pressure group networks having exerted their influence, since huge investments were involved in the construction of big dams and canals. It is a reflection on the functioning of the World Bank which was influenced by the Cold War politics in the region and by the interested construction lobbies. It is also a reminder that outside mediation or arbitration in bilateral disputes between India and Pakistan, as was done by the World Bank in this case, would not lead to a lasting and positive solution based on principles of equitability and just distribution of resources.

---

[45] Masahiro Murakami, *Managing Water for Peace in the Middle East: Alternative Strategies*, Tokyo: United Nations University Press, 1995, p. 52.

The Line of Control in Kashmir

Paula Banerjee

Perry Anderson once commented that in certain circumstances frontiers acquire a mythic significance. This is borne out by the emotions generated during the India-Pakistan conflict over Kargil, when the Line of Control (LoC) in Kashmir became the *mythomoteur* of whole societies in the region. The divide resulted in at least three wars and numerous war-like situations. Between 1999–2000 there were two near wars between India and Pakistan caused over the divide. The situation is particularly alarming because both countries now have nuclear capabilities. Etienne Balibar recently observed that 'borders are no longer the shores of politics but have indeed become ... objects or, let us say more precisely, things within the space of the political itself'.[1] In this paper I contend that borders should be treated as a separate category in any political analysis of relations between India and Pakistan.

Borders and divides form an independent category in politics because every border has its own compulsions and a propensity to create its own history. By designating a line on the map a border cannot be made or stabilized. Speaking of a different border Joya Chatterjee argued that demarcating a border is not merely a technical affair. It is in fact a political process and a border is 'created again and again by a number of agencies on

---

[1] Etienne Balibar, 'The Borders of Europe', in Peng Cheah and Bruce Robbins, ed., *Cosmo-politics: Thinking and Feeling Beyond the Nation*, Minneapolis/London, 1998, p. 220.

the ground through which it runs'.[2] But once demarcated a border can become ideologically sacrosanct even while remaining politically unstable, thereby containing seeds of dissensions, conflict and change. I argue, that this is what happened to the Line of Control in Kashmir. In their efforts to stabilize the LoC, the powers disregarded the politics of borders and converted a provisional cartographic expression into an ideological baggage. Politically the line remained unstable, with control being the only justification for its presence. Control cannot be maintained unless it is visibly justified. A show of force is necessary to portray control. If a line is legitimized only through control then it contains potentials for further violence. This and not the inherent 'malevolence' of the powers sharing this line has made a Siachen, a Kargil or even an Akhnoor probable and possible.[3]

Kashmir is a region with tremendous geo-strategic consequences. It flanks China to the east and north-east and Afghanistan to the north-west. It is contiguous with the Tajik Republic, which formed part of the Soviet Union. Historically the region was of great security and concern for the British Indian government. There are numerous passes in the Karakoram mountains that link it to China. From Ladakh the region is linked to Tibet. It is in this region that the LoC is located. The location of the LoC has had tremendous political ramifications.

THE BEGINNINGS OF A TENUOUS CONTROL

In October 1947, a force of invading Pathan tribesmen, with some help from the Pakistani army, crossed over from the north-west frontier and invaded Kashmir. The Hindu Maharaja of this Muslim majority state signed a deed of accession with India to gain India's help in repelling the invaders. Before accepting this accession Pundit Nehru sought the views of Sheikh Abdullah,

---

[2] Joya Chatterjee, 'The Fashioning of a Frontier: The Radcliffe Line and Bengal's Border Landscape, 1947–52', *Modern Asian Studies*, vol. 33, no. 1 (1999), p. 242.
[3] Such views were reflected in Indian and Pakistani newspapers during the conflict in Kargil. See *The Telegraph*, 17 June 1999.

the leader of the National Convention, which was the strongest political party of the state. The next day Indian troops landed in Srinagar and within a short time the situation had escalated into open warfare between India and Pakistan. India internationalized the problem by taking the question of Kashmir to the United Nations on 1 January 1948. A cease-fire line was drawn under the auspices of the United Nations on the same date next year. The line left Pakistan in control of Gilgit, Baltistan and a narrow strip of the western part of the vale of Kashmir, Poonch and Jammu. India occupied Ladakh and the remainder of the vale of Kashmir, Poonch and Jammu. This line more than any other has continued to bedevil Indo-Pakistani relations. Pakistan has traditionally considered this line as temporary and provisional but India desires to give it permanence. The difference in perceptions has led to three wars and numerous near war situations. After the three wars there were efforts to stabilize the line. But the format chosen contained roots of destabilization which further vitiated the relationship.

In the first few years, after the line dividing India and Pakistan was drawn, Pundit Nehru consistently upheld the provisional nature of this line. He reiterated on a number of occasions his desire to refer the issue to the people of Kashmir. On 30 October 1947 he sent a telegram to the Pakistani Prime Minister Liaquat Ali Khan stating that:

> Our assurance that we shall withdraw our troops from Kashmir as soon as peace and order are restored and leave the decision about the future of the State to the people of the State is not merely a pledge to your Government but also to the people of Kashmir and to the world.[4]

In a radio broadcast on 2 November during the trouble over Gilgit, he declared that the people of Kashmir will decide their political future through a plebiscite which may be held under the auspices of the United Nations.[5] That Nehru's sentiments had a wider base is apparent from Sheikh Abdullah's comments that 'the Dominion Government made it clear that once the

---

[4] Quoted in K. Sarwar Hasan (ed.), *Documents on the Foreign Relations of Pakistan: The Kashmir Question*, Karachi, 1966, p. 71.
[5] Ibid., p. 75.

soil of the state had been cleared of the invader and normal conditions were restored, the people would be free to decide their future by recognized democratic method of plebiscite or referendum'.[6]

While speaking on a different border I had argued that this Nehruvian flexibility was born out of India's perception of herself as a world power.[7] In one of his first speeches Nehru had declared that India 'is a great country, great in her resources, great in manpower, great in her potential in every way. I have little doubt that a free India on every plane will play a big part on the world stage, even on the narrowest plane of material power'.[8] In such a scheme of things India had to be responsive to world opinion and flexible over regional issues. For this reason Nehru stressed in his telegram to Liaquat Ali Khan, mentioned earlier, that his pledge to hold a plebiscite in Kashmir was made not only to him and his people but also to the world at large. One of Nehru's biographers has said that Nehru was aware of 'how much India was being judged by her conduct in Kashmir and Hyderabad'.[9] This resulted in greater flexibility towards the question of mediation regarding the cease-fire line. It was reflected in India's attitude towards third party mediation as well. India showed willingness to discuss the issue with representatives of UNCIP be it McNaughton, Dixon or Graham. It was Frank Graham who initiated direct negotiations between India and Pakistan when he declared that:

Instead of the United Nations' representatives continuing to report differences to the Security Council, may the leadership of over 400,000,000 people, with the goodwill and assistance of the United Nations, join in negotiating and reporting an agreement on Kashmir

---

[6] Sheikh Mohammed Abdullah, 'Kashmir, India and Pakistan', *Foreign Affairs*, vol. 43, no. 3 (April 1965), p. 530.

[7] Paula Banerjee, 'Borders as Unsettled Markers in South Asia: A Case Study of the Sino-Indian Border', *International Studies*, vol. 35, no. 2 (1998), p. 183.

[8] Jawaharlal Nehru, *India's Foreign Policy, Selected Speeches, September 1946-April 1961*, New Delhi, 1961, p. 13.

[9] Sarvepalli Gopal, *Jawaharlal Nehru: A Biography*, Oxford, 1989, p. 191.

and thereby light a torch along the difficult path of the people's pilgrimage to peace.[10]

Thus began a period of direct negotiations. This period was marked by Indian flexibility over discussions with Pakistan. For the Indian leaders the region was of little importance. They were making strides towards leadership of the post-colonial world. Pakistan's knee-jerk reactions for defence preparedness spelt out by Liaquat Ali did not alter India's position. On 8 October 1948 Liaquat declared the 'defence of the State is our foremost consideration . . . and has dominated all other governmental activities. We will not grudge any amount on the defence of our country'.[11] Such declarations seemed of little consequence to India as they stemmed from Pakistan's own insecurities. In this initial phase the Indian leadership was confident of its own position. Even the mighty Americans were seeking an alliance with India. However, soon this optimism changed.

It was after Pakistan assumed the role of the most allied ally of the United States that the situation altered. Pakistan became a member of SEATO and signed the Baghdad Pact. In 1955, the Indian prime minister made an offer to Ghulam Muhammad. He asked that the international boundary be stabilized at the cease-fire line. He said that India had no desire to take 'the part of Kashmir which is under you (Pakistan)' by force.[12] The Indian offer may have been made due to the fear that Pakistan might use its military alliance to change the course of the divide and China might accept such changes. Panchsheel notwithstanding, Bandung portrayed that a Sino-Pakistani pact was in the offing. Zhou Enlai went so far as to accept Pakistan's US connections by stating that 'the two countries had achieved a mutual understanding on the question'.[13] Whatever the rationale the Indian leadership felt it was time to consolidate its position in Kashmir.

---

[10] S/2967, paragraph 57, UN Security Council Official Record 8, Supplement no. 1 (1953) p. 14.
[11] Liaquat Ali quoted in Chaudhri M. Ali, *Emergence of Pakistan*, New York: Columbia University Press, 1967, p. 376
[12] *The Hindu*, 15 April 1956, p. 1.
[13] Abha Dixit, 'Sino-Pakistan Relations and their implications for India', *Strategic Analysis*, December 1987, p. 1068.

India realized that by accepting the cease-fire line as the international border it would not only have taken care of its vital strategic interests but would also increase their chances of controlling a Kashmir which was not as ethnically diverse as undivided Kashmir had been. In fact the CFL marked an ethnic divide and the Kashmiri Muslims had little control over the territory beyond the border. Ethnically Muslim Kashmiris on the Indian side 'are different from the Punjabis, Sindhis, Baluchs, Pathans, Mohajirs, and Bengalis—the main ethnic groups in Pakistan— in spite of their common religious faith'.[14] It was perfectly acceptable then for the Indian leadership to convert the CFL into an international border and consolidate that part of Kashmir over which they had already established control.

The situation was different for Pakistani leaders because, as Yunas Samad has argued, political failures of the post-Independence decade in Pakistan led to the emergence of centrifugal tendencies. Heavy-handed attempts at centralization by the state encouraged their reappearance. Samad, like Ayesha Jalal, argues that US aid at this juncture gave a boost to the centralizing forces. As a result of this Ghulam Muhammad dissolved the Constituent Assembly and tilted the 'equilibrium in the Centre's favour'.[15] But this equilibrium was tenuous. At such a time the Pakistani leaders could ill afford to accept Nehru's offer and convert the CFL into a border. In fact they had to justify their centrist position through victories elsewhere. Accepting the CFL as a border would seem more like a defeat. And a defeat, even a symbolic one, at this juncture might prove catastrophic. Therefore, over the next few years Pakistan made a number of proposal to change the status quo which the Indians did not want changed.[16] Herein lay the crux of the problem. Hence,

[14] Rajat Ganguly, *Kin State Intervention in Ethnic Conflict: Lessons from South Asia*, New Delhi/ Thousand Oaks/ London, 1998, p. 57.

[15] Yunas Samad, *A Nation in Turmoil: Nationalism and Ethnicity in Pakistan, 1937–58*, New Delhi, 1995, p. 169.

[16] The Indian refusal to change the status quo was pointed out by Noon when he complained to the Security Council in 1957 that a number of proposals (eleven) were made by the United Nations to solve the Kashmir impasse but India accepted almost none of these. Further, in 1958 Nehru made an offer to Noon to refer the disputes in the east to outside arbitration. But the initiative faltered when Noon refused to accept arbitration

border issues between India and Pakistan remained unresolved and control over the divide remained unstable.[17]

WHO CONTROLS THE DIVIDE?: A RHETORICAL QUESTION?

In 1958 there was a change of government in Pakistan and the country went under military dictatorship. Ayub Khan usurped power and signed a treaty with the United States which agreed to provide Pakistan with non-conventional weapons and construct launching sites for missiles. Nehru's official biographer is of the opinion that such a treaty completely changed the Indian stance toward Pakistan. The situation was further complicated due to China's growing friendship with Pakistan. The Indian leaders realized that India was pitted against China in the eyes of the Atlantic powers. Such a situation was particularly problematic because the Indian leadership realized that it was not only losing control over the Non-Aligned movement but was also increasingly being threatened by Chinese friendship with a Pakistan that was already in alliance with the West. It became apparent that to retain their position of strength the Indians had to look inward or towards the region. As their leadership of Afro-Asian states was fast becoming a dream, the Indians had to assume the leadership of South Asia to justify their claim to fame. This shift in Indian policies was reflected in the hardening of the Indian stand not just regarding the Indo-Pakistan border but also regarding the Sino-Indian border. There were indications that Ayub Khan was eager to reach a settlement with India over the border in the east which Nehru disregarded. A settlement, which the Indian leadership was perfectly willing to have a year earlier, became unacceptable. Indian insecurity over its borders grew in proportion to Pakistan's growing friendship with China. India could easily contend with Pakistan but contending with both Pakistan and China was a different matter. In 1961

---

only on one particular border and pressed for arbitration over Kashmir. This reflected Indian unwillingness to discuss the status of a region over which they perceived that they had some control, albeit tenuous. See S. Gopal, *Jawaharlal Nehru: A Biography*, vol. III, Oxford, 1984, p. 86.

[17] Rajya Sabha Debates, vol. XXII, 26 April 1958, pp. 1047–55.

Pakistan and China started negotiations over the demarcation of their borders, while Sino-Indian relations steadily deteriorated. It culminated in the 1962 border war which had serious effects on India's policy towards South Asia.

Defeat against China revealed that India could no longer consider herself a world power. It also increased Indian fear of a joint Sino-Pakistani attack across the borders. The Indian leadership increasingly became inflexible in its attitude towards the borders as control over the region became imperative for India to retain its power status. True, as a result of much prodding from the United States India had agreed to talk to Pakistan about border issues in 1963 but the talks floundered even before they commenced. The official rationale given was that Pakistan had concluded a treaty of friendship with China a day before Swaran Singh could meet the Pakistani emissary. In such a situation, more than talks, defence preparedness was given priority. In the words of Y.B. Chavan, the then Indian Minister of Defence:

In the current climate of hostility and tension, however, we have . . . to take necessary measures for defence of our territorial integrity against any aggressive threat, the more so because of our experience last year. . . . The first programme of Defence preparedness is, one of expansion of our Armed Forces.[18]

That there was a growing inflexibility in the Indian attitude towards the borders was made apparent by Krishna Menon, the Indian representative to the United Nations, a few months later. He said: 'I think we have come to a position today that any attempt, any giving away under these circumstances will be used against us. We cannot subscribe to any resolution in the Security Council. . . .'[19] All efforts at compromise had to be shelved as the Indians tried to establish total control over the borders. Sheikh Abdullah's efforts to initiate another Indo-Pakistani dialogue languished because of Nehru's death. The instability of the divide in Kashmir increased.

The next important milestone on the question of the divide in

---

[18] Lok Sabha Debates, Fifth Series, vol. XX, 9 September 1963, p. 5089.
[19] Lok Sabha Debates, Third Series, vol. XXV, 14 September 1964, pp. 854–5.

Kashmir came in September 1965 when Pakistan fought a war with India. According to Ian Talbot, the normally cautious Ayub needed a success in Kashmir to bolster his generally failing fortunes and gambled on Operation Gibraltar.[20] Actually, Kashmir gave him a ready excuse since he could argue that Pakistan had never reconciled to the present status of the cease-fire line. Therefore, crossing the line from the Pakistani standpoint was never unjustified. However, skirmishes started not on the mountains of Kashmir but in the mud of the Rann of Kutch. Then followed the incursions across the cease-fire line which went on to a full-fledged war. The war lasted for twenty-two days. A cease-fire was arranged once again under the auspices of the United Nations. Indian disgruntlement over Pakistani action was on the rise. Pakistan, at best, did not alter the status quo and at worst lost face. It could not repeat the Chinese feat and neither did the northern second front materialize. China had issued an ultimatum to the Government of India (GOI) to remove its military structures from the Tibet-Sikkim border. But before it could act on this the UN Security Council called for immediate cease-fire. This portrayed that the international community would let the Chinese proceed thus far and no further against India. Thus, Pakistan achieved no tactical advantage for its alliance with China.

According to Chester Bowles, the American Ambassador to India at the time, the GOI came away from the conflict with a new sense of confidence in its military power, its political unity and its ability to control communal sentiments. He said:

As a result of all these factors, the GOI is in no mood to present Pakistan, by negotiation, with a position in Kashmir which Pakistan failed to achieve by fighting. Nor does GOI agree that Pakistan should be rewarded by the UN for a last-minute willingness to water down a relationship with an expansionist China which Pakistan should not have entered into in the first place.[21]

---

[20] Ian Talbot, *Pakistan: A Modern History*, Oxford, 1998, p. 177.

[21] Chester Bowles, EMB Delhi, 760-Part I, India-Pakistan Working Group, Situation Report, 24 September 1965, *LBJ Papers*, NSF-India Memos (2 of 2) vol. V, 6/65–9/65.

India played up the ramifications of Sino-Pakistani relationship internationally and justified its line of action. Even the State Department urged President Johnson to recognize India as the great power of the region and 'base future policies toward India and Pakistan on what seem to be the emerging power realities on the subcontinent'.[22] Thus, much of what India lost in the 1962 war was recovered in 1965. India could no longer hope to be a world power but could assert herself as a regional giant. The consequences of giantism were many. Indian success in the war of 1965 was put down to her military preparedness. Hence, it was the National Security lobby which began to achieve primacy in politics. The success of this lobby depended on its ability to maintain control and where possible stretch Indian borders further. The effects of this became apparent to international observers soon. The UN Secretary General U. Thant, in a report to the Security Council, described the Indo-Pakistan cease-fire as 'precarious' because of numerous incursions on the cease-fire line.[23] The lines became even more unsettled.

There were numerous efforts by the international community to settle the unsettled markers of South Asia. The Soviet Premier took the initiative in calling the Tashkent meeting because, he said 'we should not be frank if we do not say that the military conflict in Kashmir arouses the Soviet Government also because it has occurred in an area directly adjacent to the borders of the Soviet Union'.[24] The discussions at Tashkent resulted in the Tashkent Declarations of 10 January 1966. It was agreed that the two powers would withdraw their forces to pre-5 August 1965 position. Thus status quo was maintained. This was a good war for India. Pakistan could not change the cease-fire line and that was what India had desired. The joint communique issued

[22] 'Chronology of India Pakistan Conflict', Research Memorandum, 21 September 1965, *LBJ Papers*, NSF-India Memos (1 of 2), vol. V, 6/65–9/65.

[23] 'A Chronology of Significant Events', Research Memorandum, June 24, 1966, *LBJ Papers*, NSC History, Indo-Pak War, vol. III, State Department History.

[24] Cited in A. Appadorai and M.S. Rajan, *India's Foreign Policy and Relations*, New Delhi, 1985, p. 98.

at the end of talks simply said that 'the Pakistan side pointed out the special importance of reaching a settlement of the Jammu and Kashmir dispute'. By this Pakistan meant that Kashmir was a disputed territory but India maintained that its sovereignty over Kashmir was non-negotiable.[25] The settlement had the further effect of highlighting India's position of strength in the region. India's emergence as a regional giant increased its preoccupation with the borders. India would now become proactive where her divides were concerned.

CONTROL LEGITIMIZED

The next war started on a different issue but ended predictably with efforts to stabilize the divide in Kashmir. India supported the secessionist movement of Bengalis in East Pakistan. Such support came in the wake of the inauguration of the ancient silk routes between China and Pakistan. The Indian policy was so successful in the East that Pakistan declared war on India. At the end of this war Bangladesh was liberated and according to the Ministry of Defence India held 479.96 square miles of territory across the 1948 cease-fire line in Jammu and Kashmir. Peace talks commenced at Simla on 28 June 1972, between the Prime Minister of India and the President of Pakistan, which resulted in the Simla Agreement of 3 July 1972. Peace, which eluded the region for years, was supposed to have been achieved in less than a week. Both the leaders had personal stakes in the matter. This was Indira Gandhi's first experience in direct diplomatic dealings with Pakistan. As for Bhutto, he had to legitimize his position of a civilian President after years of military rule. In other words both were keen for some form of settlement. The two leaders made concerted efforts to stabilize the unstable markers. But the situation was so complex that the eleventh hour agreement was completely unexpected, so much so that Bhutto had to sign the treaty with a borrowed pen.[26]

The most important provision of the Simla Agreement for India reads as follows: 'That the countries are resolved to settle

[25] *Kashmir Dispute*, p. 31.
[26] S. Taheer, *Bhutto: A Political Biography*, London, 1979, p. 1411.

their differences by peaceful means through bilateral negotiations or by any other peaceful means mutually agreed upon between them'. This has been the subject of widely differing interpretations. On the basis of this statement the GOI has contended that the issue will be settled bilaterally and not through third party mediation.[27] Such a strategy has considerable advantage for a regional giant such as India. The Indian leadership can then avoid the internationalization of contentious issues where she may have to reckon with many actors. But where the Indian leadership failed was in seeking an ambiguous no war pact and converting the divide in Kashmir into a border.

About the divide it has been stated:

In Jammu and Kashmir, the line of control resulting from the cease-fire of December 17, 1971, shall be respected by both sides without prejudice to the recognised position of either side. Neither side shall seek to alter it unilaterally, irrespective of mutual differences and legal interpretations. Both sides further undertake to refrain from the threat or the use of force in violation of this line.[28]

India's possession of some 354 square miles north and west of the cease-fire line to the line of control was thus confirmed by Pakistan. This included strategically important points in the Tithwal region and at Kargil. In Simla Indira Gandhi had bargained from a position of strength and successfully made the dispute over the divide a bilateral issue thereby robbing Pakistan of its ability to pressurize India through its alliances but where she failed was to stabilize the line by making it a border. It remained merely a line of control which is different from an international border. This difference was made more apparent because the clause on the Line of Control (LoC) was similar to that on the international border. Therefore, the accepted justification for the divide in Kashmir remained control. If a country failed to control a line then theoretically, at least, the line could be altered as it was in 1972. Although there was a clause against unilateral alteration of the line by either of the powers, yet if any one were to foster a revolt within the territory of the other power then such alterations may be justified.

[27] *Kashmir Dispute*, p. 264.
[28] Ibid., pp. 265–6.

In this context Bhutto's formal position of leaving it to the people of Kashmir to work out their own destiny acquires special significance.[29] Bhutto made a jubilant speech on arriving at the Rawalpindi airport. He said this 'is not my victory. Nor is it a victory of Mrs. Gandhi's. It is a victory for the people of Pakistan and India who have won the peace'.[30] This was exactly what did not happen. Despite hopes there was no final solution to the Kashmir problem. The offshoots of the Simla Agreement though not immediately apparent were far flung. Efforts to stabilize the LoC contained within it the roots of further instability. Henceforth, there would not be any declared wars but constant incursions into each others territories. Further, as it was an LoC two hostile armies faced each other across a line. It ushered in an age of low intensity conflicts over where the control ends?

THE LINE THAT DEFIES CONTROL

The LoC created its own history. Compulsions to control plagued the two powers. In the post-Simla Agreement period India's foreign policy became even more power and region oriented rather than seeking out a new global role. One commentator said India had no grand designs, no world visions but placed a new emphasis on 'security, territory and prestige'. There was an increased preoccupation with the need for military power, and the leadership had demonstrated a willingness to use this power boldly in their response to the Bangladesh crisis.[31] That was their moment of glory and it happened because of their reliance on the National Security lobby. There was no reason to wear the garb of flexibility in regional dealings. What India attempted to do was to become militarily even stronger by buying sophisticated weapons abroad, by keeping the nuclear option open, by conducting the first Pokhran test in May 1974, and launching in space orbit an indigenously designed and built 35 kg. satel-

---

[29] Bhutto, *Pakistan Times*, 19 July 1972, p. 1.

[30] Benazir Bhutto, *Daughter of the East: An Autobiography*, London, 1988, p. 58.

[31] Surjit Mansingh, *India's Search for Power: Indira Gandhi's Foreign Policy, 1966–82*, New Delhi/Beverly Hills/London, 1984, p. xi.

lite. Efforts to control a line led to further compulsions of control.

Internally, the borders were given highest priority. The Border Security Force was introduced in these areas. Acts like the Armed Forces Special Powers Act (1956) got its final shape in 1972 when it was amended. This Act was imposed on so-called Disturbed Areas which were largely the bordering states. Then came the National Security Act (1980) or the Public Safety Act and the Terrorist Affected Area Ordinance (1984). The national security lobby came to influence India's external affairs in a decisive manner. According to one observer,

> the growing power of the Indian military-bureaucratic complex has also greatly contributed to the expansion of India's military clout. India's intervention in East Pakistan in 1971, compounded with other military interventions ... has given the armed forces the appropriate bases to constitute themselves into a powerful lobby.[32]

Tensions near the divide created occasions for the introduction of all the previously mentioned Acts. But these Acts could remain in operation only as long as the divides remained unsettled. The beneficiaries of these Acts therefore could develop vested interest in keeping these areas destabilized.

When Indira Gandhi came back to power in 1980 she once again embarked on an aggressive policy *vis-à-vis* the borders. Its effects were immediately felt. In 1984 a small-scale undeclared war began in the Siachen Glacier area.

Siachen is a icy wasteland of no strategic value. In this highest battlefield of the world more soldiers have been killed by environmental factors than by military engagements. This meaningless and exceedingly costly military engagement in Siachen shows the absurdity of the policies followed by leaders of Pakistan and India.[33]

Siachen portrayed that control over the LoC was anything but stable. It also showed that constant efforts will be made

---

[32] Harsh Kapur, *India's Foreign Policy, 1947–92: Shadows and Substance*, New Delhi/Thousand Oaks/London, 1994, p. 99.

[33] Tapan Bose, 'Kashmir: The Theatre of Militarization', R. Samaddar, ed., *Cannons into Ploughshares: Militarization and Prospects of Peace in South Asia*, New Delhi/London/Hartfort, 1995, p. 134.

by the two countries to change the course of the LoC but it will not be called a war. At different international gatherings Mrs. Gandhi expressed concern for peace but the border policies of India reflected a different reality.[34]

In the following years India's stress on militarization of the borders paid off. The India-China military balances equalised. Rajiv Gandhi disregarded the Ministry of External Affairs advice over China. When Deng Xiaoping offered a package deal to India to discuss the Sino-Indian borders Gandhi refused to engage with it.[35] There was a feeling that 'India's conventional forces had been strengthened through the 1980s . . . as a result, India matched—indeed was perhaps superior to—China in the border areas'.[36] This could be tested when India became involved in two crises in 1986-7. The first was with China over Sumdurong Chu and the second was with Pakistan over the Brasstacks exercise conducted by India. Although there were mobilizations on both the borders a stand-off ensued.[37] Many thought it was because China and India had acquired some form of parity militarily. But this border crisis was a pointer for the future because it made it obvious how an aggressive policy regarding the markers of territoriality can result in further aggressions.[38]

Aggressive policy towards the LoC led to the militarization of areas around the borders which resulted in efforts to control this region by force if required, leading to a sense of alienation among the people living in the area. This was not the only reason for what is termed as the 'Kashmir problem', but it definitely contributed to it. In 1989 Kashmir witnessed one of

[34] For Indira Gandhi's speeches see the Ministry of External Affairs publication entitled *Disarmament: India's Initiatives*, New Delhi, 1988.

[35] *Indian Express*, 14 January 1989.

[36] Kanti Bajpai, 'CBMs: Contexts, Achievements, Functions', D. Banerjee, ed., *Confidence Building Measures in South Asia*, Colombo, 1999, p. 13.

[37] See Gary Klintworth, 'Chinese Perspectives on India as a Great Power', in R. Babbage and Sandy Gordon, eds., *India's Strategic Future: Regional State or Global Power*, New York, 1992; also see K. Bajpai et al., *Brasstacks and Beyond: Perception and Management of Crisis*, New Delhi, 1995.

[38] In Pakistani newspapers it was reported that India had violated the LoC thrice in 1984, 1986, and 1988. *The Nation*, 8 July 1999.

the worst outbreaks of secessionism. 'Islamabad has provided diplomatic and moral support to the Kashmiri secessionist and has publicised their cause internationally'.[39] That Pakistan may provide covert material support to the Kashmiri secessionists was apparent from the time of the Simla Agreement. However, it is erroneous to characterize the movement in the valley as a proxy war by Pakistan. Numerous sources reveal that Pakistan had tried to foment ethnic tensions in 1965 but failed as Kashmiriyat appeared to be stronger than ever. But this did not happen in 1989 and the onus of responsibility for destabilization in Kashmir rests on India. 'India remained primarily responsible for the continuing political crisis in the valley of Kashmir'.[40]

Pakistani activities near the LoC also caused some alarm. There was fear that if the JKLF cadres crossed the LoC there may be war. However, the situation did not deteriorate into a war and Pakistan authorities prevented the cross over. But Pakistan was successful in reviving international attention over the issue of Kashmir. Pakistan has stridently complained against India's repression of a 'just and legitimate struggle', against an 'Indian occupation force which now numbers 6,00,000'.[41] Ironically, by reviving international media attention Pakistan may have lost more in this round than it has gained. Its former allies have marked it as a state fostering terrorism in India. The Pakistani leadership has been more successful in engaging Indian forces in low intensity conflicts around the divide, thereby making it more expensive for India to hold on to Kashmir. India also has shown no inclination to look for a political solution to the border problem and its derivatives.[42] It has persisted in using repression as

[39] Rajat Ganguly, *Kin State Intervention in Ethnic Conflicts: Lessons from South Asia*, New Delhi/Thousand Oaks/London, 1994, pp. 74–5.

[40] Tapan Bose, 'Kashmir: The Theatre of Militarization', R. Samaddar, ed., *Cannons into Ploughshares: Militarization and Prospects of Peace in South Asia*, New Delhi/London/Hartfort, 1995, p. 138.

[41] Pakistani Foreign Minister's, Mr. Assef Ahmed Ali, complaints to the UN General Assembly on 5 October 1994. Reported in *The Statesman*, 6 October 1994, p. 1.

[42] Indian attitude is reflected in J.N. Dixit's comments to British author Victoria Schofield that in politics legality and reality are two different things. While speaking of Kashmir he said: 'To quible about points of law and hope

an instrument of control. Small wonder then that the borders remained unstable.

This was followed by India's efforts to fence the International Border in the Akhnoor sector in 1996. The GOI tried to raise a barbed-wire fence in that area. This was another effort to control the border. Pakistani Rangers raised objections to such fencing of what they called a 'working boundary'.[43] Apparently in a protest note in 1993 Pakistan had referred to the same area as International Border. While analysts ascribed various factors to the timing of this confrontation, it was apparent that this crisis had come in the wake of, according to one Pakistani commentator, 'Fears about a possible Indian nuclear test or the deployment of India's short-range Prithvi missiles on the Pakistan border'.[44] The area chosen was the one that was contested by the Indian forces during the 1971 war. This was popularly known as the Chicken's Neck. That Pakistan had objected to fencing was nothing new since there were similar responses to fencing in the Punjab sector. It portrayed that as a policy barbed wires may increase destabilization. Even Bangladesh had problems with Indian barbed wires. But these markers were deemed essential to the Indian hegemonic role in the region. The incident reminded observers about 'the trouble that has caused the Siachen Glacier to become the world's highest, and most costly, area of military operations'.[45] It was a sign that the scope of conflict may be enlarged.

After the end of the Cold War the military imbalance between India and Pakistan was on the increase. In terms of conventional arms 'India's military arsenal is superior to Pakistan's in all

---

that by proving a legal point you can reverse the process of history is living in a somewhat contrived utopia'. So the Indian control over the Vale of Kashmir was thus justified on the basis of real politik and not on grounds of legality or morality. This was a clear shift from the Nehruvian position. See V. Schofield, *Kashmir in Crossfire*, London, 1996, p. 146ff.

[43] *The Statesman*, 2 February 1996, p. 1.

[44] Ahmed Rashid, 'Pakistan: Trouble Ahead, Trouble Behind', *Current History* (April 1996), p. 164.

[45] *The Statesman*, 2 February 1996, p. 8.

respects'.[46] Even India's inherent strategic superiority in nuclear weapons offers, 'New Delhi a calculus in which it has an area of latitude in its military dealings with Pakistan'.[47] However, Indian compulsions were based not on the reality of the situation but on a mythical fear of a loss of control. So in May 1998 India tested for the bomb followed closely by Pakistan. Some felt that weapons may stabilize relations between India and Pakistan but there were others who argued that 'India and Pakistan are unlikely to be able to develop a stable deterrent relationship'.[48] The sceptics were more accurate in their predictions and the nuclear programme heightened regional insecurities. A logical conclusion was that the borders would become more unstable. A Kargil then was within the logic of this highly illogical situation. Part of this area came to India when the cease-fire line was stabilized into the line of control. It is ironic that incursions should have occurred.

CONTROL CHALLENGED

When undeclared war broke out in Kashmir, Pakistani officials defended their actions by saying that the LoC was 'not intended to become a permanent line of division in opposition to the wishes of the people of J and K'.[49] Pakistani Foreign Minister Sartaj Aziz repeated his country's traditional stand that the line of control was not acceptable to his country as an international border. It was merely a temporary line in a 'disputed territory'. He repeated that this divide was also not acceptable to the Kashmiris. The Pakistani stand was justified by a member of the Indian National Security Council Advisory Board, who stated

[46] Shelton U. Kodikara, 'South Asian Security Dilemmas in the Post-Cold War', K. Bajpai and S. Cohen, eds., *South Asia After the Cold War: International Perspectives*, Boulder/San Francisco/Oxford, 1993, p. 60.
[47] Sandy Gordon, 'South Asia After the Cold War: Winners and Losers', *Asian Survey*, vol. 35, no. 10 (10 October 1995), p. 893.
[48] Ambassador Thomas Graham Jr., 'South Asia and the Future of Nuclear Nonproliferation', *Arms Control Today*, May 1998, p. 3.
[49] Mr. Ashraf Jehangir Qazi in an interview to PTI. Quoted in *The Hindu*, 9 August 1999, p. 1.

that an attack across the LoC 'would not constitute an attack on the sovereignty of either nation'.[50]

Indian reactions ranged from the acrimonious about 'the malign character of a hostile neighbour which defines its very identity in anti-Indian terms', to more sentimental theories of a stab in the back.[51] The Indian prime minister stated in a press conference in Lucknow that the 'LoC is defined and identified in the maps of the two countries which are sealed and bear signatures of representative from both the sides. In this light, any change in the LoC is not negotiable'.[52] He also stated that India was always open to talks but if the purpose of these was to alter the LoC then 'the proposed talks would end before they began....'[53] In other words, what he said was that the GOI was prepared to negotiate only if status quo was maintained. But this response was more moderate than that of many from the official circles who had stated that Pakistan should not be allowed any position near the Srinagar-Leh road.[54]

The incursions in Kargil have made it clear that the purpose of the Simla Agreement has been defeated. There cannot be any peace in an area where two hostile armies face each other across a line. From the beginning Pakistan has protested against the line dividing Kashmir. After fighting three wars India tried to stabilize its position through the Simla Agreement. In the process it had to embark on an aggressive policy of control because that was what legitimized the divide. Such a policy of control led to destabilization of the whole region, which in turn lead to growing disaffection among the people inhabiting it. This brought on further repression and alienation, and then a loss of control. An unstable line led to the alienation of a whole group of people when military solutions were favoured over political negotiations.

Both India and Pakistan lived according to the letters of the

[50] Bharat Karnad to *The Telegraph*, 20 June 1999.
[51] *The Telegraph*, 17 June 1999.
[52] *The Indian Express*, 12 June 1999.
[53] *The Times of India*, 8 June 1999.
[54] J.N. Dixit quoted in 'Line of Control: Bordering on the Impossible', *The Outlook*, 12 July 1999.

Simla Agreement thereby killing its spirit. Since war could not be declared they embarked on low intensity conflict which was not quite war but it definitely was not peace. Both tried to maintain control over the LoC thereby stretching it to its extremes. Every bit of the territory had to be contested to legitimize control. Efforts were made to destabilize the region across the borders. But borders or divides are active agents of politics in South Asia. They bind the destiny of the two countries sharing it. Contests over Siachen portrayed that control had to be established militarily. Pakistan legitimized Kargil on the same ground. Recently problems over Akhnoor reveal that an unstable line can destabilize other borders. Amitabh Mattoo comments that problems over divides 'cannot be resolved on the basis of absolutes'.[55] This is what the South Asian belligerents have been striving to do. Instead of looking for political solutions to the compulsions created by the LoC the powers were trying to legitimize their authority through control. Efforts to control have led to efforts at negating other's control. This has created a vicious cycle of mistrust, war and destabilization. It is time to realize that lines are political constructs which have to be stabilized through political processes.

[55] Amitabh Mattoo, 'LOC as International Border?', *Amman Panchayat*, vol. 2, no. 1, p. 3.

Contributors

JAGATMANI ACHARYA is at the South Asia Forum for Human Rights, which is situated in Kathmandu, Nepal.

PAULA BANERJEE is at the Department of South and South East Asian Studies, University of Calcutta and is also a member of the Calcutta Research Group.

DAGMAR BERNSTOFF is a political scientist residing in New Delhi.

PRADIP KUMAR BOSE is at the Centre for Studies in Social Sciences, Calcutta, and is also a member of the Calcutta Research Group.

TAPAN K. BOSE is at the South Asia Forum for Human Rights, in Kathmandu.

SUBHAS RANJAN CHAKRABORTY is a Professor at the Department of History, Presidency College, Calcutta, and is also a member of the Calcutta Research Group.

SANJAY CHATURVEDI is at the Centre for the Study of Geopolitics, Punjab University, Chandigarh.

SAMIR KUMAR DAS is at the Department of Political Science, Calcutta and is also a member of the Calcutta Research Group.

PARTHA S. GHOSH is at the Indian Council for Social Science Research at New Delhi.

DIPAK GYAWALI is at the Nepal Water Conservation Foundation, Kathmandu.

DEVENDRA KAUSHIK is the Honorary Chairman of the Executive Council at the Maulana Abul Kalam Azad Institute of Asian Studies at Calcutta.

RITA MANCHANDA is at the South Asia Forum for Human Rights, Kathmandu.

HELMUT REIFELD is the Representative of Konrad Adenauer Foundation at New Delhi.

RANABIR SAMADDAR is at the South Asia Forum for Human Rights at Kathmandu and is also a member of the Calcutta Research Group.

K. WARIKOO is at the School of International Studies at the Jawaharlal Nehru University, New Delhi.

Index

ACTC 226
ANC Women's League 90
Abdullah, Farooq 281
Abdullah, Sheikh 287, 300, 306
Acheson, Dean 287
Act XV of 1874 256
Adenauer, Konrad 113
Agartala Agreement (1893) 243
Ahmed, Helen 266
Akaev 130
Akbar 74
Akhil Bharat Rachnatmak Samaj 201
Ali, Muhammad 287
All Ceylon Buddhist Congress 213, 216
All India Gorkha League (AIGL) 263–5, 268–9, 271–2, 275
All India Nepali Bhasa Samiti 269
All Tripura Tigers' Force 243
Allende 39
Alma Aty Declaration 122
Amsterdam, Treaty of (1997) 118
Anderson, John 262, 267
anthropology, and conflict 45–60
Arbenz 39
armed conflict, psycho-socialization of feminities and masculinities in 83–8

Armed Forces Special Powers Act 1956 312
Arusha peace talks 96–7
Asom Gana Parishad 249
Assam Accord 245, 248–50
Association of Parents of the Missing in Kashmir 94
Association of People of Asia 201
Athulathmudali, Lalith 223
Augustine, Saint 23–4
Aurangzeb 73
Aziz, Sartaj 316

Baghdad Pact 303
Bahu, Parakrama 174
Bandaranaike, S.W.R.D. 217, 219
Bandaranaike-Chelvanayagam (B-C) Pact of 1957 219
Banerjea, Surendranath 261
Basu, Jyoti 200
Bauddha Jathika Balavegaya (Buddhist National Force) 213
Behera, N.C. 73
Bentinck, Lord 254
Betrayal Buddhism 216
Beyond Boundaries 196–7
Bhandari, Romesh 222
Bhaumik, Subir 248
Bhutto, Z.A. 309, 311
Bismarck 104, 110

Bista, K.B. 266
Black, Eugene R. 288-9
Bodo Accord (1993) 243, 252
Bodo Autonomous Council 252
Bolshevik revolution 39
Bonaparte, Napoleon 105
Bowles, Chester 307
Brahman, Ratanlal 267
Briand, Aristide 108-9
Brohier, R.L. 175
Brugmanns, Henrik 108
Buddha Sasana Council 216
Buddhist Committee of Enquiry, Sri Lanka 216

CIP(M) 270-2, 274-5, 279
Calcutta Research Group 9
Carry Greenham Home 93
Cartagena Declaration of the organization of American States 1984 36
Carter 124
cartographic anxiety 69
Casey, Lord 264
Castro 39
Central Asia
  experience in regionalization 126-31
  genuine concern causes in 123-6
  holistic view on 119-35
  more towards regional integration in 121-3
  prospects of regional integration 131-5
  regionalizaiton as peace instrument 119-35
Central Asian Bank 122
Central Asian Development Bank 129
Central Asian Economic Community 126, 128-30, 132-4
Central Asian Economic Union 126, 129
Central Bank of Central Asia 131, 133

Ceylon National Congress 215
Ceylon Workers Congress (CWC) 226
Chapman 255
Chatterjee, Suniti Kumar 269
Chatterjee, Sushil 267
Chavan, Y.B. 306
Chelmsford 261
Chelvanayagam, S.J.V. 220
Chhettri, Kharga Bahadur 261
Chhettri, Maya Devi 266
Child Rights Convention (CRC) 155
Churchill, Winston 109
civil societies
  for peace 197-204
  in India and Pakistan 189-95
  link among 194-5
  meaning of 190-1
  peace initiatives by 189-94
Clinton, Bill Jefferson 39, 124
Cold War 27, 33, 38, 103, 137, 141, 143, 147, 149, 293
Committee of the Regions (COR) 116-17
Communist Party of India (CPI) 267, 269, 271-2
Communist Party Revolutionary Marxist (CPRM) 275
conflict and reconciliation 45-52
conflict resolution programmes 25-6
Convention on the Elimination of all Form of Discrimination Against Women (CEDAW) 155
Council of Europe 36
critical geopolitics 65-7
Cumaratunga, Munidasa 213
Curzon, Lord 260
Customary International Law 156
DGHC Act (Act XIII of 1988) 276-8
Damodar Valley Project 169
Darjeeling

Index | 323

after Independence 267–80
  demand for separate state 272–80
  identity crisis 253–7
  movements in 262–7
  politics of 253
  social history of 257–67
Darjeeling Gorkha Hill Council (DGHC) 253, 275–80
Darjeeling Planters' Association 262–3
De Alwis, Ananda Tissa 220
democracies, Pacific conduct of 39–40
Deng Xiaoping 313
Desai, Morarji 240–2, 247, 269
Dewan, Bhimlal 262
Dialogues 21
difference, theory of 148
Dudley Senanayake-Chelvanayagam (D-C) Pact of 1965 219
Duraiyappah, Alfred 220
Dutthugamini, King 214

ENDLF 226–7
East India Company 62
Economic Cooperation Organization (ECO) 122, 128–9
education, enmification in India and Pakistan through 73–7
Eelam People's Revolutionary Liberation Front (EPRLF) 221–2, 226
Eelam Revolutionary Organisation of Students (EROS) 221–2, 226
Eksath Buddhist Peramuna (EBP) 216
Eurasian Union 127–8
European Association 262–3
European infegration, regional policy for 112–17
Farakka Treaty of 1996 170–1
Federal Party, Sri Lanka 218, 220
federalism, and subsidiarity 105–12
forced migration 138–40

Four Mothers in Lebanon 94
Frederic the Great 104
Freedom Party Women's League 90
French Revolution 104–5

Gandhi, Indira 309–13
Gandhi, Mahatma 63, 265–6
Gandhi, Rajiv 222, 313
Ganga Barrage Project 171
Gaulle, Charles de 108, 113
geographical knowledge, politics of 65–7
Germany,
  border conflicts 102–18
  historical borders 103–5
Gewali, Surya Bijram 265
Ghising, Subhas 271, 273, 275–7
Giri, Dal Bahadur 262, 265–6
Gorkha Association 263
Gorkha Dukha Nivarak Sabha 263
Gorkha League 270
Gorkha National Empoloyees' Organisation (GNEO) 272
Gorkha National Liberation Front (GNLF) 253, 268–9, 271–6, 279
Gorkha National Students' Federation (GNSF) 274
Gorkha National Womens' Organisation (GNWO) 274
Gorkha National Youth Organisation (GNYO) 274
Government of India Act 1919 256
Government of India Act 1935 256, 262
Graham, Frank 302
Great Game thesis 125
Gujral, I.K. 190, 194
Gumilev, Lev 120
Gunathilaka, M.D. Nandana 206
Gurung, Dambar Singh 262–4

Hamal, Bhadra Bahadur 267
Hameed, A.C.S. 228
Helsinki Accord of 1975 34

Hill Development Council 276
Hill Women's Federation (HWF) 95–6
Hillmen's Association 261–8
Hmar Accord 246
Hmar People's Convention 243, 246
Ho Chi Minh 39
Hoare, Samuel 262
Hugo, Victor 108
Hydari Agreement of 1947 245
Hydraulic efficiency, concept of 174
IMF 149
IPKF 225
Iliss, W.A.B. 290
Illegal Migrants (Detection by Tribunals) Act of 1983, 251
India
  enmification through education in 73–7
  ethnic Accords 231–52
  Sri Lanka Accord 222–5
India-Pakistan Neemrana Initiative 196
Indian Council's Act of 1861 255
Indian National Security Council Advisory Board 316
Indo-Lanka Accord 221–5
Indo-Nepal Treaty of 1950 273–5
Indus Engineering Corporation 288–9
Indus Waters Treaty,
  critical review 292–8
  Indus basin 282, 285
  Lilienthal proposal 287–90
  main features 291–2
  partition of Indian subcontinent and 283–7
  perspectives of 161–3, 180, 281–98
  World Bank initiatives on 287–90
Inkatha 90
Integrated Mediferranean Programme 114
Inter-State Commission for Water Coordination 296

International Bank for Reconstruction and Development 288
International Convention for Elimination of All Forms of Racial Discrimination 155
International Court of Criminal Justice 156
International Covenant against Torture 155
International Covenant on Civil and Political Rights 155
International Covenant on Economic, Social and Cultural Rights 155
International Human Rights Law 155–6
International Law Association 296
International Refugee Organization 143
Iqbal, Mohammed 73, 190

JKLF 314
Janata Party 192
Janatha Vimukti Perumena (JVP) 175, 206, 225
Jayewardene 221, 223–4
Jehangir, Asme 202
Jinnah 73

Kant, Immanual 23, 39
Karbi Tripartite Agreement (1995) 243
Karimov, Islam 127–9, 131
Kennedy, J.S. 175
Khan, Ayub 290, 292–3, 305, 307
Khan, Liaquat Ali 287, 301–3
Khan, M. Zafrulla 287
Khan, Nusrat Fateh Ali 195
Khan, Syed Ahmed 73
Kumaratunga, Chandrika 205–7, 221–2, 229

Laden La, S.W. 261–2
League of Nations 142–3
Liberation Tigers of Tamil Eeelam

(LTTE) 205–7, 209, 221–2, 224–5, 230
Lilienthal, David E. 287–9
Lincoln, Abraham 109
Line of Control (LoC), in Kashmir
  beginning of tenuous control 300–9
  challenge to 316–19
  legitimization 309–11
  line that defies control 311–16
Lloyd 254–5
Lumumba 39
Lutsenko, L. 132

Maastricht Treaty (1992) 111, 116, 118
Madres des Plaza de Mayo, Argentina 94
Maha Bodhi Society 213
Mahabharat 207
Mahakali Treaty 163–8
Majumdar, Satyendra Narayan 267
Mangala Moonesinghe Select Committee (1991) 221, 225–9
Marwah, Ved 231
Marx 21
Mathur, H.C. 294
Mehta, Ashok 294
Menon, Krishna 306
minorities,
  and refugees 140–2
  treaties on 37–8
Mishing (Tiwa) Accord (1995) 243
Mizo Accord of 1987 243, 249
Mladjenovic, Lepa 94
Modise, Thandi 88, 90–1
Mohd., Ghulam 286
Monistic water accords, pluralizing of 176–83
Monnet, Jean 112
Montague 261
Moonesinghe, Mangala 225
Morgan Commission Report of 1867 212
Mossadegh 39

Mothers' Front 82–3, 93–4
Muhammad, Ghulam 303–4
Mukherjee, Nirmal 198
Munro, Ross 131
Musharraf, Pervez 189, 202
Muslim League 189

Naga National Congress 248
Naga National Council 239
Nation-states, ideology of 138–40
National Security Act 1980 312
National Socialist Council of Nagaland (NSCN) 243, 247
Navalar, Arumuga 214
Nazarbayev 127, 129–30
negative peace 28, 88
Nehru, Jawaharlal 268, 270, 290, 292–4, 300–2, 304–6
Nepali Sahitya Sammelan 263, 265
Nibigira, Concille 97
Niyazov 134

Official Language Committee 269
Operation Gibralter 293, 307
Organization of African Unity (OAU) 36, 146

PSC 226, 228–9
Pakistan, enmification through education in 73–7
Pakistan India Peoples' Forum for Peace and Democracy (PIPFPD) 198–200, 203
Parthasarathi Plan 222
Patashkar Committee 270
Patel, Sardar 237–8
Pathak, Ananda 270
Pause, Dietrich 116
peace,
  civil society for 194–203
  contests and histories of 42–3
  definition of 34–8, 45
  democratic argument 33
  disciplinarian argument 29–32

326 | Index

double restoration of state and 40-2
gender notion of politics of 88
historicity of 33
instruments of 101-18
international institutional definition 34-5
mainstreaming gender in 95-8
meaning of 89
normative value 207
of mind 25
older definitions and new discoures 35-8
Pacific conduct of democracies and 39-40
process of 95-8
rational argument 21-4
regionalization as instrument of 101-8
security argument 25-8
studies 11-17
validation of 21-43
value of 21-43, 206-7
women and 84-98
Peace studies
conflicts and 12-17, 30
principles of 11
research needs of 29-30
uniqueness of 29
Peace Treaty of Augsburg 1555 106
Peiris, G.H. 210
People's Alliance 229
People's Association 262
People's Liberation Organisation of Tamil Eelam (PLOTE) 221-2, 226
Pethick-Lawrence, Lord 263
Philosophy of Right 23
Phizo, A.Z. 240-2
Plato 21
Ponnambalam, G.G. 220
positive peace 28, 89
Prabhakaran, Vellupillai 224-5
Pradhan, M.K. 261
Pradhan, Parasmani 262, 265

Pranta Parishad 272
Premadasa, R. 223, 225
Primabetov, Serik 123
psychie space, constructing and sustaining the 'other' in 65-7
psychological borderlands 66
Public Safety Act 312
Pujol, Jordi 108
Putin, Vladimir 127

Qasim, Mohammad Bin 73
quarrel, origin of 21

Rabbani, M.I. 73
Radcliffe 64
Radha Hajong Accord (1995) 243
Rahman, I.A. 198
Rai, D.P. 270
Rai, I.B. 269
Rajna, Branka 89
Ramdas, L. 198
Rawl, John 13
reconciliation
anthropology of 45-80
conflict and 45-52
process of 53-6
tradition and 56-60
refugees,
absence of protective legal framework 152
Africa and South America definition of 146-7
Cartagena Declaration on 146
crisis in international regime of 147
definition of 145-7
direction of flows 148-9
harmonized national laws for 153-8
in South Asia 150
international regime 147
legal framework for 153-8
migrants and 143-5
minorities and 140-2
need for reconceptualization 145-6

non-entréé regime 148
policy of governments 153
root-cause theory 149–50
solution for 137–58
states recognize 142–3
regional policy, of European integration 112–17
regionalization as peae instrument in
central Asia 119–35
Western Europe 101–18
rejected people 138–40
Ronaldshay, Lord 261
Root cause theory, of refugees 149–50
Roy, B.C. 268
Rumer, Boris 131

SLFP 220, 225–6, 228
SLLP 228
Salmeh, Dalal 87
security as peace 25–8
Sharif, Nawaz 189
Sharma, Dharanidhar 265
Shillong Accord of 1975 231–3, 240, 247–8, 251
Shmelov, N. 132
Simla Agreement 309, 311, 314, 317–18
Singh, Iqbal 294
Singh, Swaran 306
Sinhala-Tamil, ethnic conflict 211–13
Sinlun Development Council 243
Smith, Dan 85
Societies Registration Act of 1860 191
South Asia,
civil society for peace 194–204
critical geo-politics 65–7
history through education 73–7
mental borders in 61–78
perceptual blockage and enemy mythology in post colonial period 67–77

refugees problem and solution 137–58
water accords in 159–83
spatial socialization 66
Sri Lanka,
Buddhist chauvinism in 217
Chandrika Plan 229–30
conflict in 211–13
equality of claim in 208–9
ethnic compromise in 205–30
ethnicity and nationalist movement in 215–16
Independence of 216
India accord 222–5
linguistic chauvinism in 213
Mangala Moonesinghe Select Committee 225–9
PSC Concept Paper 226–7
PSC Option Paper 227
peace in 206–8
political Buddhism 213–14
riots of 1983 221–2
Tamil extremism 220–1
Tamil nationalism 215
Tamil resurgence 214, 218–19
territorial integrity 211
territorial politics 209–11
Thimpu Talks 222
Sri Lanka Muslim Congress (SLMC) 226, 228
Stalin 104
States' Reorganization Commission 238
States Reorganization Committee 269
Stresemann, Gustav 109
Stroev, E. 130
Subba, G.L. 267
Subba, Randhir 263
subsidiarity, and federalism 105–12

Tamil Congress 220
Tamil Eelam Liberation Organization (TELO) 221–2
Tamil United Liberation Front (TULF) 219–22, 226–7

Tenessee Valley Authority 287
Terrorist Affected Area Ordinance (1984) 312
Thakurta, Chinmoy 169
Thant, U. 308
Thimpu Talks (1985) 221–2
Thomas, Saint 109
Tinkar, Hugh 37
tradition and reconciliation 59–60
Tribal National Volunteers 245, 247
Truman 287
two-nation theory 64
Tulbul Navigation Project 297

UNCIP 302
UN Declaration on Persons Belonging to National or Ethnic Linguistic and Religious Minorities 141
US Atomic Energy Commission 287
United Liberation Front of Assam (ULFA) 242, 247
United Nation Environment Programme (UNEP) 145
United Nation High Commissioner for Refugees (UNHCR) 36, 137–8, 143, 147–8
United National Party (UNP) 205–6, 216, 219, 225–6, 228–30
Universal Declaration of Human Rights (1948) 34, 38

Vajpayee, A.B. 190
Vajpayee-Koirala joint communique 2000 164
Veerappan 170
Versailles Treaty 103–4
Vishwa Hindu Parishad 194

Wall of Tears 93
Wallerstein I 178
war, causes of 21–2

War Crimes Tribunal 156
Washington consensus 27, 33
water, society in 159–60
water accords, in South Asia
  Bihar and 171–3
  Farakka Treaty 170–1
  Indus Treaty 161–3
  Mahakal Treaty 163–8
  pluralizing monistic accords 176–83
  Sri Lanka and 173–5
West Bengal Official Languages Act 268
Western Europe, regionalization as peace instrument in 101–18
Westphalian Peace Treaty 1648 61 104
Wickremasinghe, Ranil 205
Wilson, Woodrow 39
Women,
  ambivalent politics of motherhood 91–5
  cultural language of support and resistance 91–5 in conflict 81
  mainstreaming gender in political activity of peace building 95–8
  making peace 81–98
  meaning of peace for 89
  notion of peace and political violence 88–91
  peace activism 82–3
  peace and 84–8
Women in Black 93–4
Women's Bust for Peace 202–3
Woolf, Virginia 95–6
World Bank 145, 164–5, 287–90, 294, 296, 298

Young Men's Buddhist Association (YMBA) 213
Zhou Enlai 303
Zia-ul-Haq 73